Ways to
Think About
MATHEMATICS

Ways to Think About MATHEMATICS

Activities and Investigations for Grade 6-12 Teachers

Steve Benson with Susan Addington, Nina Arshavsky,
Al Cuoco, E. Paul Goldenberg, and Eric Karnowski

A Joint Publication

CORWIN PRESS

EDC

CORWIN PRESS
A Sage Publications Company
Thousand Oaks, California

For information:

Corwin Press
A Sage Publications Company
2455 Teller Road
Thousand Oaks, California 91320
www.corwinpress.com

Sage Publications Ltd
1 Oliver's Yard
55 City Road
London EC1Y 1SP
United Kingdom

Sage Publications India Pvt. Ltd.
B-42, Panchsheel Enclave
Post Box 4109
New Delhi 110 017 India

Printed in the United States of America

Library of Congress Cataloging-in-Publication Data

Ways to think about mathematics : activities and investigations for grade 6-12 teachers / by Steven Benson with Susan Addington . . . [et al.].
        p. cm.
Includes index.
ISBN 0-7619-3104-X (cloth) — ISBN 0-7619-3105-8 (pbk.)
    1. Mathematics—Study and teaching (Elementary)—Activity programs.
2. Mathematics—Study and teaching (Secondary)—Activity programs.
I. Benson, Steven. II. Addington, Susan. an.
QA135.6.W39 2005
510'.71—dc22

                                    2004007970

This book is printed on acid-free paper.

05 06 07 08 09 10 9 8 7 6 5 4 3 2 1

Acquisitions Editor:	Rachel Livsey
Editorial Assistant:	Phyllis Cappello
Production Editor:	Kristen Gibson
Proofreader:	Liann Lech
Typesetter:	C&M Digitals (P) Ltd.
Cover Designer:	Michael Dubowe

Table of Contents

Ways to Think About Mathematics:
Activities and Investigations for Grade 6-12 Teachers

Overview of the materials

Professional development for teachers has always been important in keeping them fresh, up to date, and intellectually alive. Increasingly, the calls for professional development have been backed by state requirements and by programs funded, organized, or run at national, state, and local levels. *Ways to Think About Mathematics: Activities and Investigations for Grade 6-12 Teachers* was written with a very particular perspective on the content and structure of professional development in secondary mathematics, grades 6 to 12. Our experience—as teachers, teacher educators, and mathematicians ourselves—has been that the most effective professional development in mathematics for teachers is immersion in the mathematics itself, and the most engaging and ultimately useful mathematics is the very mathematics that the teachers use or teach every day. There is depth in that mathematics, even at the sixth-grade level—one need not go beyond it to find new ideas and fresh connections. There are also important connections between that mathematics and the college mathematics courses that teachers may have taken and that often seem so very far removed from what they do in class on a day-to-day basis.

With these two kinds of connections in mind—connections within the mathematics that teachers teach, and connections between that mathematics and the seemingly more abstruse courses they may have taken—we proposed the *Connecting with Mathematics* project to the National Science Foundation. The materials created by the *Connecting with Mathematics* project team led to this book.

Each of the chapters takes problems directly from secondary curricula, lets teachers plumb the mathematics behind them through their own problem-solving and investigation, and emerges in some unexpected mathematical territories along the way. The course remains practical because it is focused on the mathematics of the classroom, and though the problems are designed for teachers, many of them can be adapted for classroom use.

One chapter explores the notion of mathematical investigation itself—the process of modifying a problem in various ways to explore its edges and depth without changing it so radically that one is simply off topic, and the process of moving from an experimenting, idea-gathering, and conjecturing stage to a stage in which one systematizes and explains through proof. Other chapters explore particular topics, including ones in algebra, combinatorics, geometry and measure, and number theory.

Outlines of the chapters

- **What is Mathematical Investigation?**

  In this chapter, participants take a mathematical investigation (which counting numbers can be expressed as the sum of at least two consecutive counting numbers?) from start to finish—from exploratory stages through reporting logically connected results—learning strategies that they can use with their students to develop their investigative skills. New mathematical facts and relationships may well be encountered, but the real purpose of this chapter is to investigate investigation.

- **Dissections and Area**

  This chapter provides a new approach to learning and teaching area, and mathematical ideas related to area. Participant teachers will rethink the concept of area through hands-on activities that involve the dissection and rearrangement of various geometrical figures. Using dissections, they will derive area formulas for various polygons and explore the meaning and properties of area in depth. This chapter also uncovers connections between area, geometrical transformations, algorithms, functions, coordinate geometry, and fractals. Interesting applications, such as tessellations of the plane, tangrams, and jigsaw puzzles, are discussed.

- **Linearity and Proportional Reasoning**

  This chapter explores the gamut of proportional thinking from its elementary origins through generalizations in several directions and dimensions. The first section explores absolute and relative comparisons. The second section links sequences with interpolation. The third section explores functions satisfying the property $f(a + b) = f(a) + f(b)$ (for all a and b). Participants will ask, for which functions is this actually true? In the fourth section, functions of two variables emerge from old-fashioned and new style word problems, and their graphs are investigated. The final section explores higher dimensional analogues of linear functions.

Did you know that the book The Pythagorean Proposition *contains 366 proofs of the Pythagorean Theorem?*

- **Pythagoras and Cousins**
  This chapter delves into the Pythagorean Theorem and related topics. Some of the topics include various proofs and generalizations of the Theorem and properties of Pythagorean triangles (right triangle with integer-valued legs and hypotenuse). Some proofs involve dissecting and reconstituting areas (as in the Dissections chapter), while others are chosen for their originality, beauty, or historical context, or to illustrate a method or idea that will be useful later. Another section asks teachers to derive an algorithm for producing all Pythagorean triples [ordered triples of positive integers (a, b, c) so that $a^2 + b^2 = c^2$] and use this algorithm to solve a variety of problems. The last section brings teachers back to the classroom to investigate the mathematics behind creating problems that "come out nice."

- **Pascal's Revenge: Combinatorial Algebra**
  Participants engage in combinatorial investigations while they work on concrete problems that encourage them to search for patterns and to create and confirm/disprove conjectures about more general situations. Through hands-on activities, teachers reflect on and discuss a variety of mathematical contexts all tied together by Pascal's Triangle and binomial coefficients. In the first section, participants work with partitions of a positive integer n (the number of different ways to express n as a sum of positive integers) through activities with number rods. Section 2 uncovers facts about graphs on the coordinate plane (specifically taxicab geometry) by asking questions like, How many ways are there to go a total of 5 blocks north and 8 blocks west? In sections 3 and 4, participants will discover explicit connections between Pascal's Triangle, binomial coefficients, and the Binomial Theorem, while section 5 introduces the capstone notion of generating functions, introduced through an analysis of dice rolls.

Organization of this book

The materials come in three pieces:

- *Activities and investigations:* Each chapter of the main text contains 5 sections, each consisting of 5-10 pages of problems for teachers to work on. Many sections start with a rich exploratory problem from one of the standards-based curricula. They continue with related problems that lead teachers to explore new mathematical territories or delve more deeply.

- *Problems for the classroom:* It is generally impossible for teachers to take off their "teaching hat," but it is important to keep in mind that, even though many of the problems might be appropriate—or adaptable—for student work, the text problems are designed for *you* to ponder, struggle with, talk about, and eventually solve with the help of your fellow participants and facilitator. As a reward for your participation, the *Problems for the Classroom* section includes problems, with solutions, for use in grades 6-12 classrooms.

- *Answers to selected problems:* Where appropriate, brief answers are given to some of the text activities. Complete solutions to all of the problems are available on the supplementary CD-ROM (see page xi for more information).

How to use this book

The materials in this book, the product of the *Connecting with Mathematics* project at Education Development Center, are designed to give you an experience with exploratory mathematics. You will work on a number of problems designed to get you thinking, conjecturing, and problem solving (i.e., *doing* mathematics). Being an effective teacher is one of the hardest jobs there is, and mathematics is a topic that has long been seen as difficult to teach and learn. A good mathematics teacher is part child psychologist, part motivational speaker, part mathematician, and any number of other "parts"! While the goal is to help you become an even better *teacher*, the strategy of the materials is to get you to do mathematics. In experiencing open-ended problems, making and checking conjectures, and evaluating your own problem-solving strategies, you become better prepared to deal with day-to-day classroom decisions:

Creation of the Connecting with Mathematics *materials was made possible by grant #ESI-9731244 from the National Science Foundation.*

> *Hmm, some of my students are approaching this problem in a different way than I expected. Is it OK to let them pursue this line of reasoning? Thinking through some of the possibilities, I see that this might be a fruitful pursuit. Should I pursue the line of thinking that Sally suggests, or will that lead us toward a dead end? Maybe that dead end will serve as a "jumping off" point for another activity. Or will it just leave them running around in circles and cause too much frustration?*

Sometimes, a little frustration is a good thing. It can motivate students (and ourselves) to dig deeper to gain more understanding.

Some directions are fruitful to pursue; some are dead ends not worth spending time on (although sometimes it *can* be valuable for students to see a dead end, just to know that there are strategies for backing up and taking another track). To make sound pedagogical decisions for your class, you need to be sensitive to the needs of your class, but you *also* need to know how to recognize the path markers along the problem-solving trail. This involves familiarity with doing mathematics. Confidence in your own mathematical understanding of the topic, gained through *doing* mathematics, will help you make these pedagogical decisions based on what is best for your class that day.

The sections within each chapter are variations on a single theme (which varies from chapter to chapter), and we encourage you to think about the connections between problems, sections, and chapters. Some of these connections are obvious, while others are quite subtle. In any case, it is essential to keep in mind that the problems have been carefully designed to tell a *story*. It is therefore important to work on all of them—in the order given—even if you think you know the answers already.

Some problems might require extra reflection and/or discussion time, in which case they are formatted as follows:

Reflect and Discuss

2. With your partner(s), devise a set of directions that explains how to *list* all trains of any given length.

Other "big picture" problems are further set apart (with a title and special formatting) as illustrated below:

PROBLEM

3. THE TRAIN PROBLEM:
   Given any positive integer, n, derive a formula for the number of trains of length n. Explain your solution, the process you used to find it, and how you know it's correct *for all n*.

In other situations, we provide a problem — or problems — that provide practice with a newly discussed concept:

Check Your Understanding

Pas(n,k) *is used to denote entry* k *of row* n *in Pascal's Triangle, which is defined recursively.*

2. Compute $Pas(6, 2)$ and $Pas(8, 5)$ using only the definition.

3. Use the $Pas(n, k)$ notation to *express* the fact that each row of Pascal's Triangle is a *palindrome* (that is, it reads the same forward and backward). More to the point, what other entry in the nth row of Pascal's Triangle is equal to $Pas(n, k)$?

4. Express the hockey stick (or sock) property (mentioned in problem 5 in section 2) in "Pas" notation.

Ways to think about it

If you stumble or hit a roadblock, you can refer to *Ways to think about it* for ideas to help you get back on track. *Ways to think about it*, included at the end of each section, provides suggestions and additional questions to help you organize strategies for solving the problems posed during the class or session. Be sure to read it when you are finished. We also hope that you'll find the marginal notes useful. They usually provide supplementary information (or an occasional humorous anecdote), but when we *really* want you to read it, we will provide one of the visual clues (▷ or ◁) to remind you to "look over" at the note in the margin. So take a few minutes to get to know the members of your group and then dive in—the water's fine!

If you'd rather dip your toes in and slowly edge your way in, that's OK, but you'll get wet sooner or later!

Supplementary materials

The *Facilitator's Guide* offers a variety of support materials to help facilitators implement the text. Each section of the *Facilitator's Guide* typically includes

- An overview section that describes the main focus and the story line of a section and puts them into the context of the whole chapter.

- Specific guidance on problems presented in the text that describes the goals and the purposes of the problems, suggests possible approaches to the problems, and gives a facilitation timeframe.

The *Further Exploration CD-ROM* (accompanying the Facilitator's Guide) extends the content of the main text with materials that can serve as a resource for independent work between classes, or as a reading outside of professional development programs. Besides additional readings for teachers, these materials also feature:

- Additional activities and explorations for teachers
- Solutions to all problems from the text and the *Further Exploration* materials.

Index of key problems

Since this book is a structured collection of mathematical explorations, it is less encyclopedic than the usual textbook. Though we believe it is important to work through chapters and sections in the order the problems are presented (so that the "story line" is not lost), we realize that there might be compelling reasons to review on one or more of the big picture problems. Therefore, in lieu of an index, we provide here an annotated list of the key problems presented in the text (those labeled PROBLEM).

Some problem statements have been slightly modified in order to provide context.

It will usually be useful to also consider the activities before and after these problems, since the surrounding explorations include essential concepts and strategies for solving—or applications of—the key problems.

Arnold and Betty are farmers. Here is a map of part of their land. ⊰ They want to straighten .out the boundary between their properties without changing the amounts of land they each have. How can they do it?

Show that every triangle is a 4-reptile by demonstrating how they can be cut into four congruent triangles that are similar to the original triangle.

A function, F, has only real numbers in its domain (its inputs), and its range (outputs) also consists of real numbers. For any real numbers a and b, $F(a + b) = F(a) + F(b)$. That is, if you put in the sum of two numbers, what comes out is the sum of the outputs for the two numbers fed in separately. What does F look like, algebraically?

For example, if $F(7) = 35$ and $F(9) = 45$, then $F(16)$ would be 80.

Kathryn has a cooking pot and two measuring cups. One cup holds 4 fluid ounces, the other holds 6 fluid ounces. Neither cup has marks that allow Kathryn to measure less than these amounts. Can she measure 2 fluid ounces using these cups? Can she measure 14 fluid ounces? 7 fluid ounces? For each amount she could measure, explain how.

There are four integer-valued points on the unit circle; namely $(1,0)$, $(0,1)$, $(0,-1)$, and $(-1,0)$. Are there any other *rational* points on the unit circle? If so, find at least six rational points in the first quadrant that lie on the unit circle.

Carefully state the Pythagorean Theorem. Be sure that your statement of the theorem will be clear to *anyone*, even if they have never heard of the theorem.

The M-graph for $\overline{AB}$ is the set of all points M which are midpoints of $\overline{AC}$ where $\triangle ABC$ is a right triangle. What does the M-graph look like for a given $\overline{AB}$? Carefully explain your conclusions and reasoning.

The following paragraph (and figure) provides the gist of the argument Euclid used in *The Elements* to prove the Pythagorean Theorem (Proposition 47 from Book 1). Fill in the details.

Pas(n, k) denotes entry k in row n of Pascal's Triangle.

Acknowledgments

Ways to Think About Mathematics is the result of the contributions of a large number of people, including Susan Addington, Nina Arshavsky, Tony Artuso, Steve Benson, Peter Braunfeld, Brett Coonley, Al Cuoco, E. Paul Goldenberg (Project Director of the *Connecting with Mathematics* project), Jane Gorman, Todd Grundmeier, Michael Humphrys, Eric Karnowski, Helen Lebowitz, June Mark, and Mark Saul. Some materials and activities were motivated by previous and simultaneous work on *Connected Geometry*, a secondary geometry curriculum, and *Problems with a Point*, a searchable, online database of focused problem sets for middle and high school mathematics students.

The main authors of each chapter are listed below:

What is Mathematical Investigation?
E. Paul Goldenberg

Dissections and Area
Susan Addington
Nina Arshavsky
Steve Benson

Linearity and Proportional Reasoning
Susan Addington
Eric Karnowski

Pythagoras and Cousins
Steve Benson

Pascal's Revenge: Combinatorial Algebra
Al Cuoco

We would also like to express our gratitude to Corwin Press, especially Rachel Livsey, Kristen Gibson, and Phyllis Cappello, whose patience, assistance, and insight were invaluable. The contributions of the following reviewers are also gratefully acknowledged: Jenny Tsankova, Ed.D., Cathy Carroll, Mardi A. Gale, M. Kathleen Heid, Ph.D., Cynthia G. Bryant, Alfred S. Posamentier, Ph.D., Joani Harr, Joan Commons, and Cathy Hewson.

Last, but by no means least, thank you to all of the college and university faculty, professional development workshop facilitators, and study group leaders who used draft versions of these materials, providing us with very useful feedback, and to Joan Kenney, the evaluator for the *Connecting with Mathematics* project, for her astute observations and suggestions.

About the authors

Steven R. Benson is a Senior Research and Development Associate at Education Development Center, Inc. He received his Ph.D. from the University of Illinois, working under the direction of Leon McCulloh in Algebraic Number Theory. Before joining EDC in June 2000, he held mathematics faculty positions at St. Olaf College, Santa Clara University, University of New Hampshire, and University of Wisconsin-Oshkosh, and is currently a Co-Director of the Master of Science for Teachers program at the University of New Hampshire. At EDC, Steve has been involved in a wide variety of projects, most of which involve the development of curricula for mathematics students and teachers. He has also facilitated preservice and inservice teacher professional development workshops across the U.S., directed a research project investigating the genesis and development of mathematical talent in Mathematical Olympians, and edited the problem calendar section of the *Mathematics Teacher* journal published by the National Council of Teachers of Mathematics. Although he enjoys his work, he much prefers spending time with his wife, Jean, and daughter, Sophia.

Susan Addington is a professor of Mathematics at California State University, San Bernardino. Though her doctoral work was in arithmetic algebraic geometry (a field that includes almost every mathematical area except statistics), she now spends most of her time thinking about math education. Her educational interests include teacher preparation (elementary through college), ethnomathematics, and the use of technology to teach traditionally difficult ideas. Susan is married to David Dennis, a math educator, historian of mathematics, jazz saxophonist, and virtuoso gardener.

Nina P. Arshavsky is a Math Coach at Boston Public Schools, providing professional development to high school math teachers. She received her doctoral degree in educational psychology from the University of Wisconsin-Madison and taught mathematics in middle and high schools in both Russia and the US. Dr. Arshavsky worked on a variety of research, professional development, and curriculum development projects in the Center for Mathematics Education at EDC and is a co-author of *Impact Mathematics: Algebra and More for the Middle Grades*, a comprehensive 6-8 mathematics curriculum. She has published and presented numerous research papers, and has taught college courses in cognitive development and human development in infancy and early childhood.

Al Cuoco is Senior Scientist and Director of the Center for Mathematics Education at Education Development Center. Before coming to EDC, he taught high school mathematics for 24 years to a wide range of students in the Woburn, Massachusetts public schools. A student of Ralph Greenberg, Dr. Cuoco received his Ph.D. in mathematics from Brandeis; his mathematical interests and publications have been in algebraic number theory. His favorite publication is his 1991 article in the American Mathematical Monthly, described by his wife as "an attempt to explain a number system no one understands with a picture no one can see."

E. Paul Goldenberg is a Senior Scientist and the Principal Investigator of three recent NSF-funded projects: *Connecting with Mathematics*, materials for teacher professional development programs; *Problems with a Point*, a Web-accessible, searchable database of orchestrated problem sets; and *Math Workshop: A Comprehensive Elementary Curriculum for Skill, Mathematical Ability, and Real Thinking*, a project that will develop materials for a K-5 comprehensive mathematics curriculum that promotes rather than requires professional development. He was previously PI on the *Connected Geometry* curriculum development project, and of a 3-year, NSF-funded research project into the nature of learning with geometry software. He has over 35 years of experience in elementary, secondary, and post-secondary teaching, teacher enhancement, and education research. He is widely published and has conducted workshops and seminars on a variety of topics in mathematics education.

Eric E. Karnowski received both his BS and MS from the University of Tennessee, Knoxville, teaching high school for a year between undergraduate and graduate schools. He is currently project director for the *Learning by Doing/Math Workshop* K-5 curriculum project. Earlier work included editing mathematics textbooks (middle and high school), writing on-line teacher professional development courses for *PBS TeacherLine*, and writing for the *Mathscape* middle grades curriculum and the *Problems with a Point* database.

Chapter I
What is Mathematical Investigation?

Problem posing

Conjecture

Proof *Habits of mind*

Problem solving

What if ... ?

What if not?

$$1 + 2 + 3 = 6$$

$$10 + 11 + 12 + 13 + 14 + 15 + 16 = 91$$

$$3 + 4 + 5 + 6 + 7 + 8 + 9 + 10 + 11 + 12 = 75$$

$$8 + 9 + 10 + 11 + 12 + \cdots + 107 = 5750$$

$$125 + 126 + 127 + 128 + \cdots + 2003 = 1999256$$

$$n + (n + 1) + (n + 2) + \cdots + (n + k) = 137$$

Introduction

Current mathematics curricula ask students, from time to time, to "investigate." But how does one do that?

Another question: why all the fuss about investigation? Investigation is not the only way to learn mathematics, nor even the best way in *every* situation.

The ability to investigate a situation is, in itself, an important skill for students to acquire. In mathematics—as in science, or diagnosing the ills of an automobile, a computer, or a person— proper investigation is often the first step in successful problem solving. Furthermore, investigation helps to bring to the fore an essential feature of the subject itself.

Mathematics is a specialization of many of the most powerful thinking techniques people normally use. Part of its great power derives from the facts, formulas, and techniques it provides to the sciences. What makes it of value even to those who will someday forget the facts and formulas is that it highlights, extends, and refines the kinds of thinking that people do in *all* fields. These include investigation, pattern-seeking, and proof.

Skilled investigators in any field have strategies that go beyond poking around and hoping for the best. In investigation, as in other aspects of thinking, mathematics adds its own special features. What makes an investigation *mathematical*? What's next after finding a great pattern?

In *What is Mathematical Investigation?*, you will take a mathematical investigation from start to finish—from exploratory stages through reporting logically connected results—and you will find strategies that you can use with your students to develop their investigative skills.

You might also encounter some new mathematical facts and relationships, but the real purpose is for you to investigate *investigation*.

Proof outside of mathematics is different, in ways, from proof within the discipline, but the fact that the same word is used attests to the relatedness of the many purposes of proof, and even to similarities in the ways of thinking.

1. Problem solving and problem posing

Take 10 to 15 minutes for a preliminary exploration of the problem below—just long enough to develop some initial conjectures.

Students in the first year course of the Interactive Mathematics Program (IMP) *are given three days to explore this lovely problem. You will get the chance to explore this problem in greater depth later.*

Such a tiny amount of time is not nearly adequate for a thorough look at this investigatory problem, but even 15 minutes should give you a sense of what students begin to see as they explore it. For the moment, this glimpse is enough.

In the brief time you devote to the problem now, keep track of partial answers and any new questions that may come up.

PROBLEM

1. The number 13 can be expressed as a sum of two consecutive counting numbers, $6+7$. Fourteen can be expressed as $2+3+4+5$, also a sum of consecutive counting numbers.

Positive integers go by many aliases: the counting numbers, the natural numbers, $\mathbb{Z}^+$.

THE CONSECUTIVE SUMS PROBLEM:
Can all counting numbers be expressed as the sum of two or more consecutive counting numbers? If not, which ones can?

Experiment, look for patterns, and come up with some conjectures. Write up what you find.

Remember: For now, take only 10 to 15 minutes.

Dissecting the problem

To investigate a problem well, you should get right to its heart. The first two sentences of problem 1 just say what is meant by "sum of consecutive counting numbers," and the last two sentences are merely guidance for the student. The problem's essence is in the middle two sentences:

> Can all counting numbers be expressed as the sum of two or more consecutive counting numbers? If not, which ones can?

Even this can be boiled down. The real information is:

> ... counting numbers ... expressed as sum of two or more consecutive counting numbers ...

2. Concealed within that deceptively simple boiled-down version are at least five essential features of the problem. Two are given to you. Find *at least three* others.

(a) It is about a *sum*.

(b)

(c)

(d)

This, of course, is a feature of every problem. Learning to notice what is not stated is extremely hard for everybody.

(e) There are restrictions that the problem *could* make, but *does not*. The fact that it *fails* to make more restrictions is part of what makes it *this* problem and not another.

Feature (e) may seem almost too silly to list, but it is important! For example, the problem refers to a "sum of two or more consecutive counting numbers." A more restrictive problem might ask "Which numbers can (or cannot) be expressed as a sum of exactly three consecutive counting numbers?"

This is a new *problem, and an interesting one!*

Similarly, the problem asks which numbers can be expressed at all, in any number of ways. A more specific problem might ask "Which numbers can (or cannot) be expressed in exactly one way (or two or . . .) as a sum of consecutive counting numbers?"

This is another *new and interesting problem!*

Modifying the problem

Two great problems are listed in the previous paragraphs, but they are not the only good ones that come from changing features of the original problem.

How do you decide, before investigating, which will be a worthwhile problem to pursue? Is it intuition? Experience? What goes into your decision?

3. By yourself or with others, brainstorm to see what related problems evolve from this one as you change the features one (or at most two) at a time. Write down and share this set of new problems.

4. Pick one or more of your problems and explore them just long enough to build some preliminary conjectures.

For now, take only 10 to 15 minutes. As before, you won't have enough time for a real investigation, but you should get a rough idea of what the problem has in store.

Problem-posing strategies

Problem 3 asked you to "change the features," but *how* should that be done? Are there any reliable ways to do that and get "good" problems as a result?

As you gain experience, you'll develop your own set of tricks for modifying the features of a problem, but here are four that are almost always among the most useful.

---

i. Make a feature more restrictive: If the problem is about triangles, restrict it to right (or scalene or ...) triangles. If the problem uses a calculation that involves two or more numbers, restrict it to *exactly* two (or three or ...).

This is sometimes referred to as finding special cases.

ii. Relax a feature: If the problem is about right triangles, see how it changes if you allow *all* kinds of triangles, or maybe all polygons. If the problem uses a restricted subset of numbers (e.g., only $\{1, 2, 3, \ldots\}$), see what happens when you expand that set in various ways.

This is sometimes referred to as generalizing, or extending the domain.

iii. Alter the details of a feature: If the problem concerns right triangles, see how it changes if you choose acute triangles. If the problem calls for one set of numbers (e.g., $\{1, 2, 3, \ldots\}$), try a different set (e.g., $\{1, 3, 5, 7, \ldots\}$ or $\{0, 3, 6, 9, \ldots\}$ or $\{0.5, 1, 1.5, 2, \ldots\}$). If the problem uses arithmetic operations, see what happens if you systematically alter them (e.g., substituting $+$ and $-$ for $\times$ and $\div$ or vice versa), and if it specifies equality, see what happens if you require a specific inequality (e.g., $>$).

These modifications may change the domain of a problem, or alter a parameter.

iv. Check for uniqueness: If the problem only asks *if* something can be done, ask if (or when) it can be done in *only one way*.

Asking how many ways can this be done? is often productive.

---

5. Apply these and your own rules to generate interesting variants on the following problem:

"How many triangles with perimeter 12 and integer side lengths can you construct?"

You get to be the judge of what is an interesting variant of the problem.

6. Now, go back to the CONSECUTIVE SUMS PROBLEM. Look over the list of features you made for problem 2 and see if applying these rules to each of the features gives you any new problems.

Ways to think about it

The statement of each problem (or a paraphrased version) is provided in the margin for your convenience.

THE CONSECUTIVE SUMS PROBLEM:
Can all counting numbers be expressed as the sum of two or more consecutive counting numbers? If not, which ones can? Make a conjecture.

1. Look at a lot of examples, being sure to keep track of everything — maybe make a table. Once you get a tentative conjecture, check it out with a few more examples. Remember that you're not being asked to prove anything. Carefully write down and share your observations and predictions.

Problem: *There are at least five essential features of the consecutive sums problem. One is "It is about a sum." Find at least three others.*

2. Analyze the problem statement and context. What "kind" of sum are we talking about here (what's being added)? Is the type or number of addends restricted? How about the relationship between addends?

Problem: *Brainstorm to see what related problems evolve from this one as you change the features one (or at most two) at a time.*

3. First, think of some ways you might alter the original problem to create a new one. One possibility is by adding or removing restrictions. Can you think of other alterations?

Problem: *Pick one or more of the problems you created in problem 3 and explore them just long enough to build some preliminary conjectures.*

4. As in problem 1, we're looking for conjectures, not proofs. Try some experimentation and see what you can come up with.

Problem: *Apply these and your own rules to generate interesting variants on the following problem:*
"How many triangles with perimeter 12 and integer side lengths can you construct?"

5. Go through each of the suggested ways of altering problems and see how you might modify this triangle problem.

Problem: *Now, go back to the consecutive sums problem. Look over the list of features you made for problem 2 and see if applying these rules to each of the features gives you any new problems.*

6. Did you miss anything when you modified the consecutive sum problem in problem 3?

2. You've got a conjecture. Now what?

In the first section, you investigated a rich problem about consecutive sums and explored ways to modify it and to pose new, related problems. You also worked on exploring a problem beyond its solution. In this section, you'll continue that activity. First, you'll investigate some important—and not so important—connections these modified problems lead to. Second, you'll solve the modified problems, which will lead you to an explanation and proof of the main result (the original consecutive sums problem).

Intuition and mathematical taste

When students are asked to investigate, the ideas and difficulties that arise are inevitably less predictable than when the course is all laid out for them in advance. Some problems they pose lead to unanticipated treasures. Others seem likely to take time without giving the students much in return. Without having more than a few moments to think about the problems, you may find yourself in the position of having to decide which direction to take.

Problems 1–5:

Here are several pairs of variations on the original consecutive sums problem. Look at each pair, and try to decide, *without first pursuing the problems,* which choice seems more likely to lead somewhere.

1. (a) Which numbers can be expressed as sums of consecutive prime numbers?
    (b) Which numbers can be expressed as sums of consecutive square numbers?

2. (a) Which numbers can be expressed in exactly seven ways as sums of consecutive counting numbers?
    (b) Which numbers can be expressed in exactly one way as sums of consecutive counting numbers?

3. (a) Which numbers can be expressed as products of consecutive counting numbers?
    (b) Which numbers can be expressed as differences of consecutive counting numbers?

4. (a) Which numbers can be expressed in exactly three ways as the sum of exactly three consecutive odd numbers?
    (b) Which numbers can be expressed as the sum of consecutive odd numbers?

"Without first pursuing the problems" does not mean that you cannot think about it at all. And "seems more likely to lead somewhere" does not mean "which will surely lead to interesting consequences."

Unit fractions are fractions whose numerators are 1, such as $\frac{1}{2}, \frac{1}{3}, \frac{1}{4}, \frac{1}{5}$, etc.

5. (a) Which numbers can be expressed as the sum of unit fractions with consecutive denominators?
   (b) Which numbers can be expressed as the difference of two unit fractions with consecutive denominators?

Reflect and Discuss

6. How did you make your decision in each of the previous problems? What "rules of thumb" did you use to help distinguish between problems that are probably good and ones that are probably not worthwhile?

And so do his sisters and cousins and aunts and ...

Even good problems can't all be pursued: too many problems, too little time. One way to decide among them is to think about which mathematical connections you most want to make.

Here, reminiscent of the TV game *Jeopardy!*, problems are listed by their answers, because the answers are one way of seeing potential connections to the rest of the curriculum.

PROBLEM

Here is an example of a sister-problem whose answer is on this list: "What numbers are produced as sums of exactly two consecutive counting numbers?"

7. CONSECUTIVE SUM JEOPARDY:
   In your investigations of the sisters, cousins, and aunts of the CONSECUTIVE SUMS PROBLEM, what questions (if any) have you run across which have the following sets of numbers as *answers* or partial answers? ▷
   (a) Only even numbers
   (b) Only odd numbers
   (c) Only prime numbers
   (d) Only powers of two
   (e) Only powers of three
   (f) Only multiples of 3
   (g) Only multiples of 5
   (h) Only square numbers
   (i) Differences of two square numbers
   (j) Only triangular numbers
   (k) Only differences of two triangular numbers
   (l) Only factorials
   (m) Only quotients of two factorials (permutations)

Following up a conjecture: Proof

At the beginning of an investigation, searching for a pattern is often a sensible thing to do. Unfortunately, students' investigations too often *end* when they've found one. Finding and describing an observed pattern is only the first step of an investigation. Next comes the essence of mathematical thinking: the effort to know, and show logically, that the pattern continues, why the pattern occurs, and how it logically follows from and connects with what is already known.

This is your chance to pursue an investigation beyond the first few minutes.

Following are several conjectures people have made as they investigated the CONSECUTIVE SUMS PROBLEM (and its closest cousins). Find a proof or counterexample (an example that shows the statement is not always true) for each one. These 13 problems form a path to a conclusion, so try to justify each statement. If you want some extra guidance, talk to a neighbor or your facilitator, or consult the "Ways to think about it" section beginning on page 11.

Elementary algebra is sufficient for solving these problems, but there are often ways of giving solid proofs—logical arguments, and not just appeals to pattern—that would work for fifth- or sixth- grade students who have never had algebra. See if you can find both kinds of supports.

8. The sum of two consecutive counting numbers (CCNs) is always odd.

9. The sum of three CCNs is a multiple of 3.

10. The sum of five CCNs is a multiple of 5.

11. The sum of *any* number of CCNs is a multiple of that number.

12. The sum of any odd number of CCNs is a multiple of that odd number.

13. Odd multiples of 3 (except 3 itself) can always be expressed in at least two ways as sums of CCNs.

14. Odd primes can be expressed in only one way as the sum of CCNs.

15. The sum of an odd number of CCNs can be odd or even. It will be odd if ...

Complete, then prove the given statement.

16. The sum of an even number of CCNs can be odd or even. It will be odd if ...

Complete, then prove the given statement.

17. The sum of a sequence of CCNs is a multiple of at least one of the numbers in the sequence.

18. The sum of a sequence of CCNs is a multiple of the mean of the first and last numbers in the sequence.

19. Any multiple of an odd number greater than 1 can be expressed as a sum of CCNs.

You may have already guessed where the preceding problems were leading. Even if you haven't, you should now be ready to put it all together.

If there's time, take a few minutes to organize a self-contained proof of the theorem.

20. THE CONSECUTIVE SUM THEOREM
The only numbers which can be expressed as a sum of CCNs are the multiples of an odd number greater than 1. That is, a counting number, N, is the sum of consecutive counting numbers if and only if N is not a power of 2.

Did thinking through and proving your conclusions to the statements in problems 8–19 help you understand and prove the consecutive sums problem? Are these proofs similar or different from the proofs you encounter (or expect to encounter) in your teaching? If so, how?

Students often make conjectures that turn out to be false. As their teacher, it is important not only to help them see why the conjecture is false, but also to recognize what *correct* (but perhaps incomplete) observations led them to the false conjecture.

21. For each conjecture that you determined not to be true in problems 8–19, see if you can guess what *correct, but incomplete,* observations might have led to that conjecture.

Ways to think about it

1–5. There are a lot of considerations which might affect your decision of what problem is worth pursuing. Here are some:
   - Is the problem *interesting*?
   - Are the hypotheses overly restrictive? Not restrictive enough? Just right?
   - Can you think of methods of solution (even if you don't yet know the answer) or at least ways of gaining enough information to make an educated guess?

6. What were *your* considerations? How did they compare with those of your neighbors? Although it is often difficult to recall the problem-solving process, thoughtful reflection is an important skill to develop. It will help you on the subsequent problems.

7. Think about the investigations and conjectures you made in section 1. Did any of these answers come up then? These might also arise as solutions to your modified problems from section 1. Brainstorm with other participants. If all else fails, think about how these numbers might come up as answers to modified problems, or try some more examples!

8. Since the question mentions parity (evenness and oddness), consider the parity of any two consecutive integers: What is the sum of one odd and one even number? Symbolically, what do you know about $n + (n + 1)$?

9. Be careful not to blindly trust examples. Symbolically, such a sum can be expressed in the form $n + (n + 1) + (n + 2)$ or $(n - 1) + n + (n + 1)$. Notice how the second sum is "balanced." Even though both representations lead to a proof, the second might be considered more elegant. Sometimes it's necessary look at a problem in just the right way in order to gain the insight necessary to solve it (or to find a "slick" solution).

10. Can you "balance" this sum, too? What is $n + (n+1) + (n+2) + (n+3) + (n+4)$ or $(n-2) + (n-1) + n + (n+1) + (n+2)$?

11. Can you balance *every* sum? Another important lesson: sometimes (but not always), the reason it's hard to prove a statement is that it's *false*. If you think that might be the case, look for a counterexample.

Problem: *Here are several pairs of variations on the original consecutive sums problem. Look at each pair, and try to decide, without first pursuing the problems, which choice seems more likely to lead somewhere.*

Problem: *How did you make your decision in each of the previous problems? What "rules of thumb" did you use to help distinguish between problems that are probably good and ones that are probably not worthwhile?*

CONSECUTIVE SUM JEOPARDY: *In your investigation of the Consecutive Sums Problem, what questions (if any) have you run across which have the following sets of numbers as answers or partial answers?*

Prove or disprove: *The sum of two consecutive counting numbers (CCNs) is always odd.*

Prove or disprove: *The sum of three CCNs is a multiple of 3.*

Prove or disprove: *The sum of five CCNs is a multiple of 5.*

Prove or disprove: *The sum of any number of CCNs is a multiple of that number.*

Prove or disprove: The sum of any odd number of CCNs is a multiple of that odd number.
It might help to recall that we have a formula for the sum of the first n counting numbers:
$$\sum_{i=1}^{n} i = \frac{n(n+1)}{2}.$$

Prove or disprove: Odd multiples of 3 (except for 3 itself) can always be expressed in at least two ways as sums of CCNs.

Prove or disprove: Odd primes can be expressed in only one way as the sum of CCNs.

Complete, then prove: The sum of an odd number of CCNs can be odd or even. It will be odd if . . . .

Complete, then prove: The sum of an even number of CCNs can be odd or even. It will be odd if . . . .

Prove or disprove: The sum of a sequence of CCNs is a multiple of at least one of the numbers in the sequence.

Prove or disprove: The sum of a sequence of CCNs is a multiple of the mean of the first and last numbers in the sequence.

Prove or disprove: Any multiple of an odd number greater than 1 can be expressed as a sum of CCNs.

12. Consider the significance of how many terms are being added. Some questions to consider (you will need to perform some symbolic manipulations to answer them): What does the sum of k consecutive counting numbers "look like"? If the *first* addend is m, the sum starts off as $m + (m + 1) + \cdots$. What is the *last* term? Can you rewrite (i.e., simplify or factor) this sum? Look back at problems 9 and 10 (as well as your earlier work) to determine which multiple you get.

13. What do you already know about odd numbers as sums of CCNs? (Maybe you ran across this context in session 1.) What about multiples of 3? In problems 8 and 9, you showed that the sum of 2 CCNs is odd and the sum of 3 CCNs is a multiple of 3. However, you probably didn't show that you could get *all* odds and *all* multiples of 3 that way. Can you? Try it!

14. How does the result of problem 12 help?

15. Try some examples. When do you get an odd sum? Show that your conclusion always works by using methods you developed for the previous problems.

16. Try some examples. When do you get an even sum? Show that your conclusion always works by using methods you developed for the previous problems.

17. Be sure you believe it (or not) by looking at some examples. If you're not sure, the examples might give you helpful insight into the problem. And if the statement is false, maybe you'll find a counterexample.

18. Try a "balanced" approach. How does the sum of the first and last addends compare to the sum of the second and next to last addends? Are there other equal sums? This can also be done symbolically, but you need to be very careful with the algebra. Does it matter whether the number of addends is even or odd? This affects whether or not there is a middle term in the sequence of CCNs.

19. What is the mean of the first and last addends when there is an odd number of terms? Look at some examples and show it generalizes.

20. First, note that the numbers which are not multiples of an odd number greater than 1 are the powers of 2 (1, 2, 4, 8, 16,...). In order to get an *even* sum, the number of addends must be a multiple of 4. (If you don't see why, refer to problems 12 and 16.)

21. Look back at problems 11 and 17. Can you see how someone might mistakenly think these are true? For instance, for what values of "the number" will the statement of problem 11 be true? Is there a pattern to the types of numbers for which it is true? The conclusion of problem 17 is often true. Try to determine when it works and when it doesn't (try some examples, using a variety of starting points and number of consecutive addends).

THE CONSECUTIVE SUMS THEOREM: *Prove that a counting number, N, is the sum of consecutive counting numbers if and only if N is not a power of* 2.

Problem: *For each conjecture that you determined not to be true in problems 8–19, see if you can guess what* correct, *but incomplete, observations might have led to that conjecture.*

3. Do it yourself

During the first two sections of this chapter, you investigated the Consecutive Sums Problem directly and by posing related problems, and you pursued some of the related problems through proof. The goal was to develop both a sense of how to open up a problem and create new ones, and why that is useful, even for the narrowest objective of solving the original problem.

In this section, you will get a chance to apply the same kinds of thinking to one or more new situations, creating, in the process, a whole host of new problems, some ways to investigate them, and probably even some preliminary results.

Two new contexts for investigation

Here are two situations—a problem and a theorem.

For each, list its features and then systematically vary each feature to create new, related problems, as you did in the first two sections. Then select what seem to be the more promising variations and perform a few minutes of exploration just to get a sense of what they might have in store. Then you will choose among the various problems you've worked on and take it further. For now, to exercise your skills at posing new problems that might support an in-depth investigation and get a preliminary sense of where, mathematically, those problems might lead.

Take some time to think and talk about how you might modify these problems. Refer back to section 1 for suggested strategies and don't forget about the *Ways to think about it* section beginning on page 16.

1. THE POST OFFICE PROBLEM:
   A particularly quirky post office clerk sells only 7-cent stamps and 9-cent stamps. Can exactly 32 cents' worth of postage be made using these stamps? Can 33 cents be made? Which amounts, if any, cannot be made?

2. THE PYTHAGOREAN THEOREM:
   This theorem, central to an enormous amount of mathematics, can be thought of as a statement about shapes. "The (area of the) square on the hypotenuse of a right triangle is equal to the sum of the (areas of the) squares on the two legs of that triangle."

   Alternatively, the theorem can be thought of algebraically, as a much more generic statement about the way some numbers are related. "The sum of two squares is equal to another square," is often written $a^2 + b^2 = c^2$. Of course, thinking about the theorem completely algebraically ignores what the three letters represent. Without saying either that a triangle whose sides are a, b, and c must be a *right* triangle, and that the sides of any right triangle must always bear this relationship, this is not really the Pythagorean Theorem, but just another arbitrary (if familiar-looking) equation.

The point of view you take in describing or thinking about a theorem will affect the features you choose to describe or alter the theorem.

What's next?

Once you've chosen one of the two problems, analyzed its features, and created some modifications, choose one (or one of its modifications) to investigate more deeply. If there is time available, prove (or disprove and salvage) the conjectures you make.

Ways to think about it

THE POST OFFICE PROBLEM
A particularly quirky post office clerk sells only 7-cent stamps and 9-cent stamps. Can exactly 32 cents' worth of postage be made using these stamps? Can 33 cents be made? Which amounts, if any, cannot be made?

1. Questions to consider when listing or altering the features of the problem:
   - What is the question being asked about these sums?
   - What are some restrictions it didn't make, but *could*?
   - What alternative problems can you think of? What can you *change*? Restrict? Unrestrict?

THE PYTHAGOREAN THEOREM: *This theorem, central to an enormous amount of mathematics, can be thought of as a statement about shapes. "The (area of the) square on the hypotenuse of a right triangle is equal to the sum of the (areas of the) squares on the two legs of that triangle." Alternatively, it can be thought of algebraically, as a much more generic statement about the way some numbers are related. "The sum of two squares is equal to another square," is often written $a^2 + b^2 = c^2$.*

2. Questions to consider:
   - What types of triangles are involved?
   - What happens if the shapes are changed?
   - What happens if other figures were built on the sides of the triangle? Will the relationship between areas be the same?
   - Are there triangles for which the side lengths are integers?

4. You know the answer? Prove it.

The next, and perhaps most important, aspect of the problem-solving process is proof. Oftentimes, the rationale given for the necessity of proof is that you don't really know that your solution (or conjecture) is correct until you've proven it. While that may be true in a strict mathematical sense, it's usually the case that you don't sit down to prove something until you *know* that it is true. In classes, for instance, a common assignment is to have students prove that a given statement is true (i.e., that two given triangles are congruent). There seems to be no problem solving, since they are told that the triangles are congruent. For this reason, students often think that proof is something separate from problem solving. So, instead of thinking of proof as necessary to show *that* something is true, let's think of it as helping us understand *why* it is true and giving us insight into what else might be true. In fact, the construction of a proof is a form of problem solving itself.

Learning to write proofs can be a difficult process. One of the reasons for this is that most of us don't have much experience with reading—and understanding—written proofs. Well-written proofs can serve as useful examples for someone who wants to write his or her own proof. Even though you shouldn't think of one proof as a *template* for another, the main ideas of proofs are often the same: Start with the given information, from which you draw conclusions based on what you know, aiming toward the final conclusion, which is what you wanted to prove.

In this session, you will read and critique several different attempts at proving a fact that may have come up in earlier sessions (that the sum of the first n counting numbers is $\frac{n(n+1)}{2}$). Keep an eye out for convincing arguments which leave no doubt that the statements are correct (as well as for arguments that are less convincing). You will also tinker with and modify the alleged proofs. Your tinkering will be another version of the *Variations on a Theme* theme, aiming at modifying these arguments to prove some new facts.

By no means is proof the end of problem solving. As George Pólya said, "Even fairly good students, when they have obtained the solution of the problem and written down neatly the argument, shut their books and look for something else. Doing so, they miss an important and instructive phase of the work. ... A good teacher should understand and impress on his students the view that no problem whatever is completely exhausted. There remains always something to do; with sufficient study and penetration, we could improve any solution, and, in any case, we can always improve our understanding of the solution."—How to Solve It, 2nd ed., Princeton University Press, 1945, pp. 14-15

Four proofs for the price of one

If you are not familiar with $\sum$ notation, try to come up with your own definition of this symbol based on what you know about the problem.

There are many ways in which the sum of the first n counting numbers was connected to the CONSECUTIVE SUMS PROBLEM. Below are four proposed proofs of the conjecture:

$$\textbf{Conjecture:} \ \sum_{k=1}^{n} k = \frac{n(n+1)}{2}$$

1. As you read each alleged proof, do the following:

    (a)   Decide whether the argument is a genuine, acceptable proof. If you feel it is not, fix it.

    (b)   Rewrite the argument to make it fit a conjecture about the sums of consecutive *odd* numbers starting at 1.

    (c)   What if the numbers were not consecutive counting numbers but, say, consecutive multiples of 3, or not starting at 1, or . . .

You know the game now. What if things were different? But as you change things, be careful not to destroy the essential elements of the structure of the original proofs. Then your new statements will be new proofs.

Do you see why this proof attempt is divided into two cases? How does the argument in case 1 fail when n is odd?

Proof Attempt i: We'll consider two cases.

Case 1: Suppose n is even. Then we can rearrange the terms to create pairs like this

$$[1+n] + [2+(n-1)] + [3+(n-2)] + \ldots$$

Each of the pairs adds up to $n+1$, and there are $\frac{n}{2}$ pairs. So, in this case, the sum is $(n+1)\frac{n}{2} = \frac{n(n+1)}{2}$.

Case 2: Suppose n is odd. Then $n-1$ is even, so we can use the formula for the sum $T = 1 + 2 + \cdots + (n-1)$, and we get $T = \frac{(n-1)n}{2}$.

$$[1 + 2 + \cdots + (n-1)] + n = T + n = \frac{(n-1)n}{2} + n,$$

which simplifies to $\frac{n(n+1)}{2}$.

QED is an abbreviation for "quod erat demonstrandum," which is Latin for "which was to be demonstrated."

Either way, the sum is $\frac{n(n+1)}{2}$.   **QED**

Proof Attempt ii: Define $1 + 2 + \cdots + n = S$. Of course, it doesn't matter what order I add these integers, so it's also true that $n + (n - 1) + \ldots + 1 = S$. Now place these two sums in rows and add "column-wise":

$$
\begin{array}{ccccccccccc}
 & 1 & + & 2 & + & \cdots & + & n-1 & + & n & & = S \\
+ & n & + & n-1 & + & \cdots & + & 2 & + & 1 & & = S \\
\hline
 & n+1 & + & n+1 & + & \cdots & + & n+1 & + & n+1 & & = 2S
\end{array}
$$

As each of the upper rows is S, the bottom row—their sum—is $2S$. But that bottom row also shows that $2S$ is the sum of n terms, each of which is $(n + 1)$.

In other words, $2S = n(n + 1)$, so $S = \frac{n(n+1)}{2}$.   **QED**

Proof Attempt iii: This attempt tries to use proof by mathematical induction.

Suppose you find *some* number for which the conjecture is true. This must be a *particular* number, like 43, for which you can verify the conjecture, perhaps using a calculator.

Let's call that number m.

$$1 + 2 + \cdots + (m - 1) + m = \frac{m(m + 1)}{2}.$$

Adding $m + 1$ to both sides of this equation, we get

$$1 + 2 + \cdots + (m - 1) + m + (m + 1) = \frac{m(m + 1)}{2} + (m + 1).$$

Using algebra to simplify the above equation, we see that

$$1 + 2 + \cdots + (m - 1) + m + (m + 1) = \frac{(m + 1)(m + 2)}{2}.$$

This is what we get if we substitute $m + 1$ for n. What this says is that if we already *know* that the conjecture is true for a given m, then we can be certain it is also true for $m + 1$.

We know that the conjecture is true for 43—we presumably checked that—so now we know that it must be true for 44. And then 45. And 46. And 47. And so on, forever.

What about 1 through 42? Our proof applies only to numbers *after* the one we checked. So let's start at $n = 1$. The conjecture says that 1 should equal $\frac{1 \cdot 2}{2}$, which it does, so the

We omit algebraic steps in this (and the next) proof. Fill in whatever steps you feel are important.

Even though the number is particular, we name it generically to help us see if the conjecture will generalize to numbers other than 43. So, in the new statement, we substitute m, not 43, for n.

Again, we may think 44, but we write $(m + 1)$ so that "the next number" is generic.

By doing the calculation generically, we have shown that if the conjecture is known to be true for any m, like 44, we know it is true for the next number.

conjecture is true when $n = 1$ But then (thinking of m as 1) we know that the conjecture must also be true for $n = 2$. But this implies that the conjecture is true when $n = 3$, so it's true when $n = 4$, so it's true when $n = 5 \ldots$. This process will continue forever, so we may conclude that the conjecture for all counting numbers, n.   **QED**

Proof Attempt iv: Represent the sum $S = \sum\limits_{k=1}^{n} k$ as the area of a stairstep figure like the one shown below (Pictures are *always* particular. In this one, $n = 6$, but the *argument* works for any n—*imagine* what the figure would look like in the general case).

Now fit a duplicate of the figure on top of the original, as shown below (left), to complete the $n \times (n + 1)$ rectangle shown in the figure on the right.

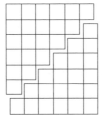   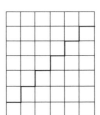

As in proof 2 above, we see that $2S = n(n + 1)$, so $S = \frac{n(n+1)}{2}$, as conjectured.   **QED**

Life after proof

You have developed or encountered several conjectures, including the one that answers the original problem—which numbers can be made?—and you have even proved them. What else is there to a mathematical investigation?

Sometimes, all that is needed is a careful re-organization of what you know into a form that can be presented coherently.

Sometimes, in the course of organizing what you know, you see that the mathematical investigation is really not quite over, and that you *might* want to map the territory more fully, take some side excursions, or fill in some gaps.

How do you choose the direction in which to guide your students? That depends partly on the students and what they've already done, partly on your goals for your class, partly on what else is competing for the time, and partly on the mathematics itself. This fact—the fact that, when students investigate, your own decision making depends partly on the mathematics—places extra demands on you to know not only the central point of the investigation, but all of its cousins and aunts.

Sometimes, putting more time into a problem has such great payoff—either in the mathematical learning or the discipline of pursuing a problem deeply—that it may be worth sacrificing other important things for it. But sometimes there's little more to be gained, and it is time to move on. *Nobody* knows in advance every mathematical problem's cousins and aunts and best-hidden secrets, so it pays to play with the problems a bit— much as you have here—and see what's beneath their surface.

Presenting a mathematical investigation can also be extremely valuable to your students. Partly, it is one contributor to the development of their ability to communicate. Most students will not need to discuss mathematical investigations, per se, for much of their lives, but mathematics, as a technical subject, *is* an ideal place to begin honing the skills of technical communication. And, the fact is that an increasing number of people do have to write and speak about technical matters. A further benefit of learning to do this in mathematics is that math is not *just* a technical subject, but a discipline that is about thinking. Learning to present a mathematical investigation is, in part, learning to express clearly a line of reasoning.

2. Enough of the pep talk. Now it's your turn. You have generated many problems and partial or complete results to some of them (in this section, as well as earlier ones). Pick one, or a group of closely related ones, and organize a presentation of your work to share with other members of your class or workshop (or just for your own intellectual satisfaction).

Ways to think about it

*Problem: As you read each alleged proof, do the following: (a) Decide whether the argument is a genuine, acceptable proof. If you feel it is not, fix it.
(b) Rewrite the argument to make it fit a conjecture about the sums of consecutive odd numbers starting at 1.
(c) What if the numbers were not consecutive counting numbers but, say, consecutive multiples of 3, or not starting at 1, or ...*

1.   In answering part (a), ask yourself whether you understand and agree with each statement. It's OK if you have to ponder some statements or even work out the details to convince yourself that the statements are true. However, it should be relatively straightforward to work them out.

In part (b), try to maintain the structure of the particular proof you're adapting to the odd consecutive integer case. Which features of the proof will change due to your focus on odd numbers? Which will remain the same? When writing a proof, you need to keep a number of things in mind. One of them is exactly what audience you're writing for. You might not write the same proof for your students that you would write for a college course, for example. Some questions to ask yourself are: *What assumptions can I make about what the readers already know and are able to do? Will the readers of this proof follow each explanation? If not, should I provide more details, or can I assume that the readers will work on it themselves?*

In part (c), you don't have to answer the specific questions (about multiples of 3 or not starting at 1), although these are perfectly reasonable problems to solve. What are *you* interested in solving?

Problem: You have generated many problems and partial or complete results to some of them (in this session, as well as earlier ones). Pick one, or a group of closely related ones, and organize a presentation of your work.

2.   Your presentation can include both your methods and your results, but, to feel coherent, its *focus* should probably be on only one or the other: the facts you found or the path you took in finding them. Each has its purpose. You need to decide which story you are telling.

If you decide to focus on the way you found the facts, the story will probably be richest if it includes the false starts, dead ends, unexpected discoveries, and other *unplanned* elements along with the deliberate strategies and methods. This is not because a confession of one's foibles is good for the soul, but because discovery in real life is rarely a smooth path. Success is often a combination of very good planning, and very opportunistic and intelligent use of serendipity. A focus on results need not tell all this—a clear, logically structured exposition is enough. A story about discovery should tell what the discovery was like.

Checklist: Have you stated what the driving question was? The related subquestions? Reasoning and proofs? The actual results? The implications or connections?

5. Discerning what *is*; predicting what *might be*

The methods of statistics provide mathematical investigations that are just different enough to justify separate focus in this section. Statistical ideas permeate modern adult life: the news is often presented with statistics of various sorts, and many jobs depend on or communicate through statistical methods. Even middle- and high-school students are increasingly faced with information and representations of that information that cannot be well understood without some grounding in the ideas, methods, and representational techniques of statistics. Without such grounding, people are likely to misunderstand (or entirely miss) reliable and truthful information that they need, and are also vulnerable to being misled by the faulty or fraudulent use of "data." While it's true that "numbers don't lie," it's also true that data can be presented (intentionally and unintentionally) in ways that cause incorrect or incomplete conclusions. This section only barely begins to investigate the nature of statistical investigation. We hope that this brief taste will spur you to further curiosity and investigation on your own.

The technique affects the message

Statistics is often portrayed as a collection of techniques for revealing subtle patterns and true meanings in what would otherwise remain a seemingly inchoate mass of numbers. It cooks the raw data and brings out the flavors.

In fact, like real cooking, the flavor depends not only on the raw ingredients, but also on the cooking process itself. The patterns are not "in" the data, but come from an interaction between the data and the technique used to process those data.

This is not just the old message that improper uses of statistics produce (accidentally or deliberately) misleading results. *All* uses of *any* technique for organizing or massaging data reveal a picture that is influenced partly by the data and partly by the technique. For this reason, it is important to understand the influences that the most basic and common techniques exert— how these do more than "reveal" what is "inherent" in the data.

In this first session, you will pry into the hidden lives of the most elementary statistical processes—visual representation of "unprocessed" data, the three most common measures of central tendency, and the very notion of boiling down a set of data. This hard-hitting exposé will reveal all. You may learn nothing new

about how to *perform* these techniques, but you are likely to see something new about their personalities.

Some of the problems you will solve are bad news, mathematically speaking—statistical questions that should never be asked. But because they are paraphrases or subtle variants of commonly encountered problems, the features that make them bad news are important to recognize and understand.

Stem-and-leaf plots and histograms

1. Work through problem **A** below. Also, decide:
   (a) which items (if any) seem to require little more than using definitions and procedures (how to read a stem-and-leaf plot, how to compute a mean, and so on);
   (b) which items (if any) require some judgment, as well;
   (c) which items (if any) are ambiguous or meaningless.

The stem-and-leaf plot takes raw data—in this case, ages—and "plots" them. The top row shows that four people in their thirties entered the store during that 15-minute period: ages 33, 34, 38, and 39. The bottom row records three children under 10.

A. To help decide what kinds of items to keep in stock, a store kept track of the ages of its customers. This stem-and-leaf plot shows the data for one 15-minute period.

```
3 | 3  4  8  9
2 | 5  8  8  8  8  8  9  9  9
1 | 0  1  1  1  2  2  3  4  4
0 | 6  7  8
```

(1) How many people entered the store during that 15 minutes?

(2) Which is the most common age group?

(3) Five customers were the same age. How old were they?

(4) Is 25 a typical age for a customer?

What could be more innocent than these questions? Part **A4** may be a bit ambiguous—it's hard to answer without knowing exactly what's meant by "typical"—but the others seem quite straightforward. Parts **A1** and **A3** test whether a person knows how to read stem-and-leaf plots. This is just convention: Either you know what this representation is intended to mean, or you don't; no real mathematical reasoning is involved.

Part **A2** also seems straightforward, but this time there's something lurking beneath the surface. To see what that is, do the following two problems.

2. Plot the data as histograms in these two ways.

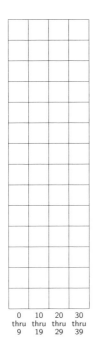

0   10   20   30
thru thru thru thru
9   19   29   39

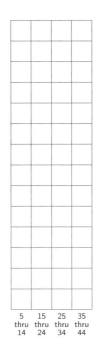

5   15   25   35
thru thru thru thru
14   24   34   44

These two graphs are inspired by applying a "what-if-not" (or WIN) strategy to the features of stem-and-leaf plots.

The WIN strategy systematically asks what happens if characteristics of a problem or situation—in this case, a stem-and-leaf plot—are varied. What features of the stem-and-leaf plot are altered in each of these graphs?

Of course, the WIN strategy begins by asking what are the features of a situation. List some characteristics of a stem-and-leaf plot.

Reflect and Discuss

3. What patterns of customer ages are "revealed" in these two histograms, and what inference might you draw about the clientele of the store based on each pattern? Which corresponds to the stem-and-leaf plot? What, if anything, about the data might you use to help decide which pattern better reflects the Truth about the store's customers?

Stem-and-leaf plots are often used to give a quick sense of the "shape" of the data, so that we can infer what that shape might tell about the data. But because problem **A** gives you only the numbers, and no information about the store to help you interpret those numbers, the question "What might that shape let you infer about the store's clientele?" is a bad question.

Surgeon General's Warning: Interpreting data from the numbers alone may be hazardous to your conclusions. To minimize the risks, try more than one appropriate way to analyze the numbers, and be sure to know as much as possible about the context from which the numbers were drawn.

The main purpose of this problem set is to show you the hazards of using statistical techniques when you have no theory about the context that the statistical techniques are testing.

4.   The box below contains another problematic problem. Like in the previous problem, as you work through it, decide:
(a) which items (if any) seem to require nothing more than definitions and procedures;
(b) which items (if any) require some judgment, as well;
(c) which items (if any) are ambiguous or meaningless.

This stem-and-leaf plot might start out like this:

```
15 | 0  2  2
14 |
13 |
12 |
11 |
10 |
```

B. Students recorded their weights to the nearest pound as they tried out for the school's track team. This is the full list: 138, 103, 135, 115, 143, 105, 112, 115, 125, 150, 125, 120, 101, 152, 149, 152, 137, 114, 119, 128, 125, 104, 110, 108, 144, 115, 144, 125, 133, 136, 144, 117, 125, 132.

(1) Make a stem-and-leaf plot to display these weights.

(2) Find the mean, median, mode, and range of these data.

(3) Describe a pattern you see in the data.

5.   Again, after working through all parts of problems **B** and **4**, make histograms in the two ways called for below.

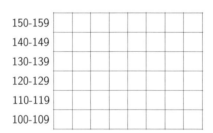

Horizontal histogram by decade   Horizontal histogram by rounding

6.   What do the histograms "reveal" about the data?

7.   What do these experiments reveal about *histograms*?

Parameters of a histogram

Problem 9 identifies a second feature of histograms, and applies the WIN strategy to vary it.

As you have seen, stem-and-leaf plots are essentially histograms made in a very particular way. You have seen a couple of trivial variations on the theme of histogram—they can be horizontal or vertical, and the "frequency" can be represented by shaded boxes (the graph-like form) or by digits to the right of a vertical line (the stem-and-leaf form).

You have also seen variations that one might superficially expect to be equally trivial but, on closer inspection, turn out to have consequences that really matter.

8. Problem 5 asked you to make two histograms. A change in one parameter distinguished the two histograms. What was varied?

Interval width—the range of values in any bar of the graph or row of the stem-and-leaf plot—is another feature of histograms. That was kept constant in the four histograms you've just done.

In the plots you've made, the interval width was always 10.

9. Experiment with this parameter *in your head*. When altering this parameter—making intervals narrower or wider—how does it affect the visual pattern you see?

If you have appropriate graphing software, try varying the interval width on a histogram of a large data set. Fathom^{TM} is a particularly intriguing tool to use for this experiment, as it allows you to change the interval width dynamically, and watch the results as you push or pull on the width of the bars. There are also a number of applets available on the Internet. Try a search with keywords `histogram applet`*.*

Reflect and Discuss

10. Is there a way to determine the "right" interval width for a particular data set?

The Meaning of Mean ... (and Mode, and Median...)

Problem **B2** (on page 26) asked you to find the mean, median, mode, and range of the data. These four measures of a data set are among the simplest to calculate and understand, but they, too, have properties that are important, yet can be hard to notice.

11. Here are three ways a student might think about the request to "find the mode" in problem **B2**. Each answer is based on a different interpretation of "find the mode." What interpretation leads to each answer? What is *correct* about each interpretation?
(a)   The mode is 125.
(b)   The mode is "110 to 119."
(c)   People's actual weights can't have a mode.

12. Suppose that the weights had been recorded to the nearest tenth of a pound, instead of to the nearest pound. Further suppose that the mean, median, mode, and range were calculated with these new, more accurate data. By how much, *at the very most*, could each of the measures differ from the ones computed with the nearest-pound data?

13. A shoe store owner keeps a record of sizes as each purchase is made and wishes to use this list to help decide what sizes to stock. Which, if any, of the following measures might be most helpful in making this decision? Explain.
(a) mean   (b) median
(c) mode   (d) range
(e) midrange (halfway between the extremes)

14. For each of the five measures in problem 13, invent a context and question for which that measure is better suited to answering the question than the others. Explain why it's the best.

This comes from Ruma Falk's Understanding Probability and Statistics *(Wellesley, MA: A.K. Peters, 1993). The entire book is a collection of wonderful problems.*

15. Create a set of 8 numbers that will simultaneously satisfy these requirements:
- mean: 10
- median: 9
- mode: 7
- range: 15

16. Eleven servers at a restaurant collect their individual tips in a pocket of their uniforms. At the end of the evening, they dump their pockets into a single bucket and share that money equally. Describe the computation that tells how much each person receives.

17. The eleven servers want a measure of the extent of the inequity of the tipping. What computation might they perform before dumping their pockets into the bucket?

18. The Franklin Knight and Arthur C. Morrow middle schools decided to report the mean score their seventh grade students achieved on a district-wide math test. The mean score of the students who go to Knight was 86; the students who go to Morrow achieved a mean of 82. Under what circumstances could the combined mean of these two schools be anything other than 84? Give a specific example and compute the correct mean for your example.

19. If all you know is that the *median* scores of students at two schools are 86 and 82, what, if anything, can you say about the *median* score of all the students at the two schools?

20. If all of the students in Morrow improve their scores by one point, what happens to the mean score for that school? What happens to the median score?

21. If the top quarter of the students in Morrow all improve their scores by 16 points, what happens to the mean score for that school? What happens to the median score?

Ways to think about it

1. Problem **A** is copied below for your convenience:

> **A.** To help decide what kinds of items to keep in stock, a store kept track of the ages of its customers. This stem-and-leaf plot shows the data for one 15-minute period.
>
> ```
> 3 | 3  4  8  9
> 2 | 5  8  8  8  8  8  9  9  9
> 1 | 0  1  1  1  2  2  3  4  4
> 0 | 6  7  8
> ```
>
> **(1)** How many people entered the store during that 15 minutes?
> **(2)** Which is the most common age group?
> **(3)** Five customers were the same age. How old were they?
> **(4)** Is 25 a typical age for a customer?

Problem: Work through problem **A**. Also, decide:
i. which items seem to require little more than using definitions and procedures;
ii. which items require some judgment, as well;
iii. which items are ambiguous or meaningless.

Remember, in addition to answering the questions given in problem **A**, you are to analyze the types of questions being asked. What assumptions are you making? Sometimes, these assumptions alter an otherwise ambiguous question–are you making any assumptions that aren't implied by the problem statement or context? Could you make different, but still reasonable, assumptions?

3. Does your answer to the question "What is the most common age group?" depend on the histogram used? Did this surprise you? Which histogram is just a rotation of the stem-and-leaf plot? Does determining which histogram better reflects the "truth" depend on any additional assumptions? If so, what are they? Since we often can't avoid making assumptions, we must at least acknowledge when we do, in order to know whether our conclusions make sense.

Problem: What patterns of customer ages are "revealed" in these two histograms, and what inference might you draw about the clientele of the store based on each pattern? Which corresponds to the stem-and-leaf plot? What, if anything, about the data might you use to help decide which pattern better reflects the Truth about the store's customers?

4. Problem **B** is copied below for your convenience:

> **B.** Students recorded their weights to the nearest pound as they tried out for the school's track team. This is the full list: 138, 103, 135, 115, 143, 105, 112, 115, 125, 150, 125, 120, 101, 152, 149, 152, 137, 114, 119, 128, 125, 104, 110, 108, 144, 115, 144, 125, 133, 136, 144, 117, 125, 132.
> **(1)** Make a stem-and-leaf plot to display these weights.
> **(2)** Find the mean, median, mode, and range of these data.
> **(3)** Describe a pattern you see in the data.

Problem: The box contains another problematic problem. Again, as you work through it, decide:
i. which items seem to require nothing more than definitions and procedures;
ii. which items require some judgment, as well;
iii. which items are ambiguous or meaningless.

Of course, this is very similar to problem 1. In what ways is it different? As before, be aware of your assumptions, and whether or not they are necessary.

Problem: What do the histograms "reveal" about the data?

Problem: What do the histograms reveal about histograms*?*

Problem: Problem 5 asked you to make two histograms. A change in one parameter distinguished the two histograms. What was varied?

Problem: Experiment with this parameter *in your head. When altering this parameter—making intervals narrower or wider—how does it affect the visual pattern you see?*

Problem: Is there a way to determine the "right" interval width for a particular data set?

Problem: Here are three ways a student might think about the request to "find the mode" in problem **B2**. *Each answer is based on a different interpretation of "find the mode." What interpretation leads to each answer? What* is correct *about each interpretation?*
(a) The mode is 125.
(b) The mode is 110 to 119.
(c) People's actual weights can't have a mode.

6. Does one of the histograms reveal the "truth" better than the other, or do you need to know something more?

7. Are histograms "bias-free," or do the choices you make in setting up the histogram affect the meaning that can be drawn from the histogram?

8. One way to answer "What is varied?" is to look for what remains the same. Looking for "invariants" is an important habit of mind to use in mathematical investigation. By learning what doesn't change, you can better find (and focus on) what does change.

9. Think first about extreme cases. *What if* the intervals were very wide? (How wide is possible?) What is the smallest the interval width can be? What can you say about varying interval width in the intermediate cases? Try a few variations of width and see what changes in the visual representation of the data will result.

10. Is there such a thing as the "right" width for a given set of data? If so, what properties would determine whether you found the right width? Be sure to make all of your assumptions explicit. Will the width choice always affect the interpretation?

11. Try to put yourself in the mind of the student. Alternatively, perhaps you, or someone you know, interpreted the problem in this way. What were you thinking about that led you to the stated conclusion? Remember to look for what is *correct* about each answer.

12. First, determine by what amount each measurement could have varied, then figure out how much of an effect that has on the calculations of mean, median, mode, and range. It might help to consider extreme cases (maximum and minimum) first, but it's important to consider other, intermediate, cases as well.

Problem: Suppose that the weights had been recorded to the nearest tenth of a pound, instead of to the nearest pound. Further suppose that the mean, median, mode, and range were calculated with these new, more accurate data. By how much, at the very most, could each of the measures differ from the ones computed with the nearest-pound data?

13. In each case, try to imagine what information could be gleaned from the calculation. Is it useful information for the stated context?

Problem: A shoe store owner keeps a record of sizes as each purchase is made and wishes to use this list to help decide what sizes to stock. Which, if any, of the following measures might be most helpful in making this decision? Explain.
(a) mean; (b) median;
(c) mode; (d) range;
(e) midrange

14. You'll probably have to choose a context other than the shoe store (or at least needing to know which shoe sizes to keep in stock). Think carefully about exactly what each of the calculations measures in order to find contexts that fit the measure. Don't forget to explain why the measure is best for the stated context.

Problem: For each of the five measures in problem 13, invent a context and question for which that measure is better suited to answering the question than the others. Explain why it's the best.

15. There are many ways to pursue this. Is it possible to plan out the choice of the numbers in advance, or should you start with some numbers, then change them, if necessary, in order to meet the requirements of the problem. Think about what each of the quantities measures. If your eight numbers have a mean of 11, how can you change one of the numbers so that the set will have a mean of 10? Try experimenting with altering a single number, keeping track of the effect on each of the measures. Is it possible to change a number in order to fix one measure, but leave the other measures unchanged?

Problem: Create a set of 8 numbers that will simultaneously satisfy these requirements: mean= 10; median= 9; mode= 7; range= 15.

Problem: Eleven servers at a restaurant collect their individual tips in a pocket of their uniforms. At the end of the evening, they dump their pockets into a single bucket and share that money equally. Describe the computation that tells how much each person receives.

Problem: The eleven servers want a measure of the extent of the inequity of the tipping. What computation might they perform before dumping their pockets into the bucket?

Problem: The Franklin Knight and Arthur C. Morrow middle schools decided to report the mean score their seventh-grade students achieved on a district-wide math test. The mean score of the students who go to Knight was 86; the students who go to Morrow achieved a mean of 82. Under what circumstances could the combined mean of these two schools be anything other than 84? Give a specific example and compute the correct mean for your example.

Problem: If all you know is that the median scores of students at two schools are 86 and 82, what, if anything, can you say about the median score of all the students at the two schools?

Problem: If the top quarter of the students in Morrow all improve their scores by 16 points, what happens to the mean score for that school? What happens to the median score?

16. Start by thinking about how you would informally do this if you were one of the servers. If you introduce notation, be sure to explain the meaning so that your answer is clear to everyone.

17. What is meant by "inequity" in this case? Under what circumstances should one server get more (or less) of the tips than another? How can you change the tip distribution so that fairness is restored?

18. Think about this abstractly first, then try some sample data sets. Be careful to avoid unjustified assumptions. For example, you don't have to assume that the scores are distributed systematically. Also, since the two classes are in two different schools, you shouldn't assume that the score distributions are similar, nor should you assume that the two classes have the same number of students. As suggested before, consider some extreme cases.

19. Must the median of the two classes' scores be between 82 and 86? Could it be *exactly* 82 or 86? Could it be smaller than 82 or greater than 86? How do you know? Look at some examples, being sure to consider extreme cases, if you're not sure. Once you've got an idea of what the answer is, try to carefully explain the reasons you know your answers are correct.

21. Does your answer depend on the results of the other students? Is there a minimum or maximum amount by which the mean will increase, or does that depend on the other students' results, too?

Chapter II

Dissections and Area

1. Be a mathematical cut-up

People have different understandings of *area*. As you work through this section, you might think about the areas of the figures you encounter and how you would calculate them.

PROBLEM

1. THE HORSE PROBLEM
Using the horse's tail as a unit—a square of side 1—find the area (the black parts) of the horse below.

2. (a) Find a way to cut this parallelogram into pieces that can be rearranged to form a rectangle.

   (b) Provide an exact description of the steps you've made. Ask someone else (a classmate, colleague, friend, or relative) to follow this description to test its accurateness.

The mathematician Han Sah, who did important and recent research in this area, called two figures "scissors congruent" if one could be cut apart and reassembled to make the other. This problem asks you to find a rectangle that is "scissors congruent" to the parallelogram.

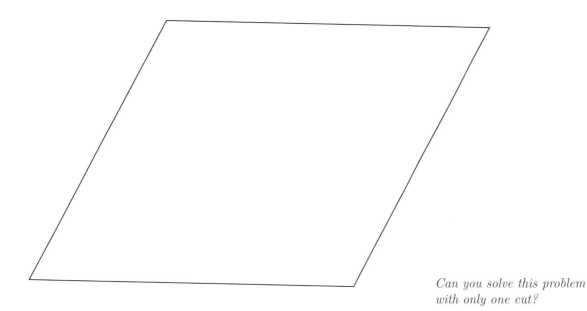

Can you solve this problem with only one cut?

It's important to be able to carefully and accurately explain your methods and the reasons they produce the intended construction. When describing your steps, you might find it helpful to label vertices and any other points on the figure that you use.

If you present your solution to others, be sure to explain how you know that the resulting figure is a rectangle.

How can you explain why the following is true? "If you can dissect a figure into a parallelogram, then you can dissect it into a rectangle."

3. Find a way to dissect this triangle into pieces that will form a parallelogram. Describe your steps.

1. If you were using this problem with your students, what would you like them to learn from it?

2. If you were using this problem with your students, how might you modify this problem or create an additional problem to extend the thinking involved?

4. (a) Dissect this trapezoid so that the pieces form a rectangle. Describe your steps.

(b) Analyze your procedure and prove that your final figure is a rectangle.

When you're proving what shape a final figure is, pretend your cuts are exact, even though that's not really possible.

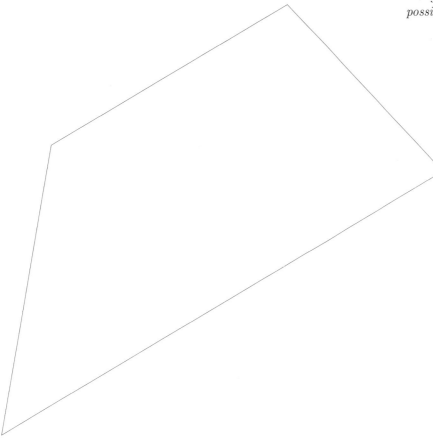

Reflect and Discuss

5. Were any of the strategies you used when you dissected the parallelogram, triangle, and trapezoid the same (or similar)? If you didn't use similar strategies, try to modify one of your strategies and apply it to a different type of polygon.

6. Devise an algorithm that will turn a parallelogram, triangle, or trapezoid into a rectangle.

7. One student gave the following solution for cutting a parallelogram into a rectangle. It seems to work perfectly, but there are times when it fails. Try to find this subtle failure. What would you say to this student?

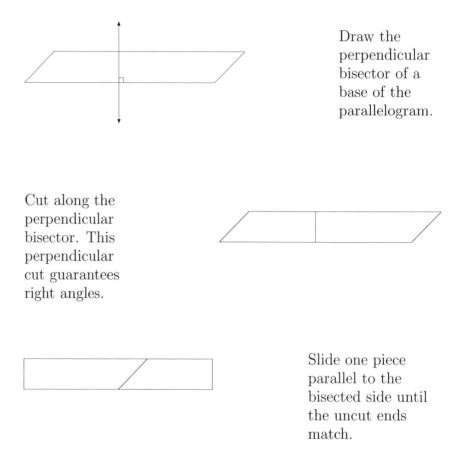

Draw the perpendicular bisector of a base of the parallelogram.

Cut along the perpendicular bisector. This perpendicular cut guarantees right angles.

Slide one piece parallel to the bisected side until the uncut ends match.

The sides *will* match—the properties of parallelograms guarantee that opposite sides must be congruent and adjacent angles will sum to 180°.

8. Look back over problems 2–7. How does the area of each initial figure compare to the area of the final figure?

Reflect and Discuss

To answer problem 8, you probably made the following critical assumption. Is this a reasonable assumption?

> **Assumption: Area is invariant under dissection.** If a figure is dissected and the parts are rearranged, the area of the new figure will be the same as the area of the original.

9. One of the big questions of this chapter is whether the converse of this assumption can be made. Is it reasonable to assume this?

> **Assumption's converse: Equidecomposability of polygons.** If two rectilinear (straight-sided) figures have the same area, it is always possible to cut either figure into a finite number of pieces and reassemble the pieces to form the other figure.

Ways to think about it

For your convenience, the problems are restated in the margin.

THE HORSE PROBLEM:
Using the horse's tail as a unit, find the area of the horse.

Problem: Find a way to cut this parallelogram into pieces that can be rearranged to form a rectangle.

Problem: Find a way to dissect this triangle into pieces that will form a parallelogram. Describe your steps.

Problem: Dissect this trapezoid so that the pieces form a rectangle.

Problem: Were any of the strategies you used when you dissected the parallelogram, triangle, and trapezoid the same (or similar)? If you didn't use similar strategies, try to modify one of your strategies and apply it to a different type of polygon.

Problem: Devise an algorithm that will turn a parallelogram, triangle, or trapezoid into a rectangle.

Problem: One student gave the following solution for cutting a parallelogram into a rectangle. Try to find this subtle failure.

1. One way to solve the problem is to cut the picture into pieces and compare the areas of the pieces to the square that forms the tail.

2. Make a cut that will create two right angles.

3. Make a cut with a line parallel to one of the sides.

4. Draw a line parallel to the bases of the trapezoid.

5. If necessary, look back over the work of previous problems. Alternatively, think about the problems again and see if you can apply similar strategies to their solutions.

6. Use the results and strategies of the previous problem to see if you can devise a general algorithm. Is it possible to "cycle" from one shape to another?

7. Can you draw a perpendicular in such a way that it does not intersect both bases? Consider parallelograms of different shapes.

2. Making assumptions, checking procedures

This entire chapter examines both a mathematical *topic* (area) and a mathematical *method* (analyzing various mathematical objects and processes). The first section, for example, focused on inventing and analyzing an algorithm for dissecting a figure into a rectangle. In this section, you will analyze your assumptions and derive area formulas based on dissection algorithms.

In the first section, you probably made an assumption that seemed reasonable enough: Cutting a figure and rearranging the pieces doesn't change its area.

Obvious restrictions apply: All pieces must be used, no overlaps are allowed, and a finite number of cuts must be used.

One important question to ask about making assumptions is, "What is reasonable?" Many people—including probably most students at some stage in their learning—find it reasonable to assume that rearranging a fixed amount of perimeter also leaves area unchanged. What is "reasonable" or "intuitively obvious," it would seem, depends on what you already believe at the time.

1. It is fairly easy to show that the commonly held assumptions "roughly equivalent perimeter corresponds to roughly equivalent area" and "greater perimeter means greater area" are false. But is it *unreasonable* for someone to make these assumptions?

History tells of times and places where the perimeter of a city or plot of land was used as the official and accepted measure of its size for taxing, exchange, and so on.

(a) First, find an example that would make clear to the average 8-year-old (don't use formulas) that this assumption is false: that two fields with the same perimeter do not necessarily have even close to the same area, and that if field *A* has greater perimeter than field *B*, it does not follow that it must also have greater area.

(b) On the other hand, there are commonplace situations in which *longer around* does reliably mean *bigger inside,* and these help explain why people tend intuitively to link area and perimeter. Describe the conditions under which this popular notion really is true.

Problem 1 (a) asked you to find convincing evidence that a reasonable-sounding assumption was wrong, and to trust the evidence over the intuition. The following famous construction works in the opposite direction. It provides a concrete example that seems to fly in the face of intuition, and yet virtually anybody—with or without a background in mathematics—is so strongly wedded to their intuitive sense of what *should* be that, instead of trusting the evidence in front of their eyes, they find it baffling, or even magical, and start looking for the trick!

Nicholas Falletta's book The Paradoxicon *is full of examples of situations that seem to work this way.*

In the Further Exploration *materials, you will find problems that will help you to create similar paradoxes and that you can use with your students for fun and learning.*

Lewis Carroll, author of Alice in Wonderland *and* Through the Looking Glass, *was a mathematician with a strong interest in logic and logical puzzles. The puzzle shown here is said to have been one of his favorites.*

With some work, you can find a geometric explanation for the "paradox" raised by the following construction, but the real question is why people find this construction a paradox, rather than accepting it as a counterexample to the conjecture that dissecting and rearranging does not change area. That is, why do we trust what we *expect* more than what we *see*?

2. Start with the eight-by-eight square shown below.

(a) Cut along the lines as shown in the figure below.

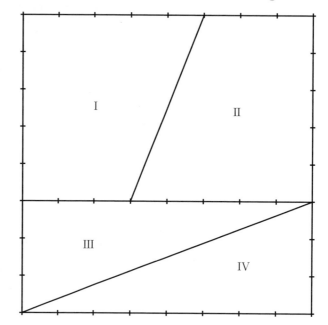

(b) Rearrange the parts to produce a five-by-thirteen rectangle.

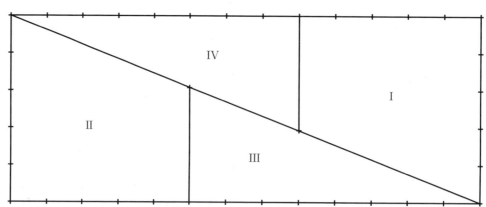

(c) This dissection appears to be a counterexample to the assumption that area is preserved under dissection. Did your cutting really change the area involved?

Reflect and Discuss

3. What's the trick? Specifically, find the error in the explanation of how a square with an area of 64 can be dissected into a rectangle with an area of 65.

Why would mathematicians waste time trying to prove something they did not believe to be true? Proof is often more to provide explanation than to establish certainty. It shows why *things are as they are.*

Problem 2 is truly an issue of mathematics, and not just psychology, because one *must* make assumptions in mathematics. The issue is to pick foundations that one trusts enough to build upon.

Whether one is testing a piece of software before its release or trying to understand (or check) an algorithm for dissecting one shape into another, one certainly wants to know, at the very least:

- Can the steps of the algorithm be executed for all the cases the algorithm claims to cover? (For example, will the software continue to run properly regardless of the user's inputs, or will it, for some inputs, get caught in a loop or stop in some unexpected way before completing its steps?)
- Does the algorithm actually do what it claims to do?

4. Choose one of your dissections of a trapezoid into a rectangle from section 1, and analyze the algorithm by answering the following questions:
   (a) Are the steps clearly described so that there are no judgment calls that must be made? If not, point out and fix the flaws.
   (b) Can each step be done as claimed, regardless of the starting trapezoid? If so, explain how you checked for generality. If there are trapezoids for which some steps won't work, give the example and try to repair the algorithm.
   (c) Is the final figure a rectangle? Explain how you know.

Do any of these activities look like a proof to you? If so, how is the proof different from other proofs you have seen?

Area formulas

In this section, you will explore deriving area formulas from dissection algorithms. You've already done preliminary work for this exploration:

- You found a general algorithm for dissecting a trapezoid into a rectangle, and you proved that this algorithm works in all cases.
- You made the assumption that area is invariant under dissection, which serves as a basis for deriving area formulas.

5. Use your algorithm for dissecting trapezoids into rectangles.
   (a) Find out how the length and width of a final rectangle are related to the dimensions of the starting trapezoid.
   (b) Replace the length and width in the area formula for a rectangle with the equivalent trapezoid measurements to get a formula for the area of a trapezoid. This formula should refer only to measurements on a trapezoid, not a rectangle.
   (c) In your algorithm, did you have to choose a particular side of the trapezoid with which to work? If so, how would choosing a different side affect the resulting formula?

Special and extreme cases

By thinking in terms of special and extreme cases, the area formula for trapezoid becomes a general-purpose tool.

To derive area formulas for a triangle and a parallelogram, will you have to go through the steps of problem 5 using dissection algorithms for turning a triangle into a rectangle and a parallelogram into a rectangle? Are there other ways to get these formulas? Can you use the trapezoid area formula to derive the formulas for the area of a triangle and a parallelogram?

6. How would you describe a triangle and a parallelogram as special or extreme cases of a trapezoid?

7. Derive an area formula for a triangle by considering it a extreme case of a trapezoid.

8. Derive an area formula for a parallelogram by considering it a special case of a trapezoid.

Ways to think about it

2. Check whether all of the restrictions mentioned in the margin of the problem were met: All pieces were used, there was no overlap, and only a finite number of cuts were used.

Problem: *Cut an 8 × 8 square with an area of 64 along the lines and rearrange the pieces to produce the 5 × 13 rectangle, with area 65.*

4. Try to think about very unusual examples of a trapezoid and see whether the algorithm still works for them. Try to come up with an example of a trapezoid for which this algorithm would not work. Prove that both pairs of the opposite sides of the resulting figure are parallel, and that at least one of the angles is the right angle.

Problem: *Choose one of your group's dissections of a trapezoid into a rectangle, and analyze this algorithm.*

6. Visualize a trapezoid, and then imagine changing the length of the shorter base. What length would change the trapezoid into a triangle? If the trapezoid were to become a parallelogram, how would the length of the two bases have to compare?

Problem: *How would you describe a triangle and a parallelogram as special or extreme cases of a trapezoid?*

3. Thinking about area

In the first two sections, you derived general algorithms for dissecting certain polygons into rectangles and used these algorithms to derive area formulas. In this section, you will derive alternative algorithms for determining the area of various polygonal regions and will discuss various ways to think about area.

In this section, you will have a chance to think about the meaning of area and analyze some of the basic assumptions we sometimes make without even noticing.

You may assume that the small grid squares have unit area and the vertices are grid points.

1. Describe at least three different methods for calculating the area of each of the following polygons. Compute the areas using each of the methods you describe.

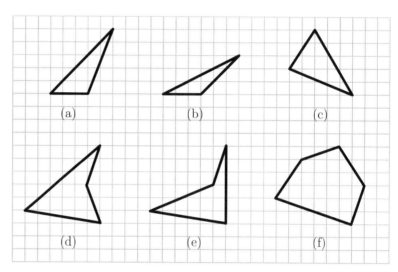

Reflect and Discuss

2. There are many ways to compute the areas of polygons, depending on the ways we think about area.

In parts (a) and (b), A, B, and C denote regions in the plane.

(a) Suppose $C = A \cup B$ and the areas of *two* of the regions are known. Can you find the area of the third? Are additional hypotheses necessary?

(b) Is there an area formula (or formulas) on which all other formulas are based?

(c) What other properties of area were you using in the previous problem?

As you probably mentioned in your solution to problem 1, one method for computing the areas of the polygons in problem 1 is dissection, the topic of the previous two sections. A related method could be described as "reverse dissection," where you imagine (or construct) a larger figure surrounding your polygon, then determine its area and the area of the region between the larger figure and your polygon.

3. The polygons from problem 1 are repeated below.

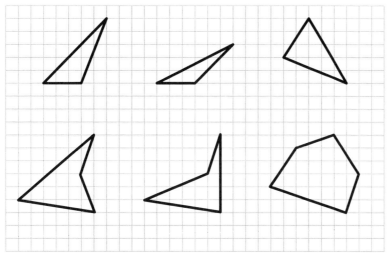

(a) For each of the polygons, sketch the smallest rectangle with horizontal and vertical sides that contains the given polygon. For each polygon, call this rectangle the polygon's *horizontal circumscribed rectangle*.

(b) Compute the areas of each of the polygons again, this time using the reverse dissection method. That is, determine the area of the polygon's horizontal circumscribed rectangle and the area of the region between the polygon and rectangle, and use that information to compute the area of the polygon.

We need to specify the orientation of the rectangle since, in general, a polygon has several circumscribed rectangles, as shown below:

4. Derive a formula for the area of a polygon's horizontal circumscribed rectangle in terms of the Cartesian coordinates of the polygon's vertices.

Formulas can be useful tools for computing areas of polygons, but these formulas usually depend on lengths of edges or altitudes of the object. Is there a way to compute the area of a polygon if you only know the coordinates of its vertices with respect to specific coordinate axes? It makes sense to start with triangles.

The method used in problems 3 and 4 seems to point to a possible formula that computes the area of a triangle as a function of the coordinates of its vertices, (x_1, y_1), (x_2, y_2), and (x_3, y_3).

Of course, the formula should work for all triangles, but it's not always so easy to check *all* possible cases.

PROBLEM

5. COORDINATE FORMULA FOR THE AREA OF A TRIANGLE

(a) Use the (horizontal) circumscribed rectangle method to derive a formula for computing the area of a triangle in terms of its vertices that works for triangles (i), (ii), and (iii), below.

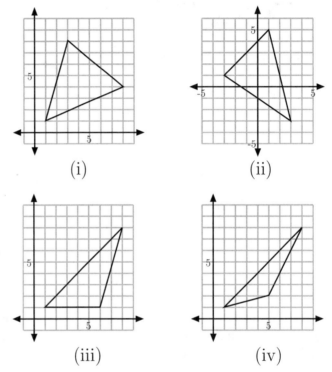

(i)   (ii)

(iii)   (iv)

(b) Does your formula work for triangle (iv)? If not, explain what goes wrong.

(c) Can you characterize the vertices for which the formula will (and won't) work?

(d) Can you "fix" your formula so that it will work for all triangles? It's OK to specify two separate formulas—one that works for triangles (i)–(iii) and one that works for those like (iv).

There's another formula that uses the fact that it's easy to compute the area of a triangle having a horizontal or vertical edge.

Reflect and Discuss

6. (a) Show that if a triangle doesn't have a horizontal or vertical edge, then it can be dissected into two triangles that share a horizontal or vertical edge, as shown in the figure below.

(b) Use the result of part (a) to derive another formula that expresses the area of a triangle in the coordinate plane as a function of its vertices.

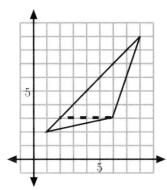 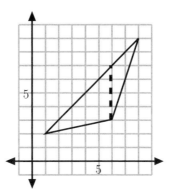

That wasn't too bad—we now have two different ways to determine the area of a triangle in terms of the Cartesian coordinates of its vertices. Is there a formula for the area of a polygon with more than 3 sides in terms of the coordinates of its vertices?

7. Sketch two different quadrilaterals with the given vertices on the grids below and compute their areas. What does this tell you about whether the area of a quadrilateral is always determined by its vertices?

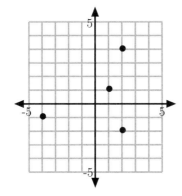 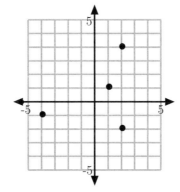

So, the coordinates of the vertices of a polygon with more than 3 sides do not always determine the area of the polygon. However, the triangle formula can be used to compute the area of particular polygons with more than 3 sides, since polygons can be partitioned into triangles whose vertices are the vertices of the polygon. To "triangulate" a polygon, pick a vertex and draw the diagonals of the polygon through the chosen vertex, being sure that all of these diagonals are contained within the interior of the polygon. The figure below demonstrates both good and bad vertex choices for a given polygon (the diagonals are shown as dotted lines).

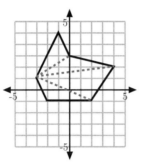

good choice for a vertex   bad choice for a vertex

8. Adapt the coordinate formula from problem 5 to the areas of the polygons below as a function of the coordinates of the vertices after first triangulating each polygon.

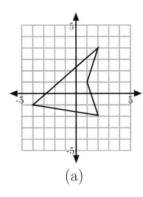 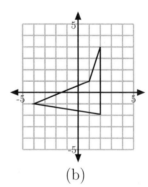 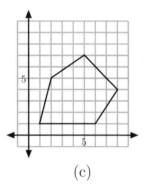

(a)   (b)   (c)

In parts (a) and (b) above, each quadrilateral has only one "good" vertex, but every vertex is a good vertex in part (c). What's the difference?

9. What property must a polygon have in order for the triangulation method to determine the area no matter what vertex you choose to work from?

Reflect and Discuss

10. Why isn't the coordinate formula (from problem 5) part of the school curriculum? Do you think it would be a good idea to ask your students to learn it? Why or why not?

In section 4, you will continue to approximate the areas of irregular regions in the plane and work to refine these approximations, finally adapting the methods you use to compute the precise areas of some irregular regions.

Ways to think about it

Problem: Describe at least three different methods for calculating the area of each of the following polygons. Compute the areas using each of the methods you describe.

1. One of the methods has been a topic of the past two sections. For another method, think about how you might have computed the areas if you hadn't yet begun this chapter. Can you make use of the coordinate system? Still another method involves surrounding the triangle with a larger polygon whose area is easily computed, then subtracting off the areas of the regions in the rectangle that are not part of the triangle. Or you can "count squares."

Problem:
(a) Suppose $C = A \cup B$ and the areas of two of the regions are known. Can you find the area of the third? Are additional hypotheses necessary?
(b) Is there an area formula (or formulas) on which all other formulas are based?
(c) What other properties of area were you using in the previous problem?

2. In part (a), consider whether any property you came up with works for all A and B. Does it matter whether A and B are polygons or whether or not they intersect (that is, if $A \cap B \neq \emptyset$)? If so, change the hypotheses in order to find a method of determining the areas of the regions in question.

   In parts (b) and (c), use a "less is more" strategy. What's the least you can assume about area in order to determine the areas of objects in the plane? Is there a "basic" unit (or a few basic units) of area?

Problem:
(a) For each of the given polygons, sketch the smallest rectangle with horizontal and vertical sides that contains the given polygon.
(b) Compute the areas of each of the polygons again, this time using the reverse dissection method.

3. (a) When sketching the horizontal circumscribed rectangle for the polygon in question, be sure that there is a vertex of the polygon on every side of the rectangle. If this is not the case, you can find a smaller rectangle.
   (b) You need to determine the area of the polygon's horizontal circumscribed rectangle, then dissect the region that lies outside the polygon and inside the rectangle. If you can dissect the region into rectangles and right triangles with horizontal and vertical legs, it makes the area calculations a lot easier.

Problem: Derive a formula for the area of a polygon's horizontal circumscribed rectangle in terms of the coordinates of the polygon's vertices.

4. Start with some specific examples (like the ones given in problem 3—in fact, be sure that the formula you derive works for these polygons). Then label the vertices with variables rather than numbers and see what you get. When trying to derive the formula, it might help to "talk out loud" before getting specific with coordinates. Which vertices and which coordinates of these vertices play a role in computing the area? How would you describe the length of the horizontal sides of the rectangle? It depends only on the y-coordinates of some of the vertices, but which ones? What about the vertical sides? Their length depends only on the x-coordinates of certain vertices (which ones?).

5. There are several ways to think about a formula—maybe it's obvious to try to use the formula you developed in the previous problem for the triangle's horizontal circumscribed rectangle, since in triangles (i)–(iii), the region outside the triangle can be seen to be the union of right triangles, each having easily computable areas. Can you express the dimensions of these triangles in terms of the coordinates of the original? When answering parts (b) and (c), think about how triangle (iv) differs from the first three. Investigate the relationship between the vertices and see if you can predict when the formula from part (a) will fail to work. Note that you can always put the *x*-coordinates in either ascending or descending order and you can do the same with the *y*-coordinates. What does it mean to say you can put the *points* in order? Is that good or bad?

After finding the area of the triangle's horizontal circumscribed rectangle, you can still compute the area of the region that is outside of the triangle, but inside the rectangle and you can dissect this region into right triangles and a rectangle. Why does the "extra" rectangle appear and how can you come up with a formula for dealing with this situation?

COORDINATE FORMULA FOR THE AREA OF A TRIANGLE
(a) *Use the (horizontal) circumscribed rectangle method to derive a formula for computing the area of a triangle in terms of its vertices that works for triangles (i), (ii), and (iii).*
(b) *Does your formula work for triangle (iv)? If not, explain what goes wrong.*
(c) *Can you characterize the vertices for which the formula will (and won't) work?*
(d) *Can you "fix" your formula so that it will work for all triangles? It's OK to specify two separate formulas—one that works for triangles (i)–(iii) and one that works for those like (iv).*

6. In part (a), play the "what if" game. *What if* you couldn't do this? Then that would mean that every horizontal and vertical line from every vertex of the triangle would fail to intersect an opposite side. Why is that impossible? In part (b), the "trick" is to determine the coordinates the point at which the horizontal or vertical line drawn through the "middle" point intersects the opposite side. It requires a little bit of algebra, using the slope of the opposite side (which can be determined since you know the coordinates of its endpoints).

Problem: (a) *Show that if a triangle doesn't have a horizontal or vertical edge, then it can be dissected into two triangles that share a horizontal or vertical edge.*
(b) *Use the result of part (a) to derive another formula that expresses the area of a triangle in the coordinate plane as a function of its vertices.*

7. There aren't very many ways to connect the dots and even fewer ways to make an honest-to-goodness quadrilateral (with edges that only intersect at vertices), so try it out and see what you get. Then compare areas. You can save yourself some time by comparing the quadrilaterals you found to the quadrilaterals in problems 1 and 3 (you've already computed their areas). You've probably guessed what's going to happen. If you don't get the answer you expect, see if there's another quadrilateral with the given vertices. In general, how many quadrilaterals are there with 4 given vertices? Are their areas *ever* the same?

Problem: *Sketch two different quadrilaterals with the given vertices on the grids below and compute their areas. What does this tell you about whether the area of a quadrilateral is always determined by its vertices?*

Problem: Adapt the coordinate formula from problem 5 to the areas of the polygons below as a function of the coordinates of the vertices after first "triangulating" each polygon.

Problem: What property must a polygon have in order for the triangulation method to determine the area no matter what vertex you choose to work from?

Problem: Why isn't the coordinate formula (from problem 5) part of the school curriculum? Do you think it would be a good idea to ask your students to learn it? Why or why not?

8. Once you find a "good" triangulation, use the formula from problem 5 to determine the area of each triangle. This can be done as long as the vertices of each triangle in the triangulation are vertices of the polygon. If the sides of the triangles are diagonals of the polygon, will the triangle's vertices always be vertices of the polygon? Is it always possible to create a "good" triangulation?

9. The difficulty in finding a quadrilateral area formula that depends only on the coordinates of the vertices arises because you can't use all vertices to make a good triangulation in all quadrilaterals. In order to be a good vertex, what should be true about each of the diagonals? In what type of quadrilaterals (or other figures) will each of the vertices have this property?

10. What do you think about this? Do you think you would have found this formula useful when you were a student? Is it convenient? Is it easy to use and remember? Is it essential? Are there other considerations for determining what should be in the curriculum? How do you decide whether to tell students a specific formula or to help them derive area calculations themselves?

4. Areas of nonpolygonal regions

In previous sections, you dissected various polygonal regions, rearranged the pieces to construct rectangles with the same area, derived area formulas, and considered the use of alternative units for measuring area. In this section, you will consider various strategies for approximating and computing the areas of regions in the plane having curved boundaries.

The figure below on the left is called a *lune*. The inner curve of this lune is an arc of a circle and the outer curve is a semicircle of another, smaller circle containing the larger circle's center. The figure on the right provides more information about the lune's construction.

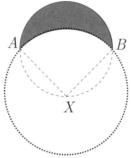

The lune   Construction of the lune

1. Suppose X is the center of the larger circle. In order to construct the lune, where must you place A and B, the endpoints of the diameter of the smaller circle? In particular, what must the measure of angle AXB be?

Imagine you're given the larger circle. How would you construct the smaller circle?

The next figure is known as *Leonardo's claws*. The top part of the larger circle is a 90° arc, which is folded down. Then a smaller circle is inscribed.

Named after Leonardo Da Vinci

Can you construct these figures, using straightedge and compass or dynamic geometry software? Give it a try!

The claws   Construction of the claws

PROBLEM

2. COMPARING THE LUNE TO THE CLAWS
Assuming the smaller circle in the lune's construction is congruent to the larger circle in the claws' construction, which is bigger—the lune or the claws? Make a guess, then check by computing the two areas.

Around Euclid's time in ancient Greece and in Alexandria, Egypt (the major intellectual center of the time), people didn't think of finding a number to represent area; to find an area meant to find a simpler figure (such as a square or rectangle) with the same area. Often, "find" meant to construct, not just to reach the conclusion by reasoning. The *rectification* of figures was a popular type of problem. To *rectify* a figure means to construct a rectangle with the same area as the given figure. To *square* a figure means to construct a square with the same area. From what you just showed about their areas, it's not hard to square the lune and claws, but other objects are difficult or impossible to square.

The impossibility of squaring the circle is due to the fact that π is a transcendental number—i.e., it is not a root of any polynomial equation with integer coefficients. This was proved in 1882 by the German mathematician Ferdinand Lindemann.

One famous problem from this era is "squaring the circle": constructing a square (using only an unmarked ruler and compass) having the same area as a given circle. This problem was unsolved until the 19th century, when it was finally proved that it can't be done.

Each of the objects you've considered so far in this chapter has been made up of polygons or circles, and therefore its area was computable. Is it true that any figure in the plane, no matter how complicated, has a number associated with it that specifies its area? Is it always possible to determine an object's area?

3.   Is it possible to determine the area of the figure below? How would you go about it?

You don't have to actually compute the area—just describe a method that would allow you to compute it.

OK, that was a hard one. You'll return to more complicated shapes in the *Further Exploration* materials. For the present, let's move back to familiar territory—circles. You know the area of a circle, but *how* do you know?

Circular reasoning

Reflect and Discuss

4. How would you respond to the following question from student in one of your classes?

> *I know you told us that the area of a circle is the square of the radius times π. But how do we know that's right?*

You don't have to give a rigorous proof for the area formula. An informal justification is fine here.

In this section, you will use a variety of methods to think about the formula for the area of a circle. It is likely that your work in problem 4 will overlap with some of the methods used, but other techniques may be new to you.

Here's a dissection method for approximating the area of a circle:

5. Explain how the figure below can be used as a "proof without words" to describe a method for implying that the area of a circle is equal to (or is at least *close to*) the radius of the circle times half its circumference.

Proofs without Words is a regular feature of the American Mathematical Monthly, *a journal published by the Mathematical Association of America. You'll see more proofs without words in Chapter IV.*

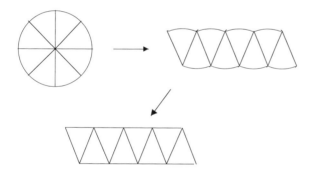

What is the (approximate) relationship between the height and base of the parallelogram and the dimensions of the circle? What about the length of its base?

6. Is the area of the parallelogram in the figure larger or smaller than the area of the circle? Does this relationship remain when the circle is dissected more finely?

Let's now think about this method of approximation a little more carefully. You've probably noticed that if you dissect the circle into more and more slices, the area of the corresponding parallelogram gets closer and closer to the area of the circle. Let's look at what the parallelogram approximation looks like back inside the circle. Since the parallelogram was constructed by connecting arc endpoints with segments, the parallelogram could be dissected and placed back inside the circle as shown in the margin. You just explained why the area of this inscribed

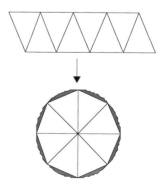

octagon is close to the area of the circle, but what, exactly, is the area of the octagon?

7. What is the area of the regular octagon inscribed in a circle of radius r?

Instead of inscribing an octagon inside the circle, we could inscribe the circle inside a regular octagon. The octagon is then said to be circumscribed about the circle:

8. What is the area of the regular octagon circumscribed about a circle of radius r?

As is evident from their definition (and the figures), the inscribed octagon's area is smaller than the area of the circle, which is smaller than the area of the circumscribed octagon. And there's nothing special about octagons. If I_n is the regular n-gon (polygon with n sides) inscribed in the circle and C_n is the regular n-gon circumscribed about the circle, then

$$\text{Area}(I_n) < A < \text{Area}(C_n),$$

where A is the area of the circle. It's also true that $\text{Area}(I_n)$ and $\text{Area}(C_n)$ will get closer and closer to A as n increases. But what do $\text{Area}(I_n)$ and $\text{Area}(C_n)$ equal, and how can you know how close either is to A?

PROBLEM

9. EASY AS π

Use the information and methods from the previous problems to express the areas of the inscribed and circumscribed n-gons as functions of n (and r), then use that information to approximate the area of the circle to within $0.001r^2$, being sure to explain your reasoning.

So, you've devised a way to approximate the area of a circle of radius r as closely as you like. Now, go one more step to *compute* the area.

10. Using the expressions you got for $\text{Area}(I_n)$ and $\text{Area}(C_n)$ in the previous problem, what *should* you get when you compute $\lim_{n\to\infty} \text{Area}(I_n)$ and $\lim_{n\to\infty} \text{Area}(C_n)$? Compute each of these limits to show that your guesses were correct.

What about circumference?

Yes, this chapter is about area, but aren't you itching to see if you can apply these methods to determine the *circumference* of a circle, too?

PROBLEM

11. DERIVING THE CIRCLE'S CIRCUMFERENCE
Use the perimeters of the inscribed and circumscribed n-gons, I_n and C_n, to approximate, then compute, the circumference of a circle of radius r. In the process, explain how you may conclude that the area of a circle is r times half its circumference.

The method of inscribed and circumscribed polygonal approximations to the circle goes back at least to the time of Archimedes and influenced the development of calculus many centuries later. You'll learn more about this in the *Further Exploration* materials.

In the next—and final—section of this chapter, you'll consider various transformations and their effect (if any) on the lengths and areas of transformed objects.

Ways to think about it

Problem: Suppose X is the center of the larger circle. In order to construct the lune, where must you place A and B, the endpoints of the diameter of the smaller circle? In particular, what must the measure of angle AXB be?

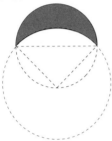

COMPARING THE LUNE TO THE CLAWS *Assuming the smaller circle in the lune's construction is congruent to the larger circle in the claws' construction, which is bigger—the lune or the claws? Make a guess, then check by computing the two areas.*

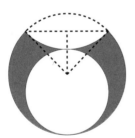

1. The figure is repeated in the margin for reference. Recall that the inner curve is an arc of a circle and the outer curve is a semicircle of a smaller circle that contains the center of the larger circle.

    Start by constructing the larger circle and labeling its center X. In order to determine the location of A and B, which will be the endpoints of a diameter of the smaller circle, you need to determine the measure of $\angle AXB$. This angle subtends a semicircle, so what does that imply about its measure? Once you've determined what the measure of $\angle AXB$ must equal, you can construct an angle with the specified measure (with X at the vertex), which allows you to place A and B. Once you've completed that, though, you still have the construct the semicircle. How do you construct a circle given a diameter?

2. Take the figures one at a time and denote the radius of the common circles r. In order to determine the area of the lune, refer to the figure in the margin above and try to compute the area of the original circle that is outside the lune. One way to characterize this is as the region made up of a quarter of the big circle (what is its radius?) that is above the triangle along with the region below, which is a semicircle of the smaller circle. To determine the radius of the larger circle (and therefore the area of the triangle), note that the triangle is a right triangle with hypotenuse equal to a diameter of the smaller circle.

    In order to determine the area of the claws, you'll need to determine the area of the piece that is folded over, then removed, as well as the radius (and therefore area) of the smaller circle (remember, the larger circle's radius is r). The region that is folded is the part of the quarter circle that is outside of the triangle. The sides of this right triangle are radii of the original circle (what's its hypotenuse?). To determine the radius of the smaller circle, note that its diameter is contained in a diameter of the original circle. In fact, the smaller diameter is less than the diameter of the original circle by an amount equal to twice the difference between the original radius and the length of the altitude to the hypotenuse of the triangle.

Are you surprised by how the two regions compare? When you think about it, isn't this the answer to nearly *every* "Which is bigger?" question?

3. You can probably come up with several approximation methods, but can you come up with a strategy for *computing* the area of the region? What if, rather than lying on the page, it was cut out of a 2-inch-thick piece of wood? Could you determine the area of the figure by comparing the piece of wood to another piece of wood? Remember, you don't have to actually compute the area—just describe a method that would allow you to compute it.

Problem: Is it possible to determine the area of the figure? How would you go about it?

4. Remember, you don't have to give a rigorous proof here. Do you know any ways to derive the formula or provide an informal justification?

Problem: How do you know that the area of a circle is the square of the radius times π.

5. Remember that you're not being asked to provide a proof here. Give a (possibly informal) argument that might convince someone that
   i.   the area of the circle is approximately the area of the parallelogram;
   ii. the area of the parallelogram is approximately half the circle's circumference times the circle's radius.

Problem: Explain how the figure can be used to describe a method for implying that the area of a circle is equal to (or is at least close to*) the radius of the circle times half its circumference.*

The following figure, similar to the one given in the problem, might help get you started. The main difference in the new figure is that the circle has been dissected into 16 pieces, rather than 8.

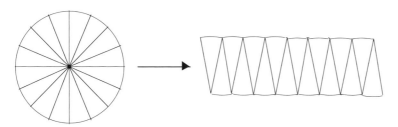

6. Think about how the parallelogram was constructed in the first place. The isosceles triangles that were created from the pieces of the circles have side lengths equal to the radius of the circle. What does that say about the height of the parallelogram? How does the length of the base of each triangle compare to the arc length of each sector?

Problem: Is the area of the parallelogram in the figure larger or smaller than the area of the circle? Does this relationship remain when the circle is dissected more finely?

Does your solution (bigger or smaller) depend on how many pieces the circle is originally dissected into?

Problem: *What is the area of the regular octagon inscribed in a circle of radius r?*

7. The octagon is the union of 8 congruent isosceles triangles, so you need only determine the area of one of the triangles (and then multiply by 8). Using the figure below, what is the apex angle of each triangle? Can you express h and b in terms of this angle (and r)? You'll probably need at least one trigonometric function, too. Try to get an exact answer, if possible. It's OK to approximate your answer, but wait until the last possible moment before approximating to reduce error.

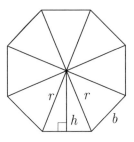

Problem: *What is the area of the regular octagon circumscribed about a circle of radius r?*

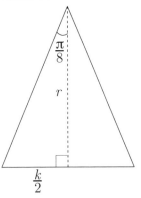

EASY AS π

Use the information and methods from the previous problems to approximate the area of the circle to within $0.001r^2$ (being sure to explain your reasoning).

8. Note that the octagon is tangent at the midpoints of the edges of the octagon (you can show this using the Side-Angle-Side Theorem along with the fact that the distance from the center to each vertex is constant). In any case, the edge length, k, and therefore the area of each subtriangle can be computed in terms of the radius, r.

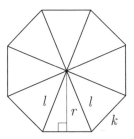

9. You should be able to apply the methods you used in the previous two problems, but this time, the angle isn't $\pi/8$—what is it? Of course, any formula for Area(I_n) or Area(C_n) will depend on n and r. It might help to draw a picture or use the figures you created for the previous two problems. As you discussed earlier, as n increases, the area between the n-gons and the circle decreases. How big must n be in order to be "close enough"? You'll probably want to leave your answer in terms of π/n. Then, it might help to make a table of values, like the one shown here:

n	Area(I_n)	Area(C_n)
8		
16		
32		
64		
128		
256		

Once the table is filled in, compare the inscribed and circumscribed areas. How should the area of the circle compare to these areas for a given n?

10. You'll need to compute $\lim\limits_{n\to\infty} n\sin\left(\dfrac{\pi}{n}\right)$ and $\lim\limits_{n\to\infty}\cos\left(\dfrac{\pi}{n}\right)$. These particular limits aren't in a familiar form, but they can be computed by using the following limits:

   - $\lim\limits_{\theta\to 0}\dfrac{\sin(\theta)}{\theta} = 1$;   *Do you know why these*
   - $\lim\limits_{\theta\to 0}\cos(\theta) = 1$.   *limits are correct?*

   The first limit can be used to determine

   $$\lim_{n\to\infty} n\sin\left(\frac{\pi}{n}\right) = \lim_{n\to\infty}\frac{\sin(\pi/n)}{1/n} = \pi\lim_{n\to\infty}\frac{\sin(\pi/n)}{\pi/n};$$

   the second limit can be used to determine $\lim\limits_{n\to\infty}\cos\left(\dfrac{\pi}{n}\right)$.

   Problem: Using the expressions you got for Area(I_n) and Area(C_n) in the previous problem, what should you get when you compute $\lim\limits_{n\to\infty}$ Area(I_n) and $\lim\limits_{n\to\infty}$ Area(C_n)? Compute each of these limits to show that your guesses were correct.

11. There are a number of ways to proceed here. Determining the perimeters of I_n and C_n is analogous to determining their areas. Focus your attention on one of the n triangles that make up the polygon and determine its contribution to the perimeter. Once you have general formulas for the perimeters of I_n and C_n, you can choose large n to get an approximation of the circle's circumference. Is it true that Perimeter(I_n) $< P <$ Perimeter(C_n), where P is the circumference of the circle? Then you can make estimates about how close Perimeter(I_n) and Perimeter(C_n) are to P. Once you have formulas for the perimeters of the n-gons, you can compute their limits as n goes to infinity.

   DERIVING THE CIRCLE'S CIRCUMFERENCE   *Use the perimeters of the inscribed and circumscribed n-gons, I_n and C_n, to approximate, then compute, the circumference of a circle of radius r. In the process, explain how you may conclude that the area of a circle is r times half its circumference.*

   Another way to approach the problem of comparing the circumference to the area of the circle is to look at their ratio in contrast to the ratios of the perimeter and area of the n-gons. Compute $\dfrac{\text{Area}(I_n)}{\text{Perimeter}(I_n)}$ and $\dfrac{\text{Area}(C_n)}{\text{Perimeter}(C_n)}$. How should these ratios compare to $\dfrac{A}{P}$?

5. Transformations and area

In this section, you'll see six transformations of the plane: shearing; two kinds of scaling (strain and dilation); and, briefly, three kinds of isometries (translation, rotation, and reflection). Which of these, if any, appear in the curriculum you are using?

While the topic of this chapter is area, the central idea is more like *how certain actions on objects affect area.* Some actions on shapes—like rotations, reflections, and translations—don't change the shapes' area at all, but that is hardly a surprise as they change nothing about the shapes except their orientation and location. The first actions you performed on shapes in this chapter—the dissections—did radically alter the shapes, and still left the area unchanged, but that, too, was not a surprise. The "common sense" notion of area is that it is the amount of "stuff" in a planar object, and that moving the object about doesn't change that amount of stuff, nor does cutting the object into parts and rearranging those parts. Children learn this "conservation of stuff" relatively early, and it forms the basis of everyone's understanding of measures of length, area, and volume.

The transformational point of view is a powerful way of looking at geometric problems.

Some actions on shapes have more surprising results. In this section, you will encounter transformations that do not preserve shape and yet do preserve area without (at first) intuitively obvious reasons, then consider transformations that leave shape unchanged, but alter area.

PROBLEM

The 1997 TIMSS (Third International Mathematics and Science Study) Video Study released a video with clips of typical 8th-grade math lessons in Japan, Germany, and the U.S. This problem is a standard lesson in Japanese classrooms. The teacher introduced the problem by recalling the previous day's lesson: two triangles with the same base and height have the same area. After about half an hour, several students presented solutions. The homework for the night was a generalization suggested by one of the students.

1. TIMSS PROBLEM
    Arnold and Betty are farmers. Here is a map of part of their land.

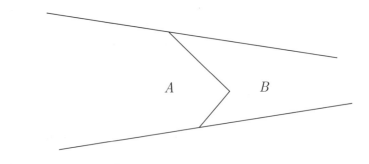

They want to straighten out the boundary between their properties without changing the amounts of land they each have. How can they do it?

Isometries

Reflections, rotations, and translations are examples of *isometries*. Sometimes called "rigid motions," these are the transformations that keep distances between points unchanged—that is, the distance between any two points before the transformation is applied is the same as the distance between the transformed points after.

Another way that this is often stated: "Isometries preserve distance."

You've probably had a lot of experience with isometries in previous courses, since it's usually the case that when any attention is given to transformations, most—if not all—of the time is spent on isometries. So much time is usually focused on isometries that we will do little with them here except to say that the proofs of many geometric theorems are made *vastly* easier if one makes good use of what features are preserved by rotations, reflections, and the like. One such theorem, an angle inscribed in a semicircle is a right angle, has an elegant symmetry proof. Think about how you might prove it, then see a sample proof in the *Further Exploration* materials.

The word isometry *is built of two parts:* iso *(same) and* metry *(measure). Isometries transform figures without changing the measured sizes of their angles or sides. Iso appears in many other scientific terms: isosceles (same sides); isomorphic (same form); isobar (equal weight, equal pressure); isomer; isotope; and so on. Where else have you run across "metry"?*

Isometries are the transformations that create congruence: Lengths, angles, and area are all preserved. What about other transformations? For instance, in problem 1, you changed the shapes of the regions, but kept the area constant. You can do this by using a transformation known as a shear.

Shears

Students often find the following demonstration that a triangle's area depends *only* on base and height quite convincing.

- Get a big stack of index cards, at least 2 inches high (200–300 cards).

The figures on the following page illustrate this procedure.

- Stack them very neatly so that they form a rectangular block. A tight rubber band or clamp will help hold them neatly as you draw on the faces of this block that is made up of the edges of the cards (next step).

- On one edge-face of the block, use a ruler and marker to draw a triangle whose base is parallel to the edges of cards. On the opposite edge-face, draw another triangle, carefully making no sides parallel to the edges of the block.

- Now remove the rubber band and shove the deck so that the cards now stack at a slant. Use a ruler, table, or book to make sure the slanted side is not curved.

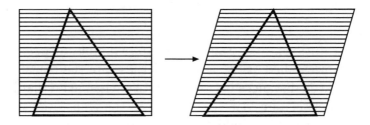

A pile of index cards, sheared

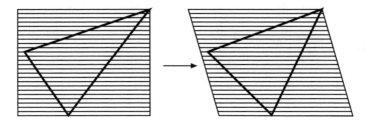

The opposite face of the cards, sheared

2.   In the index card demonstration, how does the area of the "before" triangle compare to the area of the "after" triangle? Does it matter whether a side of the triangle is along an edge of a card, or does it work for both triangles?

3.   On one triangle, the two measurements that were preserved were the base and the height. What two measurements were preserved on the *other* triangle? Invent a dissection that shows how *these* two measurements determine the triangle's area.

The action of pushing the cards to the side is not a transformation of the *plane*—it is a transformation of a pile of cards. Is it possible to extend this transformation to all of the points in the plane. A *shear* of the plane is a transformation that acts like the stack of cards transformation. That is,

- there is a line, we'll call it the *invariant line*, all of whose points are left alone by the transformation (like the bottom card on the stack);
- all other points are moved in a direction parallel to the invariant line;
- it preserves lines (that is, given A and B in the plane, if C is on the line containing A and B, then the image of C under the shear is on the line containing the image of A and the image of B).

In the following figure, three shapes are shown. The figure on the right shows the result of a shear of the figure on the left (the invariant line is the the base of shape C).

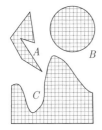 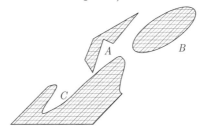

Original figures   Figures after shear

4. The figure below includes two triangles and the invariant line. A certain shear takes point A and moves it to A', four units to the right, as shown.

Note: The points F and C are on the invariant line.

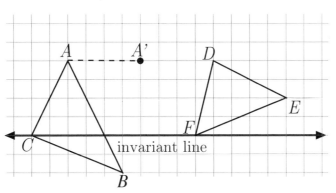

(a) Sketch the image of the triangle when the shear is applied to the whole plane.

(b) Carefully describe what happens to an arbitrary point, (x, y). Does it matter which (x, y) we choose?

(c) Suppose that a different shear moves the point $(2, 4)$ to $(10, 4)$. Where is the point (x, y) sent by this shear?

(d) Still another shear sends $(2, 4)$ to $(-10, 4)$. Where is (x, y) sent?

5. Shears preserve (leave invariant) some distances while changing others. Which? Why? And what happens to angles?

6. How is the area of an arbitrary figure affected by a shear? Prove your conjecture if possible.

Other transformations

There are many other types of transformations, notably strains (transformations that stretch or shrink the plane in *one* direction by a fixed ratio) and dilations (which "scale" a figure up or down, resulting in a figure that is similar to the original).

We finish this section, and chapter, with a few activities with similar figures. Although we won't analyze the dilations that could lead to them, we could.

7.   With a single cut (or straight line), dissect the triangle T_1 into two triangles similar to the original; call them T_2 and T_3.

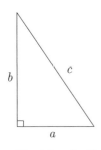

The triangle T_1

(a)   Use the hypotenuses to find scale factors for the similarities $T_2 \sim T_1$ and $T_3 \sim T_1$. (That is, a side of T_1 is what factor of the corresponding side of T_2? of T_3?)

(b)   Use the scale factors to get area factors:

$$\mathrm{area}(T_2) = ? \cdot \mathrm{area}(T_1) \quad \text{and} \quad \mathrm{area}(T_3) = ? \cdot \mathrm{area}(T_1).$$

(c)   Combine the area factor equations and the relationship between the three areas to get a single equation involving only a, b, and c.

(d)   Does this work for *any* right triangle? How do you know?

(e)   Would this proof work for non-right triangles? If so, state the theorem precisely and prove it. If not, where does the proof fail?

This is a mathematical definition, not a biological one. The idea behind this clever invented term is a self-replicating tile.

A "reptile" is a figure that can be decomposed into a finite number of congruent pieces, each similar to the original figure. What types of right triangles are 2-reptiles? (If you have time, use the results of problem 7 to investigate this.)

Here is an example of a 4-reptile, with its accompanying decomposition.

For more information about reptiles, see Transformation Geometry, *by Martin (Freeman, 1982), and* Tilings and Patterns, *by Grunbaum and Shephard (Springer Verlag, 1982).*

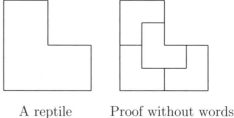

A reptile   Proof without words

PROBLEM

8. TURN ONE INTO FOUR
Show that every triangle (right or not) is a 4-reptile by demonstrating how they can be cut into four congruent triangles that are similar to the original triangle.

Ways to think about it

1. Look at the triangular piece of land belonging to region **A** that's jutting into region **B**. Is it possible to move the rightmost vertex of the triangular region and still keep the area the same? Under what circumstances will the two triangles in the figure below have the same area? Can you move the vertex to one of the "edges" but keep the area the same? Explain how.

TIMSS PROBLEM: *Arnold and Betty are farmers. Here is a map of part of their land.*

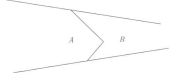

They want to straighten out the boundary between their properties without changing the amounts of land they each have. How can they do it?

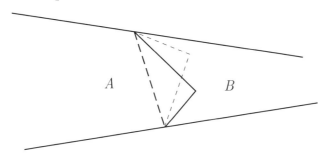

2. When one of the sides is horizontal, it's not hard to see that area remains unchanged, but it's less obvious what happens if none of the sides is horizontal. Try computing the areas of the region outside the triangle. Note that the outer regions aren't necessarily triangles (if the vertices aren't all on the edges of the cards). You can also look at the notes for problem 3 for another method to compute and compare the areas.

Problem: In the index card demonstration, how does the area of the "before" triangle compare to the area of the "after" triangle? Does it matter whether a side of the triangle is along an edge of a card, or does it work for both triangles?

3. If you're stuck, imagine constructing a horizontal segment from the middle vertex to the opposite side (as below). The length of this segment does not change, nor does the vertical distance from the topmost to lowermost vertex. If a different triangle were drawn, would this method still work?

Problem: On one triangle, the two measurements that were preserved were the base and the height. What two measurements were preserved on the other *triangle? Invent a dissection that shows how these* two measurements *determine the triangle's area.*

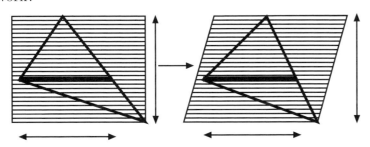

4. Start by considering where B, C, D, E, and F are sent under the transformation. What about the remaining points? Does knowing where A goes (to A') give you enough information? What gets changed and by how much? What

Problem: A certain shear takes point A and moves it to A', four units to the right, as shown.
(a) Sketch the image of the triangle when the shear is applied to the whole plane.

(b) *Carefully describe what happens to an arbitrary point, (x, y). Does it matter which (x, y) we choose?*
(c) *Suppose that a different shear moves the point $(2, 4)$ to $(10, 4)$. Where is the point (x, y) sent by this shear?*
(d) *If still another shear sends $(2, 4)$ to $(-10, 4)$, where is (x, y) sent?*

remains the same? In part (b), be sure that your "formula" for the image of (x, y) works for the vertices of the triangles.

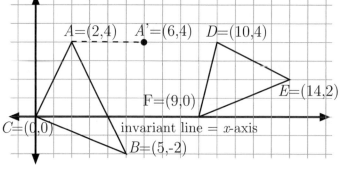

Problem: *Shears preserve (leave invariant) some distances while changing others. Which? Why? And what happens to angles?*

5. What happens to vertical lines under a shear? How does that help determine what happens to angles?

Problem: *Find a rule for how the area of an arbitrary figure changes after a shear. Prove it if possible.*

6. Are there any figures whose areas change under a shear? How do you know? Think back to the example with the stack of cards. Did areas change then? Does that result still hold? First, consider triangular areas—which figures can be split up into triangles?

Problem: *With a single cut, dissect triangle T_1 into two triangles, T_2 and T_3, similar to the original*
(a) *Use the hypotenuses to find scale factors for the similarities $T_2 \sim T_1$ and $T_3 \sim T_1$.*
(b) *Use the scale factors to get area factors:*
$area(T_2) = ? \cdot area(T_1)$;
$area(T_3) = ? \cdot area(T_1)$.
(c) *Combine the area factor equations and the relationship between the three areas to get a single equation involving only a, b, and c.*
(d) *Does this work for* any *right triangle? How do you know?*
(e) *Would this proof work for non-right triangles? If so, state the theorem precisely and prove it. If not, where does the proof fail?*

7. You may have seen a proof of the Pythagorean theorem that relies on this dissection. You need to dissect the original right triangle into two similar right triangles, so the line you draw must be perpendicular to one of the sides. In addition, then two triangles must have the same three angles as the original triangle, T_1. From where should you "drop" a perpendicular? Once you've found the dissection, compare corresponding lengths in order to determine the scale factors. The relationship between the area scale factors should be familiar, but you may not have thought about this relationship in this way before.

When considering whether this dissection will work with all triangles, be careful about making any unwarranted assumptions.

8. If you *could* dissect the original triangle into 4 congruent equilateral triangles that were all similar to the original triangle, what would the scaling factor from small to big triangle have to be? What's an easy way to construct triangles whose lengths are correspondingly half as long as the original triangle?

    You might be familiar with a dissection of an equilateral triangle into 4 congruent equilateral triangles. Does this dissection work on all triangles?

TURN ONE INTO FOUR
Show that any triangle can be cut into four triangles congruent to each other and similar to the original triangle.

Chapter III
Linearity and
Proportional Reasoning

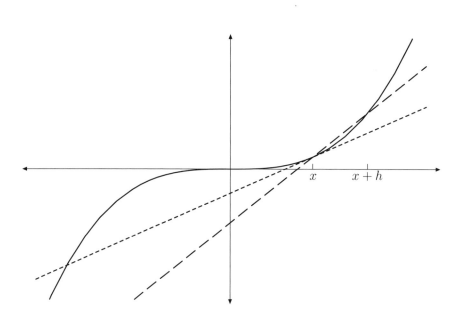

1. Mix it up

This chapter is about addition, multiplication, and combinations of those operations. These concepts start to develop in elementary school and continue into middle school. The study of the properties of those operations and combinations, though, is important from elementary school through higher mathematics. In this module, you'll explore those properties and the connections between early and more advanced mathematics.

The mixture blues

The following situation is one that can be—and has been—given to middle school students (and younger).

Product developers in the research lab for Whodunnit Jeans are trying to decide on a shade of blue for a new line of jeans. They have been mixing blue dye and clear water together, trying to find just the right shade.

In each of the problems below are two sets of blue-clear beaker combinations to mix. Each rectangle represents one beaker, and all beakers have the same volume of liquid in them. Decide which set is bluer, and explain how you made your decision. Find a way to decide *without* finding common denominators of two fractions!

In other words, which mixture has more blue in it?

1. $A = \{ \blacksquare\ \square \}$ $B = \{ \blacksquare\ \square\ \square\ \square \}$

Make believe that black is blue in these problems.

2. $A = \{ \blacksquare\ \blacksquare\ \blacksquare\ \square\ \square \}$

   $B = \{ \blacksquare\ \blacksquare\ \square\ \square \}$

3. $A = \{ \blacksquare\ \blacksquare\ \blacksquare\ \square\ \square \}$

   $B = \{ \blacksquare\ \blacksquare\ \blacksquare\ \square\ \square\ \square \}$

Notice how ambiguous the question "Which mixture is bluer?" becomes.

4. $A = \{ \blacksquare\ \blacksquare\ \blacksquare\ \blacksquare\ \square\ \square \}$

   $B = \{ \blacksquare\ \blacksquare\ \square \}$

Reflect and Discuss

Three of the developers used different methods to make their predictions.

Nancy: I figured how many blue parts were used for each clear. If mixture A uses more blue for each clear than mixture B, then mixture A will be bluer. For example, in problem 1, mixture A uses 1 blue for 1 clear. Mixture B uses 1 blue for 3 clear, or $\frac{1}{3}$ blue for 1 clear. So Mixture A is bluer.

Terry: I calculated the number of blue minus the number of clear. The mixture with a greater difference is bluer. For example, in problem 1, mixture A's difference is 0 and mixture B's difference is -2. So mixture A is bluer.

Sid: I looked at how much blue there is compared to the total amount of liquid. For example, in problem 1, mixture A has 1 blue out of 2 beakers while mixture B has 1 blue out of 4 beakers. Mixture A is bluer.

5. Do two of the developers always agree with each other?

6. Some students may have trouble accepting that one of these methods is incorrect. Find an extreme example: two mixtures for which the methods don't all agree, but it's very clear which is incorrect.

Nancy decided she preferred this mixture over all the others:

Sid wanted to make a big vat the same shade as Nancy's mixture.

7. If Sid used 45 beakers filled with blue dye, how much water (clear) was needed to get the same shade as Nancy's mixture?

8. If the total amount of liquid in the vat was 1000 units, how much dye and how much water were needed?

If possible, connect each problem with a particular developer.

9. How is the reasoning needed to answer each of problems 7 and 8 related to the developers' methods described above?

Reflect and Discuss

As you might know, *proportional reasoning* was required to answer the problems in this section. This may have been more evident in problems 7–9, but even in problems 1–4, that reasoning was helpful. Sid and Nancy compared quantities as ratios or rates. However, they used the parts and the whole of the mixture in different ways.

10. How might making the distinctions between the two methods (part-to-part ratio or part-to-whole ratio) help students in their understanding of proportional reasoning?

Putting it together

Proportional reasoning involves multiplication: When one quantity is multiplied by a factor, the other quantity must also be multiplied by that factor to maintain the proportion. Although this reasoning is developed extensively throughout middle school and high school, many students fail to connect the different ways this reasoning is used, especially when small twists are introduced.

The developers at Whodunnit jeans decided to see what would happen if they took two different mixtures and mixed them together. They called this the "union" of the two mixtures. For example, they took the two mixtures A and B from problem 2:

They made a mixture by mixing mixtures.

$$A = \left\{ \blacksquare\blacksquare\blacksquare\square\square \right\}$$

$$B = \left\{ \blacksquare\blacksquare\square\square \right\}$$

and formed the union of the mixtures (they named it $A \cup B$):

$$A \cup B = \left\{ \blacksquare\blacksquare\blacksquare\square\square\ \blacksquare\blacksquare\square\square \right\}$$

11. In this example, which is bluest: A, B, or $A \cup B$?

12. Can $A \cup B$ ever be bluer than *both* A and B? If not, why? If so, when?

Can $A \cup B$ ever be less blue than both A and B?

13. Given two (possible different) mixtures A and B, can $A \cup B$ ever be just as blue as one of A or B? If not, why? If so, when?

14. Suppose you could combine several vats of the mixture A above with one or more vats of the mixture B above. (For example, three of mixture A would have 15 total parts, 9 blue and 6 clear.) Could such a combination ever be bluer than mixture A? If not, why? If so, when?

Sid invented a term called the "blueness quotient" (BQ) for a mixture, which is the ratio of blue beakers to total beakers. In the mixture in problem 2, the BQ for A is $\frac{3}{5}$, and the BQ for B is $\frac{2}{4}$ or $\frac{1}{2}$.

A mixture with 6 blue parts and 4 clear also has a BQ of $\frac{3}{5}$, so the BQ's meaning should suggest a way in which this mixture and mixture A in problem 2 are the same.

15. Interpret the BQ as a percentage. What does this percentage mean for the mixture with a BQ of $\frac{3}{5}$? ▷

16. Do the BQs of two mixtures tell you anything about the comparison of the two mixtures?

17. Nancy preferred a shade created by mixing 3 beakers of blue dye with 2 beakers of water, and she kept a large glass container of this mixture on her lab table. Terry filled a vat with that shade by using 60 beakers of blue dye and 40 beakers of water. For a (very bad) practical joke, Sid added 3 beakers of blue dye to Nancy's container and another 3 beakers of blue dye to Terry's vat. Do the mixtures still have the same shade? Explain.

18. Is it possible to give an algorithm for computing the BQ of $A \cup B$ if you know the BQs for A and B? For example, suppose you combined a mixture with a BQ of $\frac{1}{2}$ with a mixture with a BQ of $\frac{1}{4}$. If so, how? If not, could you do it if you had more information?

19. Suppose you want to combine 7 ml of a mixture with a BQ of A and 12 ml of a mixture with a BQ of B. Could you find the BQ of the result? If so, how? If not, why?

Reflect and Discuss

20. Why can't you add fractions in the usual way (that is, $\frac{a}{b} + \frac{c}{d} = \frac{ad+bc}{bd}$) to get the BQ of the union? Does this strange fraction addition appear in any other mathematics topics for middle school and high school students?

And mix some more

Traditional algebra textbooks, particularly those published before the National Council of Teachers of Mathematics released its *Curriculum and Evaluation Standards for School Mathematics* in 1989, often included "word" or "story" problems. In contrast to the regular exercises, which were generally computational or procedural in nature, these word problems required students to apply their computations and procedures to problems presented using a context.

Often, the contexts became a way to classify the problems: coin problems, train problems, and mixture problems were only a few of the types. Students learned to do the problems by rote: They recognized the type of problem and then inserted the numbers into equations associated with the type. Years later, most would probably say, "I don't remember how to do mixture problems."

That is, a few of them learned it. Most never could solve these problems at all.

Students would be better served if they could reason about the problems, much in the same way you reasoned through the problems in this session.

Here is one example of a classic mixture problem (sometimes called a "solutions" problem):

> Five ounces of a 30% alcohol solution is mixed with ten ounces of a 50% alcohol solution. What is the percent of alcohol in the result?

21. Which of the blue-dye problems in this session does this seem to be the most like? Write a new blue-dye problem that uses the amounts in this solutions problem and would give the same result.

22. A related, but more difficult, problem might ask how much of each solution (30% and 50%) should be used to create 100 ounces of a 45% solution. Rewrite this new problem to be more like a blue-dye problem. (Algebra would probably be needed to actually solve this problem.)

Other contexts can be solved in the same way. For each of these, write a corresponding dye-mixture problem that gives the same result.

23. Speed A traveler has a 60-mile journey ahead. If he drives half the distance at a speed of 30 miles per hour and the rest of the way at a speed of 60 miles per hour, what is the average speed for the trip?

24. Weighted average Ms. Callahan calculates final grades in her class using five tests and an exam, which counts as three tests. Lon averaged 83 for the five tests and earned a 78 on the exam. What is his final grade?

Some textbooks refer to all *of these problems as weighted averages.*

25. Mixed nuts Peanuts cost $3 a pound, while cashews cost $7 a pound. If you mix 2.5 pounds of peanuts with 0.7 pounds of cashews, how much should the mixture cost per pound?

Ways to think about it

For your convenience, the problems are restated in the margin.

Problem: Do two of the developers always agree with each other?

Problem: Find an extreme example: two mixtures for which the methods don't all agree, but it's very clear which is incorrect.

Problem: If Sid used 45 beakers filled with blue dye, how much water (clear) was needed to get the same shade as Nancy's mixture?

Problem: If the total amount of dye in the vat was 1000 units, how much dye and how much water were needed?

Problem: How is the reasoning needed to answer problems 7 and 8 related to the developers' methods described on page 74?

Problem: Can $A \cup B$ ever be bluer than, or just as blue as, both A and B? If not, why? If so, when?

Problem: The BQ is defined in a somewhat abstract way, but it has a concrete meaning in the situation. What does it mean?

Problem: Do the BQs of two mixtures tell you anything about the comparison of the two mixtures?

Problem: Sid added 3 beakers of blue dye to Nancy's container and another 3 beakers of blue dye to Terry's vat. Do the mixtures still have the same shade? Explain.

Problem: Is it possible to give an algorithm for computing the BQ of $A \cup B$ if you know the BQs for A and B? If so, how? If not, could you do it if you had more information?

5. The three methods do not give identical numerical results, but two use basically the same type of reasoning.

6. Extreme examples might include a mixture that's all clear, or all blue. Other examples might be mixtures that have a large number of one type of liquid but only one of the other type.

7. If Sid made several copies of Nancy's mixture, how many blue beakers would be included in two copies? Three? Four? How many copies would give 45 blue beakers?

8. Try a similar tactic to what you did for problem 7, but focus on the total number of beakers needed.

9. Each of the two problems requires the same focus as one of the two correct methods.

12–13. You might try looking at examples. Include extreme examples, but also try examples for which A and B are nearly (or exactly) identical.

15. The BQ is a fraction or ratio. The fraction describes what part of what whole?

16. Each BQ represents a fraction with a concrete meaning. When you compare those two fractions, what does that tell you?

17. Compare the BQs of the two resulting mixtures.

18. Be sure to test any algorithms you create, using a variety of mixtures. Be wary of making assumptions about the mixture based on the BQ. Look back at problem 17 and use the mixtures given there.

If you find you are making assumptions, what assumption are you making? Can you turn that assumption into a question to ask about the mixtures?

If you think you're not making assumptions and you know whether an algorithm is possible, consider what extra information about a mixture might be lost when calculating the BQ. Could that extra information help you create an algorithm or make the one you have more efficient?

19. Note that the actual volume of a beaker of liquid has never been established. Can you assume a particular volume? Could you assume different size beakers for each mixture? You might want to try this with examples for the two mixtures.

Problem: Suppose you want to combine 7 ml of a mixture with a BQ of A and 12 ml of a mixture with a BQ of B. Could you find the BQ of the result? If so, how? If not, why?

20. Recall what information is lost when you calculate the BQ of some mixtures.

Problem: Why can't you add fractions in the usual way to get the BQ of the union?

21. It may help to rewrite the percentages as ratios. For example, 30% alcohol is how many parts alcohol to how many parts water? Draw a parallel between that and a blue-dye mixture.

Problem: Write a new blue-dye problem that uses the amounts in this solutions problem and would give the same result.

22–25. For each of these problems, identify what kind of ratios are being used, and how they are being combined. Draw parallels between the situations and the blue-dye problems.

2. Filling in the gaps

In section 1, you looked at situations which required proportional reasoning. This type of reasoning is important in many different contexts. In this session, you will explore how proportional reasoning can be helpful even in situations for which this type of reasoning doesn't necessarily lead to exact solutions.

Interpolate means literally "to polish in between."

One of the main themes of this section is *interpolation*: filling in values of a function between two known values. Before cheap pocket calculators were available, people used tables to find values of functions such as logarithms and trigonometric functions. Often, the value wanted would not be listed on the table, so the person would interpolate from the surrounding values. For example, the value of $\sin 45.7$ could be interpolated from a table that gave values for $\sin 45$ and $\sin 46$.

Reflect and Discuss

What is wrong with using "the next term" in this sentence?

1. A common type of elementary math problem is to find the next term in a sequence such as $1, 2, 4, \ldots$. Discuss possible answers for this problem and the reasoning used.

One common answer to problem 1 is 8; the term after 8 would be 16, then 32 . . . . Keeping this particular pattern in mind, change the problem.

2. Instead of continuing the sequence, fill in more terms between the existing ones. That is, if the sequence were $1, \_, 2, \_, 4, \ldots$, what could go in the blanks?

There are at least two reasonable answers for problem 2. One involves thinking of the sequence as additive; to get from one term to the next, you have to add something each time (but not necessarily always the *same* something). Another answer involves thinking of it as multiplicative; to get from one term to the next, you have to multiply something each time.

3. Find both an additive pattern and a multiplicative pattern that will generate a sequence $1, \_, 2, \_, 4, \ldots$.

4. In a way, you can think of the numbers you put in each blank as being "halfway" between the terms on either side. This gives at least two meanings for "halfway." Use similar processes (adding and multiplying) to find two different numbers that are (sort of) $\frac{1}{3}$ of the way between 1 and 2 in the sequence. Then use those answers to find two numbers $\frac{2}{3}$ of the way between.

5.   Can you find two numbers any (rational) fraction of the way between 1 and 2 in the sequence?

6.   Answer problems 4 and 5 for numbers between 2 and 4 in the sequence.

Reflect and Discuss

7.   How did you find your answers to problems 2–6?

Now consider a graphical interpretation of finding numbers a fractional part of the way between the numbers in the sequence. Call the term number n and the corresponding term a_n. So, for example, if $n = 1$, then $a_n = a_1 = 1$. Similarly, if $n = 3$, then $a_n = a_3 = 4$.

8.   Below is a plot of the first three terms of the doubling sequence. The term number or index, n, is on the horizontal axis and the sequence value, a_n, is on the vertical axis. Connect the points using straight lines. That is, connect $(1, 1)$ to $(2, 2)$ and $(2, 2)$ to $(3, 4)$.

Use a straightedge if you have one available.

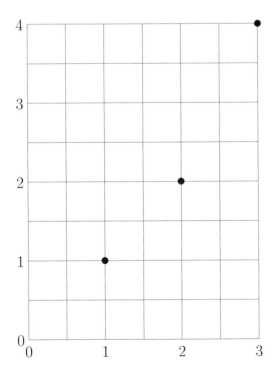

9. Mark points on the lines you just drew for which $n = 1\frac{1}{3}$, $n = 2\frac{1}{3}$, and $n = 2\frac{3}{4}$. Those points represent "between" sequence values. Use those points to find the corresponding values of a. ▷

You may get more accurate results if you use a ruler to make vertical lines and measure the distance from the axis.

One algebraic definition of the doubling sequence is $a_n = 2^{n-1}$. If you graph $y = 2^{n-1}$, perhaps on a graphing calculator, you get a nice, smooth curve through the points.

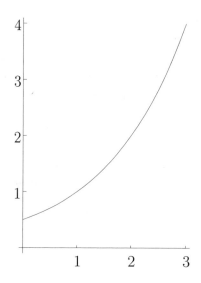

10. Here are actual values and approximations, accurate to the thousandth place, for the points on the curve corresponding to the n values in problem 9:

n	$1\frac{1}{3}$	$2\frac{1}{3}$	$2\frac{3}{4}$
a_n, exact	$\sqrt[3]{2}$	$2\sqrt[3]{2}$	$2\sqrt[4]{8}$
a_n, appr.	1.260	2.520	3.364

(a) How close were your approximations in problem 9?
(b) Explain why it makes sense that some approximations are closer than others.

11. Following is another plot of the first three terms in the sequence, along with the actual "halfway" points that lie on the curve. (Labels give approximate values, to the nearest thousandth.)

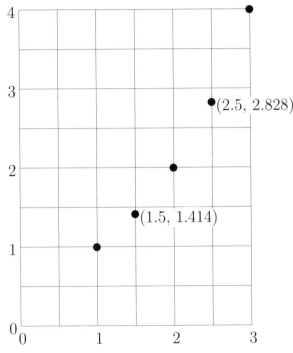

(a) Once again, draw lines on the graph and find approximate values for a_n when n is $1\frac{1}{3}, 2\frac{1}{3}$, and $2\frac{3}{4}$.

(b) You probably would expect that your new approximations are closer than the old ones. Explain why that would be true.

To move from one point to another on any graph, you have to move left or right by a certain amount (call it Δn) and also up or down by a certain amount (call it Δa). Lines, like the ones you created by connecting points in problem 8, have a special characteristic: Every time you move that Δn distance, the distance you move up or down is always the same: Δa.

This characteristic of lines allows you to work with them very easily. Think again about approximating a point $\frac{1}{3}$ of the way from $(1,1)$ to $(2,2)$, using the line you drew in problem 8. To move from $n = 1$ to $n = 1\frac{1}{3}$, you move $\Delta n = \frac{1}{3}$ unit to the right. Three of these jumps—all the same size—will land you on $(2,2)$.

12. Since you're moving along a line, each jump up is the same size (in both the n and the a directions). If you make three equal-sized vertical jumps from $a = 1$ to $a = 2$, what is the length of each jump? Where are you when $n = 1\frac{1}{3}$?

13. The following questions use the same reasoning to help you find a numerical way to make the other approximations you

The uppercase Greek letter delta (Δ) is often used in mathematics to denote a difference. For example, Δn means the difference between two n values: $n_j - n_i$.

Graphs that aren't lines don't have this characteristic. For example, when you move from $(1,1)$ to $(2,2)$ on the doubling graph, Δn is 1 and Δa is 1. When you move from $(2,2)$ to $(3,4)$, Δn is still 1, but Δa is now 2. The distances you move depend on where you are on the graph.

made graphically in problem 9. Work through the steps to approximate the value for a_n when n is $2\frac{3}{4}$.

(a) First consider what fraction of the way from one point to the next you have to jump *horizontally*. For example, to get to $1\frac{1}{3}$, you had to go $\frac{1}{3}$ of the way from 1 to 2.

(b) When you jump horizontally, you also have to jump vertically. What *fraction* of the way between two points do you have to jump? How far is that? ▷

(c) Now figure out where you land when you make that jump. Don't forget, you started at a point other than the origin.

"How far is that" is an important question to ask. If you jump $\frac{1}{3}$ of the way, that's not necessarily the same as jumping a distance of $\frac{1}{3}$ of a unit.

14. Go through the steps of problem 13 and generalize the method to give an approximation for a_n when $m < n < m + 1$ and you know a_m and a_{m+1}.

You may want to draw a picture of what's going on here!

15. Now, generalize the method further, to give an approximation for any a_n when $m < n < p$ and you know a_m and a_p. Note that m and p may be any numbers, including nonintegers.

16. The slope of a line with independent variable x (on the horizontal axis) and dependent variable y (on the vertical axis) can be defined as $\frac{\Delta y}{\Delta x}$. Does the slope of the line between (m, a_m) and (p, a_p) appear in your generalization?

This is often stated colloquially as $\frac{rise}{run}$.

In section 1, you worked with mixture or weighted average problems like the following:

> The BQ (blueness quotient) of a mixture is the ratio of the number of blue dye beakers to the total number of beakers in a mixture. Suppose you combine x ml of a mixture with a BQ of A with y ml of a mixture with a BQ of B.

17. What is the BQ of the resulting combination?

Reflect and Discuss

18. How is the blue-dye problem above related to the interpolation problem?

The weighted average you used to find the BQ of the result is a linear combination of the BQs A and B. A **linear combination** of two quantities is the sum when each is multiplied by a number or variable. For example, $3x + 2y$ can be considered a linear combination of x and y. It can also be considered a linear combination of 3 and 2.

Or, $3x + 2y$ can be considered a linear combination of x and 2, or of 3 and y.

19. Use a linear combination for the interpolation problem. That is, find a way to write a value a_n as a linear combination of a_m and a_p, where $m < n < p$:

$$a_n \approx \underline{\quad} a_m + \underline{\quad} a_p$$

Local linearity

As you saw in problem 11, having more data points (or at least, data closer together) leads to better approximations. A similar concept is often used by mathematicians working with nonlinear functions.

Using a graphing calculator, graph a polynomial or exponential function. For example, you might graph the doubling function, $y = 2^x$, or a polynomial such as $y = 3x^4 - 2x^3 + x - 1$. Try to get a function that looks "curvy."

- Find a section of the graph that looks particularly curvy—as far from a line as the graph seems to get. Zoom in on that section.

- Now find a section in that window that looks curvy and zoom in again.

- Repeat this for several zooms.

Reflect and Discuss

20. Did you find it more and more difficult to find a particularly curvy part of the graph? What did your final zooms look like?

The phenomenon you probably observed is what mathematicians call **local linearity.** If you look at the graph in a small enough "neighborhood" around a point, in most cases the graph will appear to be a line.

A line has a slope, because for a given horizontal change, the vertical change is always constant. Because a nonlinear curve can have different vertical changes depending on where you look, it can't have a single slope. You can, however, find the slope of a curve at a particular point.

The "local" means you can only assume the curve is a line "locally"—for a small neighborhood around a point. The smaller the neighborhood, the more like a line (and so the better your approximation).

21. The slope of a curve at a point can be thought of as the slope of the line tangent to the curve, at that point. A **secant line** is a line through two points on the curve. Here is a graph that includes the curve $y = x^3$, the tangent line at a point x, and the secant through two points at x and $x + h$.

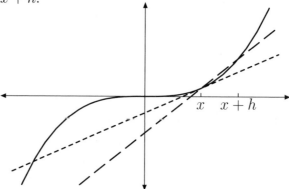

(a) What happens to the secant line as h gets smaller and eventually becomes 0?

(b) Find an expression for the slope of this secant line. What happens to the expression as h gets smaller (approaches 0)?

22. In mathematics, taking a variable to a certain value is called taking a *limit*. For example, the limit of $x + h$ as h goes to 0 is simply x (provided x and h are independent):

$$\lim_{h \to 0} x + h = x$$

(a) Write an expression for the slope of the secant line for a general function $f(x)$, through the points $(x, f(x))$ and $(x + h, f(x + h))$.

(b) The slope of the tangent line is the limit of the secant line's slope, as h goes to 0. Use the limit notation to write an expression for the slope of the tangent line.

Congratulations! You have not only found the derivative of x^3 in problem 21, you wrote the general definition of a derivative (problem 22). Derivatives are one of the fundamental concepts in calculus.

Ways to think about it

1. There are actually an infinite number of possible next terms for this sequence. The most obvious can be found by looking for patterns in ratios ($\frac{one\ term}{the\ previous\ term}$) and differences (*one term* minus *the previous term*).

    > **Problem:** *Discuss possible next terms for the sequence* $1, 2, 4, \ldots$ *and the reasoning used.*

3. You probably found one of these in your answer to problem 2, in which case your first step is to figure out if you used a multiplicative pattern or an additive one.

    > **Problem:** *Find both an additive pattern and a multiplicative pattern that will generate a sequence* $1, \_, 2, \_, 4, \ldots$.

    If you need to find an additive pattern, first figure out an additive pattern for the "parent" sequence, 1, 2, 4, 8, ... Now you have to make additions that give the same sequence with one additional value between each pair in the parent sequence. Remember, you don't have to use a different value each time, as long as you make an identifiable pattern.

    If you need to find a multiplicative pattern, consider this: In the parent sequence, you multiply by 2 to get the next term. If the sequence were $1, \_, 2, \_, 4, \ldots$, what would you multiply each time? Suppose you multiply by r. The first term is 1; the second is r. What is the third term, using r? For that to be 2, what does r have to be?

4. Use the same idea from problem 2, above. To include numbers $\frac{1}{3}$ and $\frac{2}{3}$ of the way between the original terms, the new sequence would have to look like $1, \_, \_, 2, \_, \_, 4, \ldots$.

    > **Problem:** *Find two different numbers that are (sort of)* $\frac{1}{3}$ *of the way between 1 and 2 in the sequence; find two that are* $\frac{2}{3}$ *of the way between.*

10. To explain why some approximations are closer than others, it might help to make a rough sketch of what the actual curve through the points would look like. (The curve is not a series of lines.) Where is that curve furthest from the lines?

    > **Problem:** *How close were your approximations to the actual values? Explain why it makes sense that some approximations are closer than others.*

14. Look back at your work in problem 13. For $n = 2\frac{1}{3}$, you should have used $m = 2$ and $m + 1 = 3$, with corresponding sequence values $a_m = 2$ and $a_{m+1} = 4$.

    > **Problem:** *Generalize the method to give an approximation for any* a_n *when* $m < n < m + 1$ *and you know* a_m *and* a_{m+1}.

15. Again, look back at your work in problem 13. The big new thing to remember is that the distance from m to p is not necessarily 1 unit, so jumping $\frac{1}{3}$ of the way from m to p is not jumping $\frac{1}{3}$ unit. (For example, how far do you jump if you jump $\frac{1}{3}$ of the way from 2 to 5?)

    > **Problem:** *Generalize the method further to give an approximation for any* a_n *when* $m < n < p$ *and you know* a_m *and* a_p.

Problem: Does the slope of the line between (m, a_m) and (p, a_p) appear in your generalization?

Problem: Suppose you combine x ml of a mixture with a BQ of A with y ml of a mixture with a BQ of B. What is the BQ of the resulting combination?

Problem: Use a linear combination for the interpolation problem.

Problem: What happens to the secant line as h gets smaller and eventually becomes 0? What happens to the expression for the slope of the secant line as h gets smaller (approaches 0)?

16. Look for differences $a_p - a_m$ and $p - m$ in your generalization. If you find them but they don't appear as a ratio or fraction, is it possible to create that ratio? Would doing so make your generalization look simpler or more familiar in some way?

17. Answer the following questions, then use that information to find the BQ: How many milliliters of blue dye does each mixture contribute? What is the total amount of liquid in the combination?

19. You may already have written this in your generalization from problem 15. If not, see if you can use algebra to rewrite your generalization in the form of a linear combination of a_m and a_p.

21. If you're having trouble visualizing this, place a straightedge (like a ruler or the side of a piece of paper) on the illustration, where the secant line is now. If h gets a little smaller, how does this affect x and $x + h$? Where would the points (x, x^3) and $(x + h, (x + h)^3)$ be? Move the straightedge to represent the new secant line . . . .

3. Guess my rule

In section 1, you looked at situations for which proportional reasoning and relative comparisons were important. In section 2, you looked at interpolation and how lines can be used to approximate curves.

This section explores another way of defining both linear and nonlinear functions: by identities and properties of functions. The problems have a distinctly algebraic flavor, but you may also want to try representing the functions by tables and graphs.

To begin, consider these four symbols: $\{\Box, \blacksquare, \blacksquare, \blacksquare\}$. You can "add" two symbols by superimposing one on top of the other, giving this addition table:

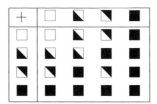

1. Suppose you add two symbols and then rotate the result 180°. (For example, add ◣ to ◣. The result is ◣, which becomes ◤ when rotated 180°.) Then, with the same original symbols, change the order: first rotate (each ◣ becomes ◤) and then add (◤ + ◤ = ◤).

   For any choice of two symbols, will you *always* get the same final answer by adding and then rotating the result as you would if you first rotate and then add the results?

For functions and operations using real numbers, students often assume that they always *can* do these things in either order. How many algebra (and even calculus) students trip up by thinking $(x + y)^2 = x^2 + y^2$?

Some college professors call this the "Freshman Dream."

Of course, adding two numbers then performing some rule on the result will not always give the same result as performing the rule on each number before adding. The next question to ask is, for what kind of rules *will* these have the same result? In this session, you will work to answer that question for real-valued functions.

PROBLEM

MYSTERY FUNCTION PROBLEM

What kind of assumptions do you want to make about F?

A function, F, has only real numbers in its domain (its inputs), and its range (outputs) also consists of real numbers. For any real numbers a and b, $F(a + b) = F(a) + F(b)$. That is, if you put in the sum of two numbers, what comes out is the sum of the outputs for the two numbers fed in separately. What does F look like, algebraically?

For example, if $F(7) = 35$ and $F(9) = 45$, then $F(16)$ would be 80.

2. Is enough information given in the MYSTERY FUNCTION PROBLEM to determine the value of $F(0)$? Is enough information given to determine the value of $F(1)$?

3. Suppose you also know that $F(1) = -\frac{5}{6}$. Fill in the table below using only the information given. That is, don't depend on finding patterns. ▷ Be sure to fill in the "Reason" column!

You'll see more about why you can't rely on patterns in problem 7.

x	$F(x)$	Reason
1	$-\frac{5}{6}$	
2		
3		
any positive integer n		
0		
-1		
-2		
any integer n		

4. Show that if $F(a + b) = F(a) + F(b)$ and c is an integer, then $F(ca) = cF(a)$ (even if a is not an integer).

5. You probably have some idea for a rule for F. Fill in the next table, again *without* using such a rule. Only use the clue that $F(a+b) = F(a) + F(b)$ and results from previous problems.

x	$F(x)$	Reason
$\frac{1}{2}$		
$\frac{1}{3}$		
$\frac{1}{n}$ where n is an integer		
$\frac{m}{n}$ where m and n are integers		

6. Show that if $F(a + b) = F(a) + F(b)$ and r is a rational number, then $F(ra) = rF(a)$ (even if a is irrational).

Reflect and Discuss

7. Can you determine a value for $F(\sqrt{2})$? For $F(\pi)$? Do problems 4 and 6 imply that $F(ka) = kF(a)$ for all real numbers k?

An *identity* is an equation that applies for all values of the variables involved. For example, if a and b are real, then $a^2 - b^2 = (a + b)(a - b)$ is an identity because it is true for all values of a and b that make sense in the equation. (In this equation, all real numbers a and b make sense. If the identity involved square roots, you might have to exclude negative numbers.) However, $x^2 - 3x + 2 = 0$ is not an identity, because it is true only for two values of x.

If a and b weren't restricted to real numbers, though, this would not be an identity. If the variables are matrices, $a^2 - b^2$ does not usually equal $(a + b)(a - b)$ because matrix multiplication is not commutative.

The equation $F(a+b) = F(a) + F(b)$ is sometimes an identity, depending on what the function F is. A function for which $F(a + b) = F(a) + F(b)$ is an identity is called an *additive homomorphism*, or an *addition-preserving* function.

The idea here is that the domain (input set) of the function is a set (in this case, the real numbers) with an operation (in this case, addition). The range (output set) of the function is another set (also the real numbers) with another operation (also addition). The identity $F(a + b) = F(a) + F(b)$ says that addition in the domain corresponds to addition in the range. Or, stated another way, if you add in the domain, then move to the range by F, you get the same result as if you first move to the range, then add.

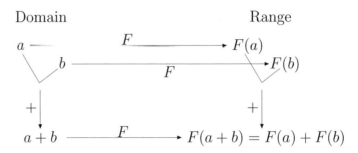

This identity, combined with the property that $F(ka) = kF(a)$ for all possible values of k, $\triangleright$ is often used as the definition of a **linear mapping**.

If our domain and range are real numbers, this includes irrational values for k.

DEFINITION

A linear mapping is a function F such that

That is, the equations are identities (they hold for all choices of a, b, and k).

- $F(a + b) = F(a) + F(b)$
- $F(ka) = kF(a)$

For a mapping from the real numbers into the real numbers, the first property guarantees the second property *if* the function is continuous—that is, as long as there are no "holes" or "breaks" in the graph.

If F is not continuous, there is no way to connect the gaps in the graph between the rational numbers, so there are many different Fs from the same rule.

8.   Are these functions linear mappings? Why or why not?
 (a) $f_1(x) =$ the cost of x pounds of beans at the health food store
      (Beans are sold in bulk; you can buy any amount you want.)
 (b) $f_2(x) =$ the area of a square x meters on a side
 (c) $f_3(x) =$ the total amount of money in your bank account after x years, if you start with $1000 at year 0, and never withdraw or deposit money, and interest is compounded annually at a constant rate of $r\%$
 (d) $f_4(x, y) =$ the cost of x pounds of beans and y pounds of rice at the health food store

Linear mappings can appear with sets other than real numbers, as you'll see in the next problem.

9. Is the described function a linear mapping? Why or why not?

(a) For an angle measure r, $f_5(r)$ is a rotation $r°$ counterclockwise about point D. Addition of rotations is their composition, that is, $f_5(r) + f_5(s)$ is the rotation through $r°$ followed by the rotation through $s°$.

(b) The function f_6 takes a point on a coordinate plane for its input and moves it 3 units to the left and 4 units up. Addition of two points (a_1, b_1) and (a_2, b_2) is defined as $(a_1, b_1) + (a_2, b_2) = (a_1 + a_2, b_1 + b_2)$.

(c) For a mixture of beakers filled with either blue dye or water, the blueness quotient (BQ) is the ratio of the number of blue-dye beakers to the total number of beakers. The sum of two mixtures is their union. Is the BQ a linear mapping? That is, is the BQ of the union equal to the sum of the BQs?

Reflect and Discuss

Here's a function that might surprise you: $f_8(x) =$ the total cost of an order of x pounds of beans from beans.com, including a $4.95 shipping charge.

10. Is f_8 a linear mapping?

11. What do you think it means to ask, "Is a function g linear?"

Standard English words can mean different things in different contexts. Mathematical terms can mean different things as well. In the case of "linear," there are two common senses which are closely related. One sense is that of high school algebra: a function is linear if its graph is a line. Function f_8 would then be considered a linear function.

The other sense is the definition of a linear mapping. This sense is used in fields such as linear algebra, which includes matrices. While the required properties exclude functions of the type $y = mx + b$ where b is nonzero, those properties allow mathematicians to do more with a linear mapping. Knowing a function is a linear mapping is much more powerful than knowing a function is a linear function.

The dual meaning for linearity can be very confusing, especially to students trying to connect this second sense to the first.

12. The following questions are based on a linear mapping T from $\mathbb{R}$ to $\mathbb{R}$, where $T(1) = -4$.

(a) Find $T(3)$.

(b) Find a so that $T(x) = ax$.

The symbol $\mathbb{R}$ denotes the real numbers, so the mapping T has real number inputs and real number outputs.

(c) Find all x so that $T(x) = 3$.

(d) Which of problems 12a–12c could you still answer if you did not know that T is a linear mapping? Why?

13. Here is a simplification of the MYSTERY FUNCTION PROBLEM: Describe all polynomials P, with real numbers for their domain and range, for which $P(a+b) = P(a) + P(b)$. Be sure to explain why you know you've described all of them. ▷

In the Further Exploration materials, you'll see how to describe not just the polynomials but all the continuous functions (with real number inputs and outputs).

Linear combinations

14. Using a linear combination, the two requirements for linear mappings can be combined into one statement:

F is a linear mapping if and only if $F(ax + by) = aF(x) + bF(y)$.

Since this is an "if and only if" statement, both directions have to be proved.

(a) Show that if F is a linear mapping, then $F(ax + by) = aF(x) + bF(y)$.

(b) Show that if $F(ax + by) = aF(x) + bF(y)$, then F is a linear mapping.

Mathematicians use two shorthand notations for "if and only if": iff is a language shorthand, and ⇔ is a symbolic notation. The ⇔ symbols indicates that the "if-then" statements must go both ways. That is, $p \Leftrightarrow q$ means both $p \Rightarrow q$ (read p implies q, or if p then q) and $q \Rightarrow p$.

15. In section 2, you found a formula for interpolating data between two points. Your formula probably looked something like this, but using subscripts instead of function notation:

$$a(n) = a(m) + \frac{n - m}{p - m}(a(p) - a(m))$$

Let $x = \frac{n-m}{p-m}$.

(a) Find an expression for n that uses x, m, and p.

(b) Replace each n in the formula above with the expression you just found. Rewrite the result using linear combinations on both sides of the formula. That is, write it in the form

a(linear combination of p and m) = linear combination of p and m

(c) What values should be used for x?

(d) Describe all polynomials for which the interpolation is exact, not an approximation. Explain why this makes sense, using both symbols and a graphical argument.

(e) Polynomials for which the interpolation is exact do not have to be linear mappings. What in the linear interpolation formula is different from the definition of linear mappings and allows this to be true?

Ways to think about it

1. You probably will find it easiest to show it works for different cases: if one symbol is □, if one symbol is ◣, and so on. For some of those cases, whether it works for every choice of the other symbol may be easy to show; for others, you might have to break it into even more specific cases.

Problem: For any choice of two symbols, will you always get the same final answer by adding and then rotating the result as if you first rotate and then add the results?

2. The only information you have is that $F(a + b) = F(a) + F(b)$. To find the value of $F(0)$, it will have to appear in such an equation. Rewrite the equation so that $F(0)$ appears somewhere, then solve for $F(0)$.

    Would something similar work for $F(1)$? If so, do it. If not, explain why not. It might help to think of some examples of F where $F(a + b) = F(a) + F(b)$ and compare $F(1)$ in each case.

Problem: Is enough information given in the Mystery Function problem to determine the value of $F(0)$? Is enough information given to determine the value of $F(1)$?

3. You should be able to fill in the value for $F(0)$. You now have function values for two input numbers, 0 and 1. The equation in the Mystery Function problem statement refers to sums. Can you write sums, using the input values for which you have function values, to create other inputs? For the negative integers, recall or read the "ways to think about" problem 2 for finding $F(0)$. Can you do something similar to find values for negative integers?

Problem: Suppose you know also know that $F(1) = -\frac{5}{6}$. Fill in the table using only the information given.

4. This proof will require more than simple algebraic manipulation, because you want to show it's true for all integers c. One way to approach the problem is to use *mathematical induction*. With mathematical induction, you show that something is true for a specific case, such as $a = 1$. Then you use the information you have to show that, assuming it's true for cases up to, say, $a = n$, then it must be true for $a = n + 1$. (Since you've shown it's true for $a = 1$, then, it must be true for $a = 2$. But that means it's true for $a = 3$, which in turn means ... .) In this case, you would have to work in two directions. Going up will prove the statement is true for positive integers but not negative integers. A second (similar) argument will be needed to show the statement is true going down, as well. (That is, assuming it's true for $a = n$, show it's also true for $a = n - 1$.)

Problem: Show that if $F(a + b) = F(a) + F(b)$ and c is an integer, then $F(ca) = cF(a)$.

Picture walking up stairs: you can touch every step by standing on the first step and then taking one step up, then the next, then the next, and so on. If you know you can get to step n, you can get to step $n + 1$. You then just have to be sure you can get to the first step!

5. The table starts with $x = \frac{1}{2}$. Again, you know the function values for integers, and you know how to find function values for inputs expressed as sums. How can you use sums with $\frac{1}{2}$ to get an integer (and so a function value you know)? To find values for rational numbers that are not unit frac-

Problem: Fill in the table. Only use the clue that $F(a + b) = F(a) + F(b)$ and information from previous problems.

tions (that is, $\frac{m}{n}$ where m and n are integers, $n \neq 0$ and $m \neq 1$), you need to use previous results. You should know how to find values for unit fractions. You know how to find function values when the input is expressed as the product of an integer and an input whose function value you know.

Problem: *Show that if* $F(a + b) = F(a) + F(b)$ *and* r *is a rational number, then* $F(ra) = rF(a)$.

6. This seems similar to problem 4, but mathematical induction would be difficult to use here. (Why?) The method you used to find function values for $x = \frac{m}{n}$ should help, though. medskip

Problem: *Can you determine a value for* $F(\sqrt{2})$? *For* $F(\pi)$? *Do problems 4 and 6 imply that* $F(ka) = kF(a)$ *for all real numbers* k?

7. For the previous problems, you found function values by using sums and products of inputs for which you already knew the function values. Can you express $\sqrt{2}$ or π using such sums and products? What kinds of values *can* you express in such a way?

Problem: *Are these functions linear mappings? Why or why not?*

8–10. Show whether the definition of a linear mapping holds for each function.

Problem: *Which of problems 12a–12c could you still answer if you did not know that* T *is a linear mapping? Why?*

12d. Look back at how you found answers to problems 12a–12c. Did you use either part of the definition of a linear mapping? If so, could you have answered the problem without using the definition?

Problem: *Describe all polynomials* P, *with real numbers for their domain and range, for which* $P(a + b) = P(a) + P(b)$.

13. By now, you should know a family of polynomial functions in which all its members are additive homomorphisms. Proving this requires some algebra. You also need to be sure that you know *all* polynomial functions that are additive homomorphisms. (How could there be others?)

Why is a constant term, a_0, *not needed here?*

There are several ways to show this. For each, suppose $P(x) = r_1x + r_2x^2 + \cdots + r_nx^n$ is an additive homomorphism.

Corresponding coefficients must be equivalent because the equivalency must hold for an infinite number of inputs.

- For two polynomial expressions to be equivalent ($P(a) + P(b)$ and $P(a + b)$ in this case), the coefficients of corresponding terms must be equivalent. What terms will $P(a) + P(b)$ have? What additional terms will $P(a + b)$ have? Since corresponding terms must have equivalent coefficients, what must those coefficients be? What does that imply about the coefficients $P(x)$?

Once you have a contradiction, one of your original premises—in this case, that there is a polynomial of the form $P(x) = r_1x + r_2x^2 + \cdots + r_nx^n$ *which is an additive homomorphism, or there is more than one distinct zero—must be incorrect.*

- How many zeroes can $P(x)$ have? Use the additive homomorphism property to show that if there is more than one distinct zero, there are an infinite number of distinct zeroes. To avoid a contradiction, there is only one possible polynomial. (What is it? Hint: It can be expressed in the form you probably identified as the family of linear mappings.) Once you know there isn't more than one zero, you can address the possibilities of one or no zeroes. What would a graph with no zeroes look like? Next, assume there is only one zero, although that zero may appear multiple times. If there is only one zero, what must $P(x)$ look like? Show that a polynomial of that form can be an additive homomorphism in only one case—that is, that it must be in the family you've already described.

For example, the graph of $y = (x+1)^2$ has only one zero, but it appears twice, once for each factor $x + 1$.

- For a graphical argument, consider two values 1 unit apart, say, a and $a + 1$, where a is some rational number. How far apart are their function values? ≺ What if you had chosen two other values, 1 unit apart—how far apart are the function values for those? What does this tell you the graph of such a function must look like? What do you know about polynomial graphs that can help you conclude which families can be additive homomorphisms?

You don't need to use $P(x) = r_1 x + r_2 x + \cdots$ for this. Only use the fact that $P(a + b) = P(a) + P(b)$.

14. To prove statements like this, first assume the "if" part is true. Then use that assumption to show the rest must be true.

    For part (a), you know that F is a linear mapping. Recall the definition of a linear mapping, and use it to find an equivalent expression for $F(ax + by)$. (You should be able to show that $aF(x) + bF(y)$ is an equivalent expression.)

    For part (b), you know that $F(ax + by) = aF(x) + bF(y)$. Can you then show that the conditions for being a linear mapping must be true for F? Perhaps some thoughtful numerical substitutions for a and b would help.

Problem: (a) Show that if F is a linear mapping, then $F(ax + by) = aF(x) + bF(y)$. (b) Show that if $F(ax + by) = aF(x) + bF(y)$, then F is a linear mapping.

15. For part (a), use algebraic manipulation on $x = \frac{n-m}{p-m}$ to get n on one side, alone.

    For part (c), recall between what points the original formula interpolated. What values of x will give those points? What values will give points between them?

    For part (d), you might approach the problem graphically, first. When you interpolated using linear combinations, what were you assuming the curve looked like (or almost like) between the two points? For what polynomials will the curve actually look like that? For a symbolic argument, you can refer to problem 13, but you have to justify why the answer here is not as restricted as the answer in problem 13. (This is also the answer to part (e).)

Problem: (a) Find an expression for n that uses $x, m,$ and p. (b) Write the formula in the form $a(\text{linear combination of } p \text{ and } m) = \text{linear combination of } p \text{ and } m$. (c) What values should be used for x? (d) Describe all polynomials for which the interpolation is exact. Explain. (e) What in the linear interpolation formula is different from the definition of linear mappings and allows the polynomials for which the interpolation is exact to not be linear mappings?

4. Functions of two variables

As you worked through the first three sections of this chapter, you may have noticed times when more than one variable was used for a function or situation. In section 1, the blueness quotient (BQ) was based on both the number of blue beakers in a mixture and the total number of beakers in the mixture. In section 2, linear combinations often use two variables, such as in the linear combination $3x + 2y$. Some of the linear mappings in section 3 involved more than one variable, like the total cost of x pounds of beans and y pounds of rice.

In this session, you will explore functions of two variables (two input variables, one output variable). Some of the big questions are: How should linearity be defined for functions of two variables? Which features of linearity of one variable still apply in this new situation? What do those functions look like algebraically, graphically, and in tables?

You can find it in Comparing Quantities, *by Kindt, Martin, et al. The curriculum is published by* Encyclopaedia Britannica.

The first problem context is adapted from the *Mathematics in Context* middle school curriculum.

1.   Four pencils and 2 erasers cost 40 cents; 2 pencils and 5 erasers cost 60 cents.
    (a) Examine this chart, and explain what it will show when completed.

number of pencils

	0	1	2	3	4	5	6
0							
1							
2					40		
3							
4							
5			60				
6							

number of erasers

(b) How can you use the chart (but no algebraic equations) to find the cost of 2 pencils and 1 eraser?

    (c) Complete the chart, again without using algebraic equations. Record the steps you take.

    (d) What is the cost of each eraser and each pencil? Could this be found from the table in more than one way?

    (e) What are all the combinations shown in the chart which you could buy for exactly 55 cents? What are all the combinations you could buy for 30 cents? For any fixed amount of money, how could you describe all the combinations you could buy?

Reflect and Discuss

2. Compare your approaches with those of others. For the approaches that worked, explain what made them work.

3. Analyze the chart with traditional algebraic methods. Can the chart methods be interpreted algebraically?

You could think of the cost of pencils and erasers as a function of the numbers of pencils and erasers: $C(p, e)$ is the cost of p pencils and e erasers.

Think about section 3, "Guess My Rule," while doing this problem.

4.   (a) Before you filled out the chart, you were given the information $C(4, 2) = 40$ and $C(2, 5) = 60$. What is $C(4 + 2, 2 + 5)$?

    (b) In general, if you knew $C(p_1, e_1)$ and $C(p_2, e_2)$, how could you find $C(p_1 + p_2, e_1 + e_2)$? Could this method have been used to fill the chart? Was it used by someone?

    (c) Since you know $C(4, 2)$, how could you find $C(8, 4)$, $C(12, 6)$, ...?

    (d) In general, if you knew $C(p, e)$, how could you find $C(ap, ae)$ for a whole number a? Could this fact have been used to fill the chart?

Think carefully—someone might have used it without really thinking in this way. What choices for p_2 and e_2 would make an efficient strategy for filling the chart?

In section 3, you learned that a linear mapping is a function F that satisfies the following conditions:

- $F(a + b) = F(a) + F(b)$
- $F(ka) = kF(a)$

As you saw, the quantities a, b, and k do not have to be real numbers. If the domain of F is a subset of $\mathbb{R}^2$ (ordered pairs of real numbers) and the range is a subset of $\mathbb{R}$ (*scalar*, or one-dimensional, real numbers), then the conditions for a linear map could be restated like this:

- $F(x_1 + x_2, y_1 + y_2) = F(x_1, y_1) + F(x_2, y_2)$
- $F(kx, ky) = kF(x, y)$

That is, $(x_1, y_1) + (x_2, y_2) = (x_1 + x_2, y_1 + y_2)$, and $k(x, y) = (kx, ky)$.

We could also define a and b to be two-dimensional vectors, and use vector addition and scalar multiplication. Abbreviate $\mathbf{v} = (x, y)$, $\mathbf{v_1} - (x_1, y_1)$, and $\mathbf{v_2} = (x_2, y_2)$. Then the two conditions are

- $F(\mathbf{v_1} + \mathbf{v_2}) = F(\mathbf{v_1}) + F(\mathbf{v_2})$
- $F(k\mathbf{v}) = kF(\mathbf{v})$

Note that this is exactly the definition of a linear mapping of one variable.

5. (a) Is $C(p, e)$ a linear mapping?

(b) In section 3, you saw that a linear mapping from $\mathbb{R}$ into $\mathbb{R}$ looks like $F(x) = mx$ for some constant m. What do you think a (continuous) linear mapping from $\mathbb{R}^2$ into $\mathbb{R}$ looks like? Write a general description.

6. Is the function $F(x, y) = 7x + y - 5$ a linear mapping of two variables?

Reflect and Discuss

7. Should the function $F(x, y) = 7x + y - 5$ be considered a linear function? Why or why not?

The chickens and the eggs

You may have heard this joke problem before: "If a hen and a half can lay an egg and a half in a day and a half, how many eggs can 3 hens lay in 3 days?"

8. Most people's first inclination is to say 3 eggs is the answer. This answer uses the idea of linearity, but incorrectly. How is linearity being used, and why is it incorrect in this case?

Be sure your thinking cap is on for this one!

9. Try looking at the problem this way: Suppose you have an egg function $E(H, D)$, which gives the number of eggs that H hens can lay in D days. Complete a table for the egg function, following the example of the pencils/erasers function. Use increments of half a hen on one axis, and increments of half a day on the other axis. What is the correct answer to the question?

10. Would you say from your table that the eggs function is linear? Why or why not?

11. In the following questions, a and b are positive. As you answer the questions, think about what they mean in terms of hens, eggs, and days. It might help to invent a barnyard scenario. Part a, for example, could be used to answer this question: If the number of hens on a farm increases by a factor of a, how does this affect the egg production?
(a) Is $E(aH, D) = aE(H, D)$?
(b) Is $E(H, bD) = bE(H, D)$?
(c) Is $E(H_1 + H_2, D) = E(H_1, D) + E(H_2, D)$?
(d) Is $E(H, D_1 + D_2) = E(H, D_1) + E(H, D_2)$?

12. Rephrase this question in terms of the egg function: How many eggs can 3 hens lay in 5 days? Use the identities you developed in problem 11 to answer it.

13. Write an explicit formula for the egg function.

14. Would you like to change your mind on whether the eggs function is a linear function? Why or why not?

15. Describe a family of functions F from $\mathbb{R}^2$ to $\mathbb{R}$ that satisfy these conditions. Be sure to show that all functions in the family will satisfy them.
- $F(ax, y) = aF(x, y)$
- $F(x_1 + x_2, y) = F(x_1, y) + F(x_2, y)$
- $F(x, by) = bF(x, y)$
- $F(x, y_1 + y_2) = F(x, y_1) + F(x, y_2)$

A function of two variables that satisfies these four identities is called a bilinear function.

Reflect and Discuss

16. In what way are the functions you described in problem 15 linear?

Graphs

The graph of a function of one variable uses two axes: one for the independent variable (input) and one for the dependent variable (output). In the same way, the graph of a function from $\mathbb{R}^2$ into $\mathbb{R}$ needs 3 axes: one for each independent variable, and one for the dependent variable. Often, the independent variables are called x and y, and the dependent variable is called z. The x-y plane is usually pictured horizontally, with the x-axis pointing towards you and the y-axis to the right; the z-axis is then pointing up. Here, the point $(-3, 4, 2)$ has been plotted.

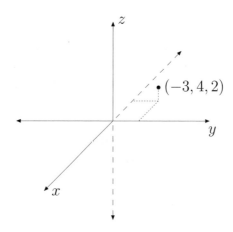

The set of all possible input variables fills up the x-y plane (or at least a region of it). The value of the function $z = F(x, y)$ is plotted at a height z above the x-y plane (or below it if z is negative), directly over the point (x, y).

17. (a) If you have graphing technology that will show three-dimensional graphs, graph the pencil-eraser cost function, $C(p, e)$.

If you don't have that technology available, make a model of the graph using manipulatives: Cuisenaire rods, centimeter cubes, Unifix or Multifix cubes, or Legos. If you use Cuisenaire rods or centimeter cubes, a rod or stack of cubes should just fit on the square of the table corresponding to (p, e). Choose your height scale carefully; if you use a centimeter to represent each penny of cost, the stack will be much too high. The top surface of the rods or stacks represents the graph of the cost function.

(b) How could you geometrically describe the graph? It helps to look at it sideways, in "profile."

(c) Does the idea of the slope of a graph seem to apply to this graph? How?

How could you include negative pencils and erasers in the story?

(d) If the function were extended to include negative pencils and erasers, what would the graph look like?

Using your graph in problem 17, consider combinations for which the total cost is 55 cents, that is, solutions to the equation $C(p, e) = 55$.

It may help if you imagine allowing fractional inputs as well as whole-number inputs.

18. What does the solution look like on the graph?

19. Compare this equation to an equation in one variable, for example, $5p = 55$.
   (a) How many solutions does each equation have?
   (b) When you graph the functions for each ($C(p, e)$ and say $D(p) = 5p$), what dimension is the result? What dimension does the graph of the solution have?

20. What would the graph of $E(H, 0)$ look like? What would the graph of $E(H, \frac{1}{2})$ look like? What about the graph of $E(H, \frac{5}{2})$? Your table from problem 9 might help you decide.

21. What would the graph of $E(0, D)$ look like? What would the graph of $E(\frac{1}{2}, D)$ look like? What about the graph of $E(\frac{5}{2}, D)$?

22. What would the graph of the egg function (E) from problem 9 look like? You might want to create a graph using manipulatives or software.

Ways to think about it

Problem: *How can you use the chart (but no algebraic equations) to find the cost of 2 pencils and 1 eraser?*

Problem: *Complete the chart, again without using algebraic equations.*

Problem: *In general, if you knew $C(p_1, e_1)$ and $C(p_2, e_2)$, how could you find $C(p_1 + p_2, e_1 + e_2)$? Could this method have been used to fill the chart?*

Problem: *What do you think a linear mapping from $\mathbb{R}^2$ into $\mathbb{R}$ looks like?*

Problem: *The answer "3 eggs" uses the idea of linearity, but incorrectly. How is linearity being used, and why is it incorrect in this case?*

Problem: *On graph paper, complete a table for the egg function, following the example of the pencils/erasers function. What is the correct answer to the question?*

1b. Consider how these quantities compare to quantities you already know. Just thinking about the situation of buying pencils and erasers, how will the respective costs compare?

1c. Again, compare quantities with those you already know (including the one you found in problem 1b).

4b. Suppose you know the cost of a single pencil and a single eraser, as well as the cost for p_1 pencils and e_1 erasers. How can you find the cost when you buy p_2 pencils? What is e_2 in this case? Is there a particular p_2 to add (over and over) that will help you fill part of the chart quickly and easily?

5b. A function from $\mathbb{R}^2$ into $\mathbb{R}$ might have a rule expressed using the two input variables. What would that expression look like? Was the cost function one? If so, how much can you change that function and still have a linear mapping? If not, is there something that can be changed that will result in a linear mapping?

8. To see how linearity is being used, consider how the input variables are being changed and how the original output is changed to get the incorrect answer. What aspect of linearity is used?

To understand why it's incorrect, it might help to consider changing only one of the input variables. For example, suppose the original number of hens work twice as long as in the original statement. How does that change the number of eggs laid?

9. This problem might be harder than you expect at first. A good strategy is to record everything that you know, including the trivial situations of 0 days, or 0 hens. Using the original numbers $E(1\frac{1}{2}, 1\frac{1}{2}) = 1\frac{1}{2}$, keep one of the numbers constant and vary the other.

It may help you to recall the interpolation problem from session 2: You have three increments between 0 and $1\frac{1}{2}$. How much will each increment need to be?

After filling in what you can from that, you have new information. For example, you might have the number that 1 hen can lay in $1\frac{1}{2}$ days. Can you use the same method to find how many eggs 1 hen can lay for other lengths of time?

13. With a full table, you have plenty of examples to try to find a pattern from, but that pattern may not be obvious.

    Again, consider fixing one of the variables (H or D) and try to find a pattern just within that column or row. Then consider if the pattern holds among other columns or rows. If not, do new (similar) patterns exist? Are they similar to the first pattern? It helps if you use a systematic approach—for example, start with the first column, then try the next column, and so on.

    If you're still getting stuck, try this. At the bottom of each column, write how the numbers in the column change. (How can you change the entry in row n to get the entry in row $n+1$?) Write a separate formula for each column: $E(H, 0)$, $E(H, \frac{1}{2})$, $E(H, 1)$, and so on. Next, how do the formulas change? Remember that for $E(H, \frac{1}{2})$, $D = \frac{1}{2}$ (and similarly so for each of the formulas). How do the formulas you wrote depend on the value of D?

    Problem: Write an explicit formula for the egg function.

16. If you used the method described for problem 13, you might have noticed some aspects of linearity in the patterns you found.

    Problem: In what way are the functions you described in problem 15 linear?

18. Remember that on the graph, the value of z at the point (p, e) is the function value, $C(p, e)$. One way to answer this question is to find the solution. Can you write an equation for $C(p, e) = 55$? What do you think the graph of that equation would look like (in three dimensions)?

    Problem: What does the solution look like on the graph?

    If you're using a graph created from manipulatives, find a way to visually identify the points for which the function value is 55.

    If you're using graphing software, you might graph the solution along with the function. This would require rewriting the equation in terms of one of the input variables, and using that variable as the output. For example, $p = \ldots$.

22. Try to use your answers to problems 20 and 21 to visualize the graph. How do the graphs change as you increase H? How do they change as you increase D? This type of visualization may be difficult for some people, so even if you think you know, you might want to check your answer by creating a graph using software or manipulatives.

    Problem: What would the graph of the egg function (E) from problem 9 look like?

5. From cups to vectors

In sections 1–4, you have looked a lot at what it means for a function to be linear. You've also looked at linear combinations of numbers. Much of what you've worked on showed connections among topics from elementary school to college-level courses.

You've probably seen variations of the following problem in many guises, including postage stamps and coins.

PROBLEM

1. THE MEASURING CUPS PROBLEM
Kathryn has a cooking pot and two measuring cups. One cup holds 4 fluid ounces, the other holds 6 fluid ounces. Neither cup has marks that allow Kathryn to measure less than these amounts. Can she measure 2 fluid ounces using these cups? Can she measure 14 fluid ounces? 7 fluid ounces? For each amount she could measure, explain how.

The connection between the MEASURING CUPS PROBLEM and linear combinations is fairly simple: Any amount that can be measured using the cups is a linear combination of 4 and 6, $4x + 6y$, where x and y are both integers.

*Equations involving linear combinations with integers, such as $4x + 6y = 14$ where x and y must be integers, are called **Diophantine equations** for Diophantus of Alexandria. Fermat wrote his famous claim, known as Fermat's Last Theorem, in the margin of a copy of one of Diophantus' notebooks.*

2. Use your answers to problem 1 to find solutions for the equations $4x + 6y = 2$ and $4x + 6y = 14$.

3. Provide a rationale to explain why it's impossible to find integers x and y so that $4x + 6y = 7$.

4. What amounts can be measured using Kathryn's measuring cups? Indicate how you might create those amounts, and explain why no other amounts can be created.

Greatest common divisors

Then again, maybe this isn't surprising.

You might be surprised to know that the Measuring Cup Problem also has connections to greatest common divisors.

5. What is the greatest common divisor (GCD) of 4 and 6? How does this GCD appear in your answer to problem 4?

6. For the following pairs of cups, find the GCD of the two amounts. Then describe all amounts that can be measured using the cups.
(a) 2 ounces and 5 ounces
(b) 3 ounces and 6 ounces
(c) 8 ounces and 12 ounces
(d) 3 ounces and 13 ounces

Reflect and Discuss

7. How do you know that you have found *all* amounts that can be measured using the pairs of cups in problem 6?

There are two theorems ⊰ that can be seen from your work with the Measuring Cup Problem:

Proofs of these theorems are in the Further Exploration *materials.*

Theorem 1 *The GCD of two counting numbers a and b can be written as a linear combination of the numbers, $ax + by$, where x and y are integers.*

Theorem 2 *A positive linear combination $ax + by$, where a and b are counting numbers and x and y are integers, is a multiple of the GCD of a and b.*

8. What do these two theorems say about a generalization of the Measuring Cups Problem: What measurements can be made using cups of *a* ounces and *b* ounces, if *a* and *b* are counting numbers?

9. Frank had only one measuring cup, which measured 3 fluid ounces. He borrowed one of Kathryn's cups, claiming that he only needed that one (along with his 3-ounce cup) to get all integer measurements. Which cup should he borrow? How do you know?

Recall that Kathryn had one cup that measured 4 fluid ounces and one that measured 6 fluid ounces.

10. What do you know about any two pairs of cups for which all integer measurements can be found?

On what basis?

In section 4, you looked at linearity in $\mathbb{R}^2$. While linearity can show up in functions that use ordered pairs as inputs, linear combinations are important, too. A **basis** for $\mathbb{R}^2$ is a special set of ordered pairs that **spans** the space—that is, a set with which all other ordered pairs in the space can be created using linear combinations. For example, $\mathbf{e_1} = (1, 0)$ and $\mathbf{e_2} = (0, 1)$ span $\mathbb{R}^2$. An ordered pair (a, b) can be expressed as $a\mathbf{e_1} + b\mathbf{e_2}$. A set of ordered triples, each of the form (a, b, c), might span $\mathbb{R}^3$—the space of all ordered triples.

Remember, $\mathbb{R}^2$ can be considered all ordered pairs, (x, y), where x and y are real numbers. Think of coordinate axes going out in all four directions, forever; $\mathbb{R}^2$ is the set of all points that can be placed on the grid.

11. If the set spans the given space, find a linear combination of the pairs or triples that produces a general pair or triple, (a, b) for $\mathbb{R}^2$ or (a, b, c) for $\mathbb{R}^3$.

    (a) $(2, 12)$ and $(3, 0)$ for $\mathbb{R}^2$
    (b) $(10, 15)$ and $(2, 3)$ for $\mathbb{R}^2$
    (c) $(1, 1, 0)$ and $(1, 0, 1)$ for $\mathbb{R}^3$

(d) $(1, 1, 0), (0, 2, 1)$, and $(1, 0, 1)$ for $\mathbb{R}^3$

(e) $(3, 5), (2, 12)$, and $(5, 17)$ for $\mathbb{R}^2$

A spanning set of pairs or triples might be called a *basis* for the corresponding space. To be a basis, the set must be **linearly independent**. A set is linearly independent if for every subset, a linear combination is 0—that is, $(0,0)$ or $(0,0,0)$—only when all the multipliers are 0. That is, if $\{\mathbf{v_1}, \mathbf{v_2}, \dots, \mathbf{v_n}\}$ is linearly independent, then

$$a_1\mathbf{v_1} + a_2\mathbf{v_2} + \cdots + a_n\mathbf{v_n} = 0$$

is true only if

$$a_1 = a_2 = \cdots = a_n = 0.$$

There's that word linear *again. Which sense—linear as in the graph is a line, as in linear mapping, or as in linear combinations—is meant here?*

To multiply an ordered pair or triple by a single number (called a scalar*), multiply each entry by the scalar: $a(b, c) = (ab, ac)$ and $a(b, c, d) = (ab, ac, ad)$. To add, just add the corresponding entries: $(a, b) + (d, e) = (a + d, b + e)$ and $(a, b, c) + (d, e, f) = (a + d, b + e, c + f)$.*

12. Which of the sets in problem 11 are linearly independent?

13. If a set is not linearly independent, it's said to be linearly dependent. (Was anyone surprised by *that* definition?)

(a) Show that if one ordered pair or triple is a multiple of another, the two are linearly dependent.

(b) Show that if an ordered pair or triple can be written as a linear combination of two others, the three are linearly dependent.

14. Suppose you have two pairs, (a_1, b_1) and (a_2, b_2). To determine if they are linearly independent, you have to consider linear combinations for which $x(a_1, b_1) + y(a_2, b_2) = 0$.

(a) Use that equation to write two equations that you can graph on a coordinate plane. Both equations will involve x and y.

(b) Where are the graphs of the two equations guaranteed to cross? Can you make a decision on the independence of the pairs based on that intersection?

(c) Suppose the two lines cross at another place as well. What does high school algebra tell you about the two lines and their equations in that situation?

(d) Show that if the two lines cross in more than one place, the pairs are linearly dependent—that is, there's a non-trivial way (a way that doesn't involve just multiplying everything by 0) to combine the pairs and get $(0, 0)$.

(e) If (a_1, b_1) and (a_2, b_2) are linearly dependent, what's true about the two lines L_1 passing through $(0, 0)$ and (a_1, b_1) and L_2 passing through $(0, 0)$ and (a_2, b_2)? Are these the same lines as the ones you found in part (b)?

Ordered pairs can be thought of as vectors, or directed segments. In this case, the vector (a_1, b_1) is the segment from $(0, 0)$ to (a_1, b_1). If the segments are parallel, so are the vectors—what does that mean about the linear independence of the vectors?

15. A set of ordered pairs or triples must be linearly independent and span a space to be a basis. Which of the sets in problem 11 are a basis for the stated space?

16. Some of the sets in problem 11 weren't a basis for the given space but were linearly independent. For each of those, describe the space for which it *is* a basis.

The results with these ordered pairs and triples can be generalized to other *vectors*, which have the form $(a_1, a_2, a_3, \ldots, a_n)$. If each a_i is real, the space is then $\mathbb{R}^n$. Each space is called a *vector space*. (There are conditions that define a general vector space, but $\mathbb{R}^n$ always meets those conditions.)

Reflect and Discuss

17. In what way is problem 16 similar to the MEASURING CUPS PROBLEM on page 106?

Ways to think about it

Problem: Provide a rationale to explain why it's impossible to find integers x and y so that $4x + 6y = 7$.

3. The *parity* of a number is the number's evenness or oddness. For this particular problem, consider the parity of the numbers involved. You want to add two numbers to get an odd number .... .

Problem: For each pair of cups, find the GCD of the two amounts. Then describe all amounts that can be measured using the cups.

6. If you had only one cup, what amounts could you measure with just that cup? Can you find a way to create the GCD of the amounts for the two cups? Put your answers to these two questions together.

Problem: How do you know that you have found all amounts that can be measured using the pairs of cups in problem 6?

7. Basically, this question is asking you to show that amounts other than the ones you answered in problem 6 cannot be measured. This is a more general version of problem 3. In that problem, the parity of the numbers was involved with the reasoning. Something similar will work here. (Remember, parity is evenness or oddness, and a number is even if it's divisible by .... . What was the GCD in the original cups problem?)

Problem: What do these two theorems say about a generalization of the MEASURING CUPS PROBLEM: *What measurements can be made using cups of a ounces and b ounces, if a and b are whole numbers?*

8. Try to connect the theorems to problem 6. For one of those cup pairs, what would a and b represent? What does a linear combination of those numbers represent? How does the GCD fit in?

The difference between the two theorems might seem subtle, but it's the same issue as in problem 7. One theorem implies what's possible, the other tells you that those are the only things possible.

Problem: What do you know about any two pairs of cups for which all integer measurements can be found?

10. Theorem 2 says that only multiples of the GCD of two numbers can be created from linear combinations of those numbers. All integers are a multiple of what number? (Depending on your mathematics background, you might be able to attach a name to this: What does it mean for that number to be a GCD?)

Problem: If the set spans the given space, find a linear combination that produces a general pair or triple.

11. Create a general linear combination for the pairs or triples. For example, for $(2, 12)$ and $(3, 0)$, the linear combination might be $x(2, 12) + y(3, 0) = (a, b)$. From this, you can write two (or in some cases, three) equations. Solve them for x and y, in terms of a and b. (If there are three pairs or triples, there will be three variables to solve for. For triples, there will be three constants, a, b, and c.)

Problem: Which of the sets in problem 11 are linearly independent?

12. Use the definition of linear independence to write an equation using the set—a linear combination set equal to $(0, 0)$ or $(0, 0, 0)$. From that equation, you should be able to write a system of two or three equations (depending on how many

coordinates there are) in two or three variables (depending on how large the set is). How many solutions does the system have? If the set is independent, how many solutions would the system have?

16. To be a basis for a space, the set has to span the space. What space does the set span? That is, what does a general pair or triple in the space look like? (Look back at the definition of *span* if necessary.)

Problem: For each set in problem 11 that isn't a basis for the given space but is linearly independent, describe the space for which it is a basis.

17. Suppose that instead of pairs and triples, the objects discussed in this section had only one coordinate, and only integers can be used for multipliers in linear combinations. What would spanning give in that case? See what parallels you can draw between the two situations in terms of linear independence as well.

Problem: In what way is problem 16 similar to the MEASURING CUPS PROBLEM*?*

Chapter IV

Pythagoras and Cousins

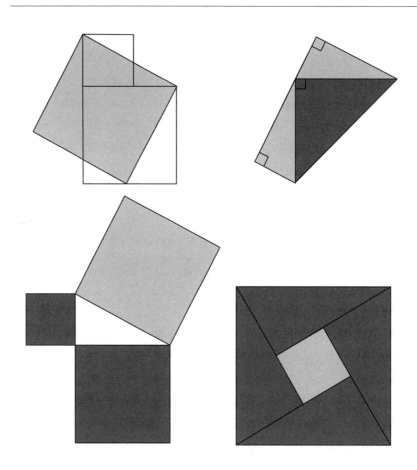

Introduction

The interplay between geometry and algebra is a theme that goes back at least to the Greek mathematicians of Euclid's time. Even without standard algebraic notation, mathematicians have always been taken with the connections between calculations and visual images. In this chapter, we'll look at some algebraic questions that are motivated by what is perhaps the most famous theorem from plane geometry, the Pythagorean theorem. Along the way, you will see how frequently it appears in the context of problem solving and become familiar with some of its mathematical cousins, which are found by tweaking the features of the Pythagorean theorem in the spirit of Chapter I, *What is Mathematical Investigation?*

A second theme weaving through the five sections of this chapter is one with which teachers are very familiar: how you can make up problems for your students that involve "nice" numbers. The search for Pythagorean triples is one example of such a "nice" number quest, but there are many others that appear in the field of Diophantine Geometry. For example:

A Pythagorean triple is a triple of positive integers (a, b, c) so that $a^2 + b^2 = c^2$.

- Can you find points A, B, and C on the plane with integer coordinates so that $\triangle ABC$ has integer side lengths?

- Are there any scalene triangles with integer side lengths and a 60 degree angle?

- Which integers are areas of right triangles whose side lengths are rational numbers?

Some of these questions are quite simple to solve and some are amazingly difficult. We will address some of them in later sections, but will leave the last for you to ponder in your free time. (It remains an open problem in mathematics, although much progress has been made in the past two decades!)

1. What would Pythagoras do?

Take some time to think about, and solve, the following "nice" number quest. Also, be sure to reflect on the methods and strategies you use.

PROBLEM

(x, y) is a rational point if both x and y are rational numbers.

The unit circle is the circle with center (0, 0) and radius 1.

1.   RATIONAL POINTS ON THE UNIT CIRCLE
There are four integer-valued points on the unit circle; namely $(1, 0)$, $(0, 1)$, $(0, -1)$, and $(-1, 0)$. Are there any other *rational* points on the unit circle? If so, find at least six rational points in the first quadrant that lie on the unit circle.

Consider the following problems, all of which share (at least) one of the big ideas from problem 1. Most of these problems were motivated by activities in the *Math Connections*, *Mathematics in Context*, and *Connected Mathematics* curricula.

2.   Find all points in the plane which are exactly 5 units away from the point $(-1, 3)$.

E–I–E–I–O!

3.   Old MacDonald has a huge cornfield ▷ which is shaped like a rectangle, with sides running north-south and east-west. He knows that the area of the field is 12 square miles and and that the distance from the northeast corner to the southwest corner is 5 miles. What are the possible dimensions of the cornfield? Be sure to confirm that you've found *all* of the possibilities.

4.   If the lengths of the sides of a triangle are 4.5, 12.3, and 13.1, is the triangle's largest angle an acute, obtuse, or right angle?

5.   Find the perimeter of $\triangle ABC$, shown below, given that $CD = 12$, $BD = 9$, and angles ADC and ACB are right angles.

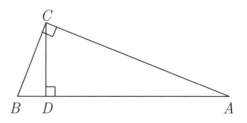

6. In the figure in the margin, the legs and hypotenuse of a right triangle are the diameters of semicircles. How does the sum of the areas of the smaller semicircles compare to the area of the larger semicircle?

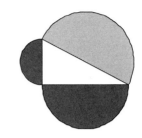

7. If you know that $\sin(\theta) = -\frac{5}{13}$, what can you say about the value $\cos(\theta)$?

Of course, the main thread that runs through each of the previous problems is the Pythagorean theorem, one of the most recognizable mathematical results. In the rest of this chapter, you will consider various mathematical cousins of this theorem, so it is important to start by carefully considering its features.

PROBLEM

8. THE PYTHAGOREAN THEOREM

Carefully state the Pythagorean Theorem. Be sure that your statement of the theorem will be clear to *anyone*, even if they have never heard of the theorem.

When asked to state the Pythagorean Theorem, many students will just say "$a^2 + b^2 = c^2$." Why isn't this correct? What's missing?

The Pythagorean Theorem is such a recognizable part of the curriculum that it is often taken for granted. Did you find that your initial statement of the theorem was incomplete? In mathematics, it's important to be very clear about your underlying assumptions. After all, if you're not completely clear on the hypotheses of the theorem, you might be tempted to use it in situations in which it doesn't apply *or* to apply it incorrectly.

Where does the Pythagorean Theorem arise in your district's curriculum (or when did you see and use it when you were a student)? Where are students first introduced to the theorem and in what courses do they encounter it again?

However, there's an ulterior motive behind asking you to carefully think about what the Pythagorean Theorem says—and doesn't say. In later sections, you'll be asked to alter the hypotheses of the Theorem, and tweak it any other ways, as well, in order to make new discoveries or analyze familiar results. In the remainder of this section, though, you'll apply the Theorem to derive well-known (yet, unfortunately, easily forgotten) formulas, then use the Pythagorean theorem to solve some problems concerning right triangles with a specified hypotenuse.

Where's Pythagoras?

One of the points of doing all of the problems at the beginning of this section is to see that the Pythagorean Theorem comes up in many other mathematical contexts besides problems like *If the two legs of a right triangle are 5 cm and 8 cm long, what is the length of the hypotenuse?*

When you were a student you may have been required to memorize the formula for the distance between two points in the plane and the general form of the equation for the circle centered at the point (a, b) having radius r. The next few problems ask you to derive these formulas using only the Pythagorean Theorem. While there's nothing wrong with knowing these formulas, isn't it also useful to be able to derive them in case you—or your students—forget them? And if we make a few mathematical connections in the process, so much the better!

Try to use only the Pythagorean Theorem in your derivations and be sure to prove that your derivation is correct. Be sure that your reasoning does not depend on the point (x, y) (or (a, b) or ...) lying in the first quadrant.

9. Determine the distance between points (a, b) and (c, d) in the plane.

10. Derive the general equation for all points (x, y) lying on the circle of radius r centered at the point (a, b).

The final activities of this chapter ask you to investigate properties of right triangles having a specified hypotenuse. Start with a specific segment $\overline{AB}$, and imagine all right triangles ABC having $\overline{AB}$ for a hypotenuse. If you plotted all possible points C so that $\triangle ABC$ is a right triangle, what kind of graph would you get? Several points on the "C-graph" for one choice of $\overline{AB}$ are shown below (some with their corresponding triangles).

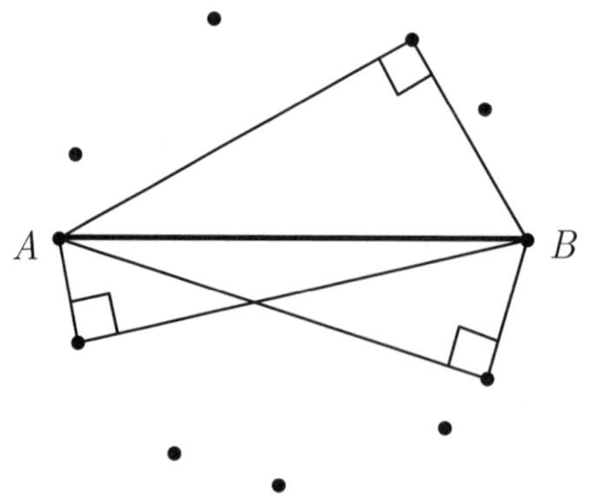

Some points on the C-graph of $\overline{AB}$

You could also experiment yourself with a dynamic software tool.

11. Using the partial C-graph above as an example, what do you think the whole graph will look like? Be as specific as possible with your description.

12. Let's check your conjecture. First, imagine that the hypotenuse $\overline{AB}$ has length 2. In particular, imagine that $A = (-1, 0)$ and $B = (1, 0)$. Derive an equation for the C-graph of $\overline{AB}$.

13. Does your conclusion in the previous problem depend on the length of $\overline{AB}$ (the segment which is the hypotenuse for the C-graph)? Is the shape of the graph the same no matter what hypotenuse you start with? Explain how you can tell.

A strategy that is often useful when dealing with geometric figures is to use coordinates to define vertices. Do you see how choosing $A = (0,0)$ and $B = (2,0)$ would be acceptable, as well? Would the algebra have come out as nicely? Try it!

You've now shown that the C-graph for $\overline{AB}$ is the circle centered at the midpoint of $\overline{AB}$ with radius $\frac{1}{2}AB$. What happens if, rather than looking at all of the points C so that $\triangle ABC$ is a right triangle, you look at M, the *midpoint* of $\overline{AC}$?

PROBLEM

14. HOW ABOUT THE M-GRAPH?

The M-graph for $\overline{AB}$ is the set of all points M which are midpoints of $\overline{AC}$ where $\triangle ABC$ is a right triangle. What does the M-graph look like for a given $\overline{AB}$? Carefully explain your conclusions and reasoning.

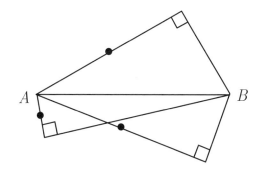

Some points on the M-graph of $\overline{AB}$

Of course, when defining the M-graph, we could have chosen the midpoints of $\overline{AB}$, instead. What will be the same and what will be different about the M-graph defined in that way? Will the two different M-graphs coincide? Will they even intersect? Think about this before continuing to the next section.

Ways to think about it

For your convenience, the problems are restated in the margin.

RATIONAL POINTS ON THE
UNIT CIRCLE: *Find at least
six different rational points in
the first quadrant which lie on
the unit circle.*

1. You're looking for points, (x, y), so that x and y are rational numbers *and* $x^2 + y^2 = 1$. There are at least two fruitful approaches to this problem. On the one hand, you can use trial and error—pick a rational value for x, then solve for y and see if it's rational. After a few trials, you'll gain some insight into how to choose x (and therefore y) so that (x, y) is rational. The other solution method involves investigating under what circumstances $\left(\frac{a}{b}\right)^2 + \left(\frac{c}{d}\right)^2 = 1$ when $\frac{a}{b}$ and $\frac{c}{d}$ are rational numbers. If you're not assuming that the fractions are reduced, you can assume that $b = d$. It will probably help to "clear denominators" first.

*Problem: Find all points in
the plane which are exactly 5
units away from the point
$(-1, 3)$.*

2. There are 4 points which are relatively easy to find—those that are 5 units to the left, 5 units to the right, 5 units above, and 5 units below $(-1, 3)$. In order to find *all* such points, suppose (x, y) was one of them. At first, imagine that it is above and to the right of the point $(-1, 3)$. How can you express the fact that (x, y) is exactly 5 units away from $(-1, 3)$? If all such points were plotted, what would the shape of the resulting curve be?

*Problem: The area of a field
is 12 square miles and the
distance from the northeast
corner to the southwest
corner is 5 miles. What are
the possible dimensions of the
cornfield?*

3. Sketch the cornfield and draw in the segment which is said to be 5 miles long. What's the relationship between the length and width of the field and this diagonal distance?

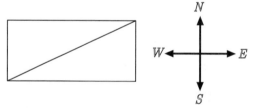

*Problem: If the lengths of
the sides of a triangle are 4.5,
12.3, and 13.1, is the
triangle's largest angle an
acute, obtuse, or right angle?*

4. If the angle were a right angle, how would you be able to tell? What relationship would be satisfied by the three side lengths? If that relationship is not satisfied, how can you tell whether the angle is smaller (or larger) than 90 degrees?

*Problem: Find the perimeter
of $\triangle ABC$, given that
$CD = 12$, $BD = 9$, and angles
ADC and ACB are right
angles.*

5. First, solve for BC. How do triangles $\triangle ADC$, $\triangle CDB$, and $\triangle ACB$ compare?

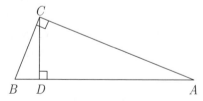

6. How does the area of a circle depend on its diameter? What's the relationship satisfied by the circles' diameters?

Problem: *The legs and hypotenuse of a right triangle are the diameters of semicircles. How does the sum of the areas of the smaller semicircles compare to the area of the larger semicircle?*

7. What's the relationship between $\sin(\theta)$ and $\cos(\theta)$? Do you recall (or can you derive) the connection between $\sin(\theta)$, $\cos(\theta)$, and points on the unit circle?

Problem: *If $\sin(\theta) = -\frac{5}{13}$, what can you say about $\cos(\theta)$?*

8. Be sure not to leave out any hypotheses. What are the key features of the theorem? To what context does it apply? Any variable you introduce should be explained.

THE PYTHAGOREAN THEOREM: *Carefully state the Pythagorean Theorem.*

9. Draw two points in the plane and build a right triangle whose hypotenuse is the segment connecting the points. Be sure that your distance formula does not depend on the locations of (a, b) or (c, d) (or both).

Problem: *Determine the distance between points (a, b) and (c, d) in the plane.*

10. The circle in question consists of all points which are exactly r units from the point (a, b). Which (x, y) satisfy that condition?

Problem: *Derive the general equation for all points (x, y) lying on the circle of radius r centered at the point (a, b).*

11. How might you "connect the dots" using the points given? Does the shape look familiar? Do you recognize any symmetry? Once you have recognized a shape, get specific–that is, describe important defining features of the shape.

Problem: *Using the partial C-graph given as an example, what do you think the whole graph will look like? Be as specific as possible with your description.*

12. Let (x, y) denote an arbitrary point C so that $\triangle ABC$ is a right triangle. Compute AC and BC in terms of x and y. What other algebraic relationship is satisfied by AC and BC? Now, derive a relationship between x and y. What does the graph of this curve look like?

Problem: *If $A = (-1, 0)$ and $B = (1, 0)$, derive an equation for the C-graph of $\overline{AB}$.*

13. This problem is the same as the previous one, except now the length of $\overline{AB}$ is not given. Try letting $A = (-r, 0)$ and $B = (r, 0)$ and proceeding as in problem 12. Is the shape of this C-graph the same as the previous one?

Problem: *Does your conclusion in the previous problem depend on the length of $\overline{AB}$ (the segment which is the hypotenuse for the C-graph)? Is the shape of the graph the same no matter what hypotenuse you start with? Explain how you can tell.*

HOW ABOUT THE M-GRAPH?
The M-graph for $\overline{AB}$ is the set of all points M which are midpoints of $\overline{AC}$ where $\triangle ABC$ is a right triangle. What does the M-graph look like for a given $\overline{AB}$?

14. Recall that the x-coordinate of the midpoint of a segment is the average (arithmetic mean) of the x-coordinates of the endpoints of the segment. The y-coordinate of the midpoint is computed analogously. It might help to first consider a specific example, as in problem 12. Let $A = (-1, 0)$ and $B = (1, 0)$. It would be reasonable to let $C = (x, y)$, but remember that you're trying to find out about M, the midpoint of $\overline{AC}$. If you let $M = (x, y)$, you can determine the coordinates of C using the relationship of the midpoint to the endpoints of the segment. Then proceed as before and determine a relationship between x and y. Once you have an answer for the case $A = (-1, 0)$ and $B = (1, 0)$, use that information to *predict* what will happen in the general situation. Then, check to see what happens when $A = (-r, 0)$ and $B = (r, 0)$.

2. Puzzling out some proofs

In section 1, you worked on several variations on a theme of Pythagoras, then showed that a number of useful formulas are due entirely to the Pythagorean Theorem. At the end of the section, you worked through activities involving right triangles with a given hypotenuse and showed that the third vertex of the triangle (in addition to the endpoints of the hypotenuse) lies on the circle centered at the midpoint of the hypotenuse. In this section, you will spend most of your time "decoding" *Proofs Without Words* by providing the details of a visual justification of the Pythagorean Theorem. These proofs will just scratch the surface, however. The book, *The Pythagorean Proposition*, by E. S. Loomis (currently out of print, but originally published by Dr. Loomis in 1940, then reprinted by the *NCTM* in 1968) contains more than 360 different proofs of the theorem!

Truth be told, *Proofs Without Words* are not always *proofs*. A more accurate description would be that they are mnemonic devices for visualizing, recalling, or reconstructing a proof of a given theorem. Here's one such "proof" of the Pythagorean Theorem.

For more Proofs Without Words, *see* Proofs Without Words I and II, *edited by Roger Nelson, published by the Mathematical Association of America.*

1. Show how the figure below can be used to provide a visual proof of the Pythagorean Theorem by showing that the area of the shaded square (the square of the hypotenuse of the right triangle shown) is equal to the sum of the areas of the other two squares (the sum of the squares of the legs of the triangle).

You may assume that the triangle at the "top" of the shaded region is a right triangle and that the quadrilaterals built off the sides of the triangle are squares.

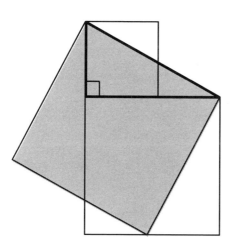

Which of these proofs would be accessible to your students?

In each of the following problems, determine how the figures provide a *Proof Without Words* of the Pythagorean Theorem. Be sure to explain all details. You may assume that the triangles with side lengths a, b, and c are right triangles, but you may *not* assume other angles are right angles (that must be proven).

The idea here is that the similarly shaded regions have equal area. As constructed, the outer border of each figure is a square and the triangles are all congruent right triangles. You'll want to show that the quadrilaterals are squares.

2.

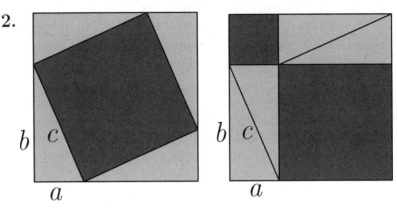

The proof that accompanies this picture is usually attributed to James Garfield, the twentieth president of the United States. It appeared in the April 1, 1876 issue of the New England Journal of Education *when Mr. Garfield was a member of the U.S. House of Representatives. However, it was likely known at least a millennium earlier to Arab and Indian mathematicians.*

3.

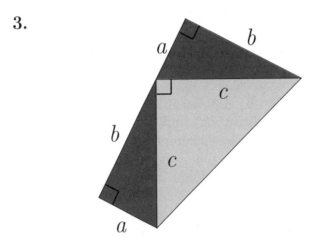

4.

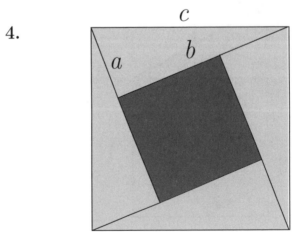

PROBLEM

5. EUCLID'S PROOF OF THE PYTHAGOREAN THEOREM
The following paragraph (and associated figure) provides the gist of the argument Euclid used in *The Elements* to prove the Pythagorean Theorem (Proposition 47 of Book 1). Fill in the details completely and carefully.

The Elements, *first published approximately 2300 years ago, is by far the most widely read mathematics book in history. In it, Euclid presented all of the mathematics known to Greek mathematicians at the time and rigorously proved all its propositions.*

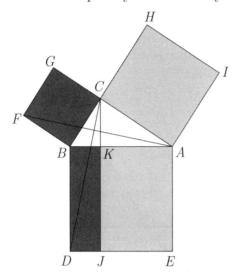

As before, $\triangle ABC$ is a right triangle with right angle $\angle ACB$, and quadrilaterals $ABDE$, $CAIH$, and $BCGF$ are squares. Let J be the foot of the perpendicular from C to $\overline{DE}$, and K is the intersection of $\overline{AB}$ and $\overline{CJ}$. Since rectangle $DJKB$ and square $BCGF$ have equal area *and* rectangle $JEAK$ and square $CAIH$ have equal area, $(AC)^2 + (BC)^2 = (AB)^2$.

Proofs *with* words

Not all proofs of the Pythagorean Theorem are *Proofs Without Words*, even those that require a picture! Here's one, which requires a little bit of work to "decode."

6. Finish the proof of the Pythagorean Theorem suggested by the following figure.

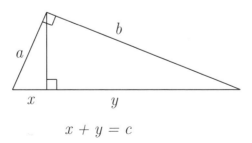

$$x + y = c$$

You'll learn about this generalization, PAPPUS' THEOREM, *in the* Further Exploration *materials.*

The last proof of the Pythagorean Theorem that you'll consider (in this section) is similar to Euclid's proof, but is chosen because it leads to a surprising generalization of the theorem.

7. Using the now familiar figure of the right triangle with appended squares, prove that the areas of the similarly shaded regions are equal, thus showing that the sum of the areas of the "*a*-square" and "*b*-square" equals the area of the "*c*-square." Note that G is the intersection of $\overleftrightarrow{HJ}$ and $\overleftrightarrow{DE}$, $\overleftrightarrow{GL}$ contains C and N, and O is chosen so that $\triangle KMO \cong \triangle ABC$.

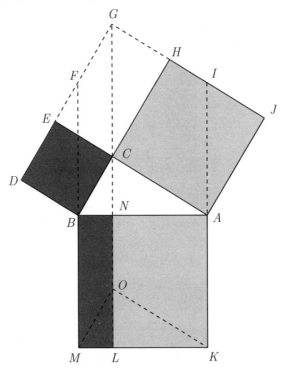

You've just gone through several proofs of the Pythagorean Theorem. It might seem like a lot, but there are 367 proofs of the theorem in *The Pythagorean Proposition,* referred to on page 121. Once a theorem is proven, why would someone want to find *another* proof—not to mention 366 *more*?

Reflect and Discuss

8. Why might it be useful for you to work through a number of *different* proofs of the Pythagorean Theorem? Would it be useful for your *students* to work through several proofs, too?

Pythagoras's *first* cousins

In mathematics, it is often very fruitful to play the "What if?" and "What if not?" games with the hypotheses and context of a known result. Let's take the Pythagorean Theorem as an example (now there's a shocker!). The Pythagorean Theorem was originally stated, by Euclid for instance, in terms of areas: *The area of the square on the hypotenuse is the sum of the areas of the squares on the legs.* In fact, mathematicians of ancient Greece did not separate numbers from geometry— products, like squares, had to denote areas. *What if,* instead of building squares off the sides of a right triangle, you built some other sort of figure? As you showed in the first section of this chapter, if you build semicircles off the sides, the area of the semicircle built on the hypotenuse is equal to the sum of the areas of the semicircles built on the two legs. This brings up an obvious question, with a less than obvious answer. Which types of figures work like squares (or semicircles) and which figures don't?

In the What is Mathematical Investigation? *chapter, you played these games with the consecutive sums problem.*

9. Construct equilateral triangles on the sides of a right triangle, as in the figure below. Is the area of the triangle on the hypotenuse equal to the sum of the areas of the triangles on the legs?

What if *the semicircles are replaced by equilateral triangles?*

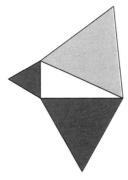

10. In the figure below, rectangles of equal height have been built off the sides of a right triangle. Is the sum of the areas of the smaller rectangles equal to the area of the larger rectangle?

What if *the semicircles are replaced by rectangles of equal height?*

__What if__ the squares are replaced by rectangles half as tall as they are wide?

11. Construct rectangles on a right triangle so that the base of each rectangle is a side of the triangle and the height of each rectangle is half the base. Is the area of the rectangle on the hypotenuse equal to the sum of the areas of the rectangles on the legs?

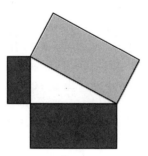

12. Among the previous few attempts at generalizing the Pythagorean Theorem by replacing squares with other figures, only problem 10 didn't "work." What about the hypotheses of that problem was different from those in problems 9 and 11? Make a conjecture, which is as general as possible, specifying the types of figures that can be placed on the sides of a right triangle so that the area of the figure on the hypotenuse is guaranteed to be equal to the sum of the areas of the figures on the legs.

That's all for now. What other Pythagorean cousins have you thought of? In section 3, you will meet some more by exploring the question,

What if $\triangle ABC$ isn't a right triangle? How does the sum of the areas of squares built off the legs compare to the area of the square built off the hypotenuse?

Ways to think about it

1. Can you imagine moving the puzzle pieces (formed by the shaded region) to fill in the two smaller squares (built off the legs of the right triangle)? Some of the pieces of the shaded square already lie in one of the smaller squares (they are shaded more darkly in the figure below). *Don't move them.* Notice that an additional segment has been drawn into the figure below. This is not an accident. Do you see how it helps with the puzzle fitting?

Problem: Explain how the figure provides a proof of the Pythagorean Theorem. You may assume that the triangle at the "top" of the shaded region is a right triangle and that the quadrilaterals built off the sides of the triangle are squares.

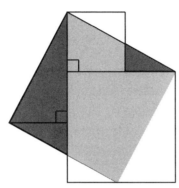

If it helps to visualize the situation, make copies of the figures provided below, then cut out and move the pieces around until they fit. (For instance, cut up the shaded square in the figure on the right, then fill the figure on the left with the pieces.) In the end, you'll want to describe which pieces fit where, so you'll probably want to add some labels to the figure.

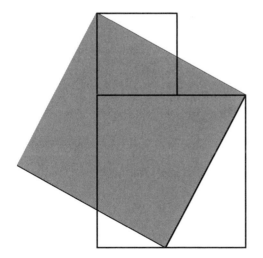
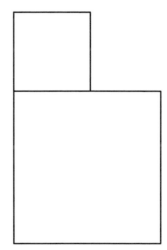

Problems 2-4: *Determine how the figures provide a* Proof Without Words *of the Pythagorean Theorem. Be sure to explain all details. You may assume that the triangles with side lengths a, b, and c are right triangles, but you may* not *assume other angles are right angles (that must be proven).*

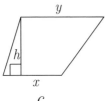

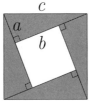

EUCLID'S PROOF OF THE PYTHAGOREAN THEOREM
Fill in the details of the proof:

As before, $\triangle ABC$ is a right triangle with right angle $\angle ACB$, and quadrilaterals $ABDE$, $CAIH$, and $BCGF$ are squares. Let J be the foot of the perpendicular from C to $\overline{DE}$, and K is the intersection of $\overline{AB}$ and $\overline{CJ}$. Since rectangle $DJKB$ and square $BCGF$ have equal area and rectangle $JEAK$ and square $CAIH$ have equal area,
$$(AC)^2 + (BC)^2 = (AB)^2.$$

2. You are given that the four triangles in the figure on the left (with side lengths a, b, and c) are right triangles. How do you know the quadrilateral in the figure on the left and the similarly shaded quadrilaterals in the figure on the right are squares?

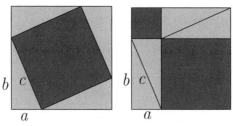

3. Compute the area of the trapezoid in two different ways. The area of a trapezoid with parallel sides of length x and y is $\frac{1}{2}(x+y)h$, where h is the perpendicular distance between the parallel sides (as in the figure).

4. You'll need to compute the area in two ways, but first, make sure the triangles fit together as drawn. You may assume that the four triangles are right triangles, but how do you know that the outer quadrilateral is a square? What's the shape of the interior quadrilateral? What are its dimensions?

5. *To show that the area of $DJKB$ is the same as the area of $BCGF$:* Show that $\triangle CBD \cong \triangle FBA$ and observe that (and explain why) the area of $\triangle CBD$ is half the area of rectangle $DJKB$ and the area of $\triangle FBA$ is half the area of rectangle $BCGF$ (what are the height and base of each of these triangles?).

To show that the area of $JEAK$ is the same as the area of $CAIH$: Repeat the above strategy with $\triangle CAE$ and $\triangle LAB$.

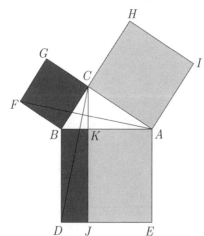

6. First, note (and prove) that the three right triangles in the figure are similar to one another. How does this fact allow us to conclude that $a^2 = x(x+y)$ and $b^2 = y(x+y)$? What does that tell us about $a^2 + b^2$?

Problem: *Finish the proof of the Pythagorean Theorem suggested by the figure.*

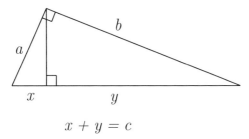

$$x + y = c$$

7. In this proof, you first need to compare the area of parallelogram $FGCB$ to the area of square $ECBD$ and the area of parallelogram $BCOM$ to the area of rectangle $BNLM$. It will help to first confirm that $\triangle GCE \cong \triangle ABC$ (what does this say about the two parallelograms?). Next, compare parallelograms, rectangles, and squares on the right side of the figure.

Problem: *Using the now familiar figure of the right triangle with appended squares, prove that the area of the similarly shaded regions are equal, thus showing that that the sum of the areas of the "a-square" and "b-square" equals the area of the "c-square." Note that G is the intersection of $\overleftrightarrow{HJ}$ and $\overleftrightarrow{DE}$, $\overleftrightarrow{GL}$ contains C and N, and O is chosen so that $\triangle KMO \cong \triangle ABC$.*

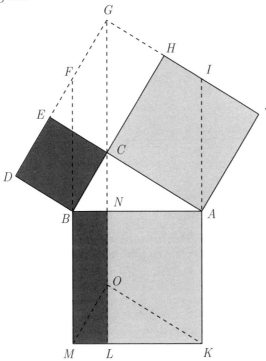

8. Did you learn anything new by considering these proofs? Are any of them *memorable* (or at least "remember-able")?

Problem: *Why might it be useful for you to work through a number of different proofs of the Pythagorean Theorem? Would it be useful for your students to work through several proofs, too?*

Problem: *Construct equilateral triangles on the sides of a right triangle, as in the figure below. Is the area of the triangle on the hypotenuse equal to the sum of the areas of the triangles on the legs?*

Problem: *Rectangles of equal height have been built off the sides of a right triangle. Is the sum of the areas of the smaller rectangles equal to the area of the larger rectangle?*

Problem: *Rectangles are built on the sides of a right triangle so that the base of each rectangle is a side of the triangle and the height of each rectangle is half the base. Is the area of the rectangle on the hypotenuse equal to the sum of the areas of the rectangles on the legs?*

Problem: *Among the previous few attempts at generalizing the Pythagorean Theorem by replacing squares with other figures, only problem 10 didn't "work." What about the hypotheses of that problem was different from those in problems 9 and 11? Make a conjecture, which is as general as possible, specifying the types of figures that can be placed on the sides of a right triangle so that the area of the figure on the hypotenuse is guaranteed to be equal to the sum of the areas of the figures on the legs.*

9. To compute the areas of the triangles, you need to know their heights (we already know the side lengths). What's the height of an equilateral triangle with side length s? If you drop an altitude from a vertex to the opposite side, where does it intersect the "base"? How do you *know*?

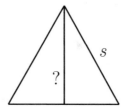

Remember that you may use the Pythagorean Theorem in your proof—we've proved it enough already!

10–11. Say the rectangles' lengths (a.k.a. the sides of the triangles) are a, b, and c. What are the areas of the two smaller rectangles? What is the area of the larger rectangle? Do you arrive at the expected result?

12. In problem 10, the heights are constant, while in problem 11, the heights are proportional to the corresponding lengths. How, then, do the figures compare to one another? Try some other figures to test your hypothesis.

3. Pythagoras's second cousins

In the previous sections, you worked through several applications of the Pythagorean Theorem, analyzed a number of different proofs of the Theorem, and began to investigate a few Pythagorean cousins—results which are related, but not identical, to the Pythagorean Theorem. In this section, you will meet some more members of the Pythagorean family as you continue to play "What if ... ?" and "What if not?"

1. Suppose $\triangle ABC$ is a triangle and that $a = BC$, $b = AC$, and $c = AB$. Fill in the table below, describing whether $(a^2 + b^2) - c^2$ is positive, negative, or zero depending on the measure of $\angle ACB$. Provide brief justifications for your choices.

What if $\triangle ABC$ *isn't a right triangle?*

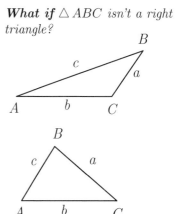

$\angle ACB$	$(a^2 + b^2) - c^2$
acute	
right	
obtuse	

2. Let's investigate the expression $(a^2 + b^2) - c^2$ a little further. If a and b stay constant and $\angle ACB$ varies from 0 to 180 degrees, describe the behavior of $(a^2 + b^2) - c^2$ by addressing the following questions.

(a) Does it increase, decrease, or oscillate?

(b) Can you think of a trigonometric function with behavior similar to that of $(a^2 + b^2) - c^2$?

As $\angle ACB$ moves from 0 to 180 degrees, $\cos(\angle ACB)$ acts a lot like $(a^2 + b^2) - c^2$. Namely, both functions decrease from positive to negative, equalling zero when $\angle ACB = 90$. Does $(a^2 + b^2) - c^2$ equal $\cos(\angle ACB)$? The table below lists the side lengths of several triangles, all containing a 60° angle between the sides of length a and b. Therefore, $\cos(\angle ACB)$ is the same in each case. However, $(a^2 + b^2) - c^2$ is clearly not constant, so $(a^2 + b^2) - c^2 \neq \cos(\angle ACB)$.

This shows that $(a^2 + b^2) - c^2$ is not a constant multiple of $\cos(\angle ACB)$, either.

You'll learn how to generate all of the triangles having integer-valued side lengths and a 60° angle in a later section.

a	b	c	$(a^2 + b^2) - c^2$
2	2	2	4
3	8	7	24
5	8	7	40
5	5	5	25
7	15	13	105

So how *do* $\cos(\angle ACB)$ and $(a^2 + b^2) - c^2$ compare?

3.   The side lengths, $\angle ACB$, and $\cos(\angle ACB)$ for several triangles are given in the following table. Fill in the final column with the value of $(a^2 + b^2) - c^2$, then make a conjecture concerning the relationship between $(a^2 + b^2) - c^2$ and $\cos(\angle ACB)$ which takes each of these examples into account.

$\angle ACB$	$\cos(\angle ACB)$	a	b	c	$(a^2 + b^2) - c^2$
$60°$	$1/2$	3	3	3	
$60°$	$1/2$	3	8	7	
$60°$	$1/2$	5	8	7	
$60°$	$1/2$	7	15	13	
$30°$	$\sqrt{3}/2$	3	5	$\sqrt{34 - 15\sqrt{3}}$	
$45°$	$\sqrt{2}/2$	3	5	$\sqrt{34 - 15\sqrt{2}}$	
$60°$	$1/2$	3	5	$\sqrt{19}$	
$30°$	$\sqrt{3}/2$	4	7	$\sqrt{65 - 28\sqrt{3}}$	
$45°$	$\sqrt{2}/2$	4	7	$\sqrt{65 - 28\sqrt{2}}$	
$60°$	$1/2$	4	7	$\sqrt{37}$	

PROBLEM

Be sure to consider both the acute and obtuse cases (the right angle case is taken care of already).

4.   THE LAW OF COSINES
Prove the conjecture you made in problem 3.

You've now succeeded in generalizing the Pythagorean Theorem to the case when $\triangle ABC$ is *not* a right triangle, showing that the difference between the sum of the areas of the squares built on two sides of the triangle and the area of the square built on the third side is a function of the lengths of the first two sides and the angle opposite the third side.

Perhaps you're more familiar with $c^2 = a^2 + b^2 - 2ab\cos(C)$.

One version of the LAW OF COSINES states that if $BC = a$, $AC = b$, and $AB = c$, then $a^2 + b^2 = c^2 + 2ab\cos(C)$, where C represents $\angle ACB$. Is this the version that you recall?

The following theorem, attributed to Pappus of Alexandria (c. 300-350), illustrates a startling fact that on the one hand provides another proof of the Pythagorean Theorem and on the other hand is a generalization of the Pythagorean Theorem. In fact, the proof of the Pythagorean Theorem discussed in problem 7 of section 2 is a special case of Pappus' Theorem. You are given the chance to prove the theorem in the *Further Exploration* materials.

PAPPUS' THEOREM:
Suppose that $\triangle ABC$ is a triangle and that quadrilaterals $BCED$ and $CAGF$ are parallelograms (not necessarily similar to one another). Let X be the intersection of lines $\overleftrightarrow{DE}$ and $\overleftrightarrow{FG}$. Construct parallelogram $ABYZ$ so that $\overline{BY}$ and $\overline{AZ}$ are parallel and congruent to $\overline{XC}$. Then the area of $ABYZ$ is equal to the sum of the areas of $BCED$ and $CAGF$.

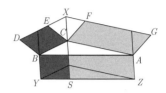

Nontriangular cousins of Pythagoras

Even though the Pythagorean Theorem is about triangles— specifically, right triangles—it has applications to other objects, in both two and three dimensions. And, as you probably guessed, the theorem has several nontriangular cousins, as well.

5. Find a relationship between the sum of the squares of the diagonals and the sum of the squares of the four sides of a rectangle.

Of course, "the square of the diagonal" is shorthand for "the square of the length of the diagonal."

6. Is there a relationship between the sum of the squares of the diagonals of a parallelogram and the sum of the squares of the sides?

Surprise!

So far, we've only delved into 2-dimensional Pythagorean cousins. Does the Pythagorean theorem have any 3-dimensional generalizations or applications? Let's see!

7. A rectangular box is 12 inches long, 9 inches wide, and 8 inches deep. What's the furthest distance apart two points on the box can be from one another?

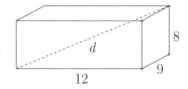

8. What's the relationship between the three dimensions of a rectangular box (length, width, and height) and the length of its "diagonal"?

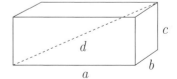

9. What's the distance between the points $(1, 2, 3)$ and $(0, 4, 5)$ in space?

10. Find an equation for the sphere of radius 4 centered at the point $(1, -1, 2)$.

In problem 6, you proved that the sum of the squares of the four sides of a parallelogram is equal to the sum of the squares of the two diagonals. Alternatively, one could say that the sum of the squares of the two different edge lengths is the *average* of the squares of the diagonals. Problem 8 shows that the same can be said of the relationship between the edges of a rectangular box and its diagonals.

Note that each edge and diagonal length appears four times in the figure.

11. Is there a relationship between the sum of the squares of the edges and the average of the squares of the diagonals in a "parallelepiped" (a slanting box, in which opposite sides are congruent parallelograms)?

A parallelepiped is the three-dimensional analogue to a 2-D parallelogram.

Were you surprised that the solutions to problems 7–10 were all integer-valued? Is it sometimes important to have answers that "come out nice"? In the next section, you'll investigate *Pythagorean triangles*, right triangles with integer-valued side lengths, and in section 5, you'll discover ways of guaranteeing "nice" solutions for more problems (and you'll learn some new, interesting mathematics along the way).

Ways to think about it

1. You can imagine that $\overline{AC}$ and $\overline{BC}$ form a hinge, allowing $\angle C$ to vary while keeping a and b constant. What happens as $\angle C$ varies?

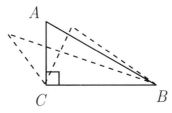

Problem: *Fill in the table below depending on whether the value is positive, negative, or zero.*

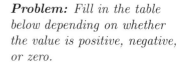

$\angle ACB$	$(a^2 + b^2) - c^2$
acute	
right	
obtuse	

If you prefer a more algebraic approach to the problem, consider the figures below. Can you compute $(a^2 + b^2) - c^2$ using the Pythagorean Theorem and the fact that the figures can be partitioned into right triangles?

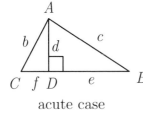

acute case

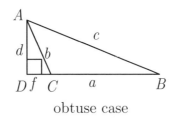

obtuse case

2. If you built or imagined a hinge to solve problem 1, then it will probably help to use it here, too. As $\angle ACB$ grows, what happens to c (the length of the hypotenuse)? Since a and b remain constant, what happens to $(a^2 + b^2) - c^2$?

   In part (b), it might help to graph the sine, cosine, and tangent functions for angles between 0 and 180°. Alternatively, think about the "unit circle" definition of sine and cosine:
   > If the ray from the origin to a point (x, y) on the unit circle makes an angle of θ with the positive x-axis (when measured in the clockwise direction), then $x = \cos(\theta)$ and $y = \sin(\theta)$.

   Problem: *If a and b stay constant and $\angle ACB$ varies from 0 to 180°, describe the behavior of $(a^2 + b^2) - c^2$:*
   (a) *Does it increase, decrease, or oscillate?*
   (b) *Can you think of a trigonometric function satisfying the same properties?*

3. Once you've filled in the column, take a look at the results. Do you notice any patterns? What do the results have to do with $\cos(\angle ACB)$? It might help to make a new table which "lumps together" triangles with the same value for $\angle ACB$. Is it significant that, when $\angle ACB = 45°$, $(a^2 + b^2) - c^2$ has a $\sqrt{2}$ in it, and $(a^2 + b^2) - c^2$ has a $\sqrt{3}$ in whenever $\angle ACB = 60°$?

   Problem: *Fill in the final column of the table, then make a conjecture concerning the relationship between $(a^2 + b^2) - c^2$ and $\cos(\angle ACB)$ which takes each of these examples into account.*

THE LAW OF COSINES:
*Prove the conjecture you
made in problem 3.*

4. There are at least two ways to prove that $(a^2 + b^2) - c^2 = 2ab\cos(\angle C)$—we'll call them the *algebraic* and *geometric* strategies.

- **Algebraic strategy:** This is a refinement of the algebraic strategy outlined in problem 1. Drop a perpendicular from A to $\overleftrightarrow{BC}$ (letting d be its length, as in the figure) and apply the Pythagorean Theorem to the two right triangles that are created.

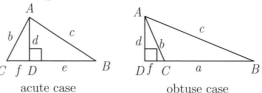

acute case   obtuse case

Use the right triangles in the figure, along with the Pythagorean Theorem, to find a relationship between a^2, b^2, c^2, and $\cos(\angle ACB)$. In the acute case, $a = e + f$, $c^2 = d^2 + e^2$, and $b^2 = d^2 + f^2$. Does this show us anything about $(a^2 + b^2) - c^2$? The identity $\cos(\theta) = -\cos(180 - \theta)$ might prove useful. What's the relationship between f and $\cos(\angle ACB)$?

- **Geometric strategy:** Use the figure below as a guide to determine the relationship between the sum of the areas of the squares built off the shorter sides and the area of the square built off the long side of $\triangle ABC$ when $\angle ACB$ is acute.

*Do you see why this identity
is true?*

*The geometric strategy is
motivated by the solution to
problem 5 of section 2. It
might help to review this
problem before proceeding.*

*You may assume that
quadrilaterals $BCHJ$,
$ABLN$, and $CADF$ are
squares, $\overline{BG} \perp \overline{AC}$,
$\overline{CO} \perp \overline{AB}$, and $\overline{AK} \perp \overline{BC}$.*

*You'll need to express
$AB^2 - (AC^2 + BC^2)$ as a
function of AB and
$\cos(\angle ACB)$. Can you show
that the areas of similarly
shaded rectangles are
congruent? (First, compare
ADB to ACN and BCL to
ABJ.) What are the areas of
$GEFC$ and $KCHI$ in terms
of $\cos(\angle ACB)$? (Note that
$\cos(\angle ACB) = \frac{CG}{BC} = \frac{CK}{AC}$.)*

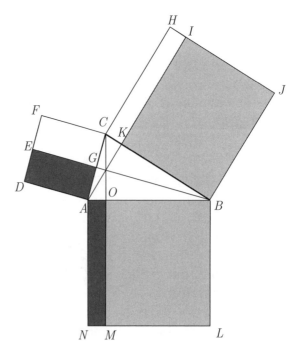

The figure for the obtuse case is given below:

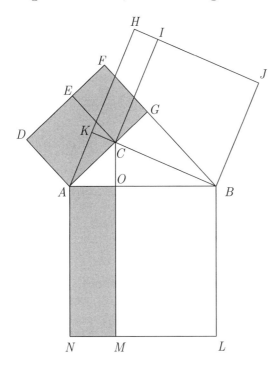

As before, the quadrilaterals built off the sides of $\triangle ABC$ are squares, $\overline{BF} \perp \overleftrightarrow{DE}$, $\overline{AH} \perp \overleftrightarrow{IJ}$, and $\overline{CM} \perp \overline{LN}$. Can you show the areas of $ADFG$ and $AOMN$ are equal? (Compare triangle ADB to ACN.) What about $OBLM$ and $HJBK$? (Compare triangle BCL to ABJ.) Finally, determine the areas of $EFGC$ and $KHIC$, in terms of $\cos(\angle ACB)$?

5. Look for the hidden right triangles in the rectangle. Recall that in section 1, you showed that the two diagonals were equal (alternatively, take a second to remind yourself why it's true!).

__Problem:__ Find a relationship between the sum of the squares of the diagonals and the sum of the squares of the four sides of a rectangle.

6. Try a few examples. If you have access to Dynamic Geometry software (*Geometer's Sketchpad, Cabri Geometry,* a *TI*-92 calculator, or *Cabri Jr.* on a TI-83, for example), use it to generate some examples, but they're also easy enough to sketch using (square) grid paper. Be sure that your proof takes all possible cases into account. Another way to think about the problem is to use the Law of Cosines (surprise!), since a diagonal partitions a parallelogram into two triangles. If you're familiar with vectors and their properties (especially lengths and dot products), you can use vector methods instead to solve the problem.

__Problem:__ Is there a relationship between the sum of the squares of the diagonals of a parallelogram and the sum of the squares of the sides?

Problem: *A rectangular box is 12 inches long, 9 inches wide, and 8 inches deep. What's the furthest distance apart two points on the box can be from one another?*

7. First, find the length of the diagonal of the base of the box. Use that information to find the diagonal we're really interested in. In the process, be sure to convince yourself (and anyone else) that this diagonal is what you're looking for.

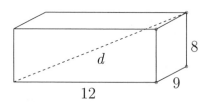

Problem: *What's the relationship between the three dimensions of a rectangular box and the length of its "diagonal"?*

Problem: *What's the distance between the points* (1, 2, 3) *and* (0, 4, 5) *in space?*

8. This is just the abstract version of the previous problem. Call the dimensions a, b, and c, and let d denote the diagonal. Can you solve for d?

9. Imagine a box with the two given points at the ends of the "diagonal." What would the coordinates of the corners be? Alternatively, what are the dimensions of the box?

Problem: *Find an equation for the sphere of radius* 4 *centered at the point* (1, −1, 2).

10. All of the points on the sphere will be exactly 4 units from the center. It might be helpful to derive and discuss the 3-dimensional distance formula (of which the work in problem 9 is a special case).

Problem: *Is there a relationship between the sum of the squares of the edges and the average of the squares of the diagonals in a "parallelepiped" (a slanting box, in which opposite sides are congruent parallelograms)?*

11. As suggested in the paragraph preceding the problem statement, this investigation is the 3-D analogue to problem 6. The methods are analogous as well. Try some examples (your facilitator may have some for you to investigate).

4. Pythagorean triples (and cousins)

In this section, the Pythagorean cousin you'll investigate led to what is probably the most famous mathematical problem of the past four centuries—perhaps of all time. In fact, this problem was the genesis of an entire branch of mathematics, Algebraic Number Theory. But we're getting ahead of ourselves. First things first.

If you ask someone to give you an example of the side lengths of any right triangle, they'll probably think you're kidding. If you're able to convince them that you're serious, then the most common response you'll get will probably be "3, 4, and 5." The ordered triple $(3, 4, 5)$ is an example of a *Pythagorean triple*, which can be defined in a couple of equivalent ways:

- *Algebraically,* we say that (a, b, c) is a Pythagorean triple if a, b, and c are integers and $a^2 + b^2 = c^2$.
- *Geometrically,* (a, b, c) is a Pythagorean triple if a, b, and c are integers and also the lengths of the legs and hypotenuse of a right triangle.

1.   You probably know several more Pythagorean triples besides $(3, 4, 5)$. List as many as you can think of.

Did you have trouble coming up with other triples? Don't worry, by the end of the section, you'll have a method to generate as many triples as you want! But first, let's consider some properties of Pythagorean triples.

PROBLEM

2.   CAN PYTHAGOREAN TRIPLES EVER BE ODD?
How many even entries can *any* Pythagorean triple have? (Are 0, 1, 2, and 3 all possible?) Can the hypotenuse ever be the only even side length in a Pythagorean triangle? Prove that you're right.

It can be useful to know some Pythagorean triples, especially when solving problems involving right triangles, since the sides often have integer lengths. Students can solve the problem below without knowing ahead of time that the side lengths are all integers, but it's even easier to solve if you know the

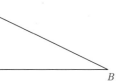

Pythagorean triples that are hidden within the problem. Here's a type of problem that occurs in many curricula.

3.   Determine the perimeter of $\triangle ABC$ (in the margin), given that $AC = 13$, $CD = 12$, and $BD = 16$. Repeat the problem assuming that $AC = 15$ (while CD is still 12 and BD is still 16).

The triple (ka, kb, kc) is said to be a multiple of the triple (a, b, c) when k is an integer.

While we're often happy for students to recognize Pythagorean triple patterns, there might also be occasions in which we *want* them to do the required arithmetic to solve for one of the values in the equation $a^2 + b^2 = c^2$. How, then, can you find more Pythagorean triples in order to construct problems like the previous one, but with side lengths that aren't part of familiar Pythagorean triples? One way would be to use triples which are multiples of the original ones by multiplying each of the given sides by a number, like 7, then ask students to determine the perimeter. It's unlikely that a student would automatically recognize that 84 is the missing entry in the triple $(35, ?, 91)$, so they'd have to solve the problem algebraically. You could also use trial-and-error: Pick two integers for a and b and see if $\sqrt{a^2 + b^2}$ is an integer. Alternatively, you could pick integer values for a and c and check whether $\sqrt{c^2 - a^2}$ is an integer. Are there any ways to narrow our search? Are there properties Pythagorean triples must satisfy that we can apply? Let's investigate.

The table below lists several related Pythagorean triples. Do you see how they are related? Can you find the next few triples in the table?

a	b	c
3	4	5
5	12	13
7	24	25
9	40	41
11	60	61
13	84	85

Check that the triples you add to the table are Pythagorean triples.

4.   Find a pattern in the above table, then determine the next 3 triples by following the observed pattern.

15		
17		
19		

5. Use the pattern found in problem 4 to create a formula that will generate infinitely many Pythagorean triples. Prove that your formula always gives a Pythagorean triple.

6. Here's another table of Pythagorean triples, which follows a different pattern. Find the pattern, then fill in the next three triples in the table by following the pattern.

Be sure that the triples you create are Pythagorean triples.

a	b	c
4	3	5
8	15	17
12	35	37
16	63	65

a	b	c
20	99	101
24		
28		
32		

7. Based on the previous table, guess another formula that will generate infinitely many Pythagorean triples. Prove that your formula always gives a Pythagorean triple.

As mentioned earlier, one of the reasons that teachers might want to know a lot of Pythagorean triples, or at least know how to find a lot of them, is that they could then create problems involving Pythagorean triangles for their students.

A Pythagorean triangle is a right triangle with integer side lengths.

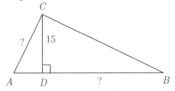

8. Find two different Pythagorean triangles with legs of length 15, to rewrite the hypotheses of the first half of problem 3 so that $CD = 15$, instead of 12. That is, find integer lengths for the sides marked with a "?".

Problems 4–7 provided some ways of finding infinitely many Pythagorean triples—some, but not all of them. There is a way of finding every single Pythagorean triple, though. In *Further Exploration*, you'll have the opportunity to work through the derivation of the following formula, which generates *all* Pythagorean triples.

A Pythagorean triple formula

$(n^2 - d^2, 2nd, n^2 + d^2)$ is a Pythagorean triple whenever n and d are positive integers and $n > d$. Not only is every triple of this form a Pythagorean triple; *every* Pythagorean triple is similar to a triple of this form.

In other words, (a, b, c) is a Pythagorean triple if and only if it looks like one of
$(k(n^2 - d^2), 2knd, k(n^2 + d^2))$
or
$(2knd, k(n^2 - d^2), k(n^2 + d^2))$
for some integers n, d, and k such that $n > d$.

Before continuing, take a moment to ponder this amazing fact. The PYTHAGOREAN TRIPLE FORMULA provides a way to find *every* Pythagorean triple there is! The next problem asks you to confirm that the formula always gives Pythagorean triples.

A practical benefit of the formula is that it can be used to write a fairly simple program for a computer or programmable calculator to list as many triples as you want.

9. Show that if n, d, and k are positive integers and $n > d$, then $(k(n^2 - d^2), 2knd, k(n^2 + d^2))$ is a Pythagorean triple.

10. Use the formula to find five Pythagorean triples that don't appear in the tables from problems 4–7.

11. Use the PYTHAGOREAN TRIPLE FORMULA to find all Pythagorean triangles with at least one side of length 12.

Properties of Pythagorean triples

Here's a list of Pythagorean triples you may have seen in the *Ways to think about it* section for problem 2.

a	b	c
3	4	5
5	12	13
6	8	10
7	24	25
8	15	17
9	40	41

a	b	c
10	24	26
11	60	61
12	35	37
13	84	85
14	48	50
15	112	113

a	b	c
16	63	65
17	144	145
18	24	30
19	180	181
20	99	101
21	220	221

That is, for what integers, d, do you think it's true that every Pythagorean triple has an entry divisible by d?

12. You've shown that every Pythagorean triple has an entry divisible by 2. What other properties involving divisibility seem to be satisfied by all of the Pythagorean triples in the table? You don't have to prove your conjectures, yet. You are given the opportunity to do that in the *Further Exploration* materials.

If (a, b, c) is a Pythagorean triple and a, b, and c share no common factors greater than 1, then (a, b, c) is called a *primitive* Pythagorean triple.

13. Suppose (a, b, c) is a primitive Pythagorean triple and b is the even entry. What can you say about the difference between b and c?

14. Is it true that if (a, b, c) is a primitive Pythagorean triple, then at least one of a, b, or c is a prime?

Using your knowledge of Pythagorean triples to construct problems for students with numbers that come out nice (as in problems 3 and 8) is one of Pythagoras' many "classroom cousins." You'll investigate some more of these in the final section of this chapter.

Ways to think about it

1. There are infinitely many possibilities here—be sure to check that your triples *are* Pythagorean triples. If you have trouble coming up with triples that work, can you think of any that are *similar* to $(3, 4, 5)$? If all else fails, try out some right triangles with integer-valued legs and check to see if the hypotenuse has integer length.

Problem: *You probably know several more Pythagorean triples besides* $(3, 4, 5)$. *List as many as you can think of.*

2. From the examples you generated for problem 1 and in the table below, there appear to be two choices: either all three entries are even or exactly one of them is even. Use the fact that every odd integer can be represented as $2k + 1$ for some integer k and every even integer can be represented as $2n$ for some integer n.

CAN PYTHAGOREAN TRIPLES EVER BE ODD? *How many even entries can a Pythagorean triple have? Can the hypotenuse ever be the only even side length in a Pythagorean triangle? Prove that you're right.*

a	b	c
3	4	5
5	12	13
6	8	10
7	24	25
8	15	17
9	40	41

a	b	c
10	24	26
11	60	61
12	35	37
13	84	85
14	48	50
15	112	113

a	b	c
16	63	65
17	144	145
18	24	30
19	180	181
20	99	101
21	220	221

Some Pythagorean Triples

Looking at the entries in the table provided, or creating some more Pythagorean triples with the help of the formula, leads to the conjecture that c can't ever be the only even entry in a triple. Why is that? Suppose (a, b, c) is a Pythagorean triple and that a and b are both odd. Then, since at least one of a, b, and c must be even, c must be the even one. Given that c is even, by what number (larger than 2) can you guarantee c^2 will be divisible? If a and b are both odd, is it possible for $a^2 + b^2$ to be divisible by this number?

3. Notice that the figure can be partitioned into a number of right triangles and that you know some of the side lengths of these triangles already. Use the Pythagorean theorem, or your memory of Pythagorean triples, to find the lengths of the other sides.

Problem: *Determine the perimeter of triangle ABC, given that* $AC = 13$, $CD = 12$, *and* $BD = 16$ *(as in the figure). Repeat the problem if* $AC = 15$ *(while CD is still 12 and BD is still 16).*

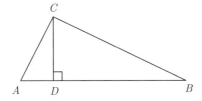

Problem: *Find a pattern in the table, then fill in the next three triples in the table by following the pattern.*

Problem: *Guess a formula that will generate infinitely many Pythagorean triples. Prove that your formula always gives a Pythagorean triple.*

Problem: *Here's another table of Pythagorean triples. Find a pattern, then fill in the next three triples in the table by following the pattern.*

Problem: *Based on the previous table, guess another formula that will generate infinitely many Pythagorean triples. Prove that your formula always gives a Pythagorean triple.*

Problem: *Find two different Pythagorean triangles with legs of length 15, to rewrite the hypotheses of problem 3 so that $CD = 15$, instead of 12. That is, find integer lengths for the sides marked with a "?".*

4. You've probably noticed that a is odd in each entry, so a^2 is odd, as well. Do you notice how b and c compare to one another in each triple listed? What do you know about the difference of two consecutive squares? In trying to find a triple corresponding to $a = 15$, think about how 15^2 can be the difference of two other squares.

5. The conjecture you make will depend on the pattern(s) you found in the table and the method you chose to fill in the next three entries in the table for problem 4. Two useful observations about the table are that a is odd and that b and c are consecutive. If a is odd, you can write a as $2n+1$. Letting n range over all positive integers will provide infinitely many triples. Once you know that $a = 2n+1$, what must b and c equal in order for (a, b, c) to be a Pythagorean triple? If b and c are consecutive, then $c = b + 1$, since c must be larger than b. What about the relationship between b and c guarantees that they can't share a common divisor greater than 1? Can you express the entries of row k in the table in terms of k?

6. Notice the pattern in the a terms of the table, as well as the relationship satisfied by the b and c terms. In addition to being equal, what is true about $b + 1$ and $c - 1$ in each case? As mentioned in the margin, it's important to check that the triples you find really are Pythagorean triples.

7. The key to the formula, as in problem 5, is representing the key features of the examples given in the table. If $b + 1$ is a square, then $b = n^2 - 1$ for some integer, n. If $c = b + 2$, then $c = n^2 + 1$. What does this say about a? Alternatively, what happens if you start with the assumption that a is a multiple of 4? What does that say about b and c? Can you express the entries of row k in the table in terms of k?

8. Find two different triples with either a or b equalling 15, then label the two triangles in the figure with the corresponding values of the other lengths. Use the tables from the session or other Pythagorean triples you know. Once you've done that, restate problem 3 with the appropriate values for AC and BD.

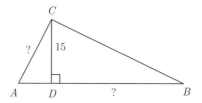

9. What does it *mean* to say that (a, b, c) is a Pythagorean triple? Is the definition satisfied by every triple of the form $(k(n^2 - d^2), 2knd, (k(n^2 + d^2)))$? You can use specific choices for k, n, and d initially, but you need to show that *every* triple of the stated form is a Pythagorean triple.

Problem: Show that if n, d, and k are positive integers and $n > d$, then $(k(n^2 - d^2), 2knd, k(n^2 + d^2))$ is a Pythagorean triple.

10. This is just a matter of carefully using the formula. While it's possible to just choose k, n, and d at random, you can save some time by choosing the values systematically. For instance, start with $k = 1$, then let n and d vary in some specific pattern which is easy to keep track of. Remember that the first two terms in a Pythagorean triple are interchangeable (since they give rise to congruent Pythagorean triangles).

Problem: Use the formula to find five Pythagorean triples that don't appear in the table on page 143.

11. Use the PYTHAGOREAN TRIPLE FORMULA. For what values of k, n, and d could $2knd = 12$? Could $k(n^2 - d^2)$ ever equal 12? What about $k(n^2 + d^2)$? It might help to *first* pick a k and try to find n and d, then pick another k, and so on. What are the possible values of k that make sense to try? If you are systematic, you can be sure that you've looked at all the possibilities, then can say with confidence that you've found all such triples.

Problem: Find all Pythagorean triangles with at least one side of length 12.

12. There are a number of possible conjectures. Look at each triple one at a time. What can you say about the entries? Must there always be an odd term? An even term? A multiple of 4? A multiple of 3? What else do you see?

Problem: What other properties involving divisibility seem to be satisfied by all of the Pythagorean triples in the table?

13. You can get some ideas from the tables. Once you have a conjecture, use the PYTHAGOREAN TRIPLE FORMULA to describe all primitive triples (what must k be in this case?) and compute the difference in question. You can create more specific triples to check your conjecture or use the algebraic formula to characterize all possible differences.

Problem: Suppose (a, b, c) is a primitive Pythagorean triple and b is the even entry. What can you say about the difference between b and c?

14. First, check to see what the tables tell you. Be sure the triples you check are primitive. Use the formula to generate some more triples. How might you prove the conjecture if you can't find any counterexamples? Do you hope it's *not* true?

Problem: Is it true that if (a, b, c) is a primitive Pythagorean triple, then at least one of a, b, or c is a prime?

5. More classroom cousins

In this section, you'll apply some of what you learned in previous sections to creating useful classroom activities for you *and* your students. But first, in the spirit of the *What is Mathematical Investigation?* chapter, let's consider what happens when we alter one of the features of another cousin. When looking for Pythagorean triples, you ask which integer squares are the *sum* of two integer squares. What about the *difference* of two squares? Although it's not obvious, this turns out to be related to a Pythagorean classroom cousin.

PROBLEM

Stated algebraically, for which k can you find m and n so that $k^2 = m^2 - n^2$?

1.   THE DIFFERENCE OF TWO SQUARES
Which counting numbers can be expressed as the difference of the squares of two counting numbers?

And now, some more classroom cousins.

You might choose to provide your students with more information, depending on the goal of the activity.

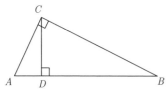

If you have taught geometry or trigonometry, the next problems are probably similar to some you've given in class. ▷ Take a few minutes to solve them in order to be aware of what's involved when students work on them. Later, we'll discuss the *creation* of these problems.

2.   Determine the perimeter of right triangle ABC (see the figure in the margin), given that $CD = 12$, and $AB = 25$.

3.   Determine the perimeter of the triangle having vertices at the points $(1, 2)$, $(10, 14)$, and $(5, 2)$.

4.   Compute the area of the triangle having side lengths 3, 7, and 8, given that one of its angles measures 60 degrees. Repeat the problem with the assumption that the side lengths were 7, 13, and 15 (and one of the angles is still 60 degrees).

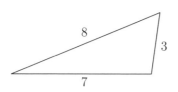

This is a rewording of problem 7 from section 3. Solve it again to remind yourself of its features.

5.   A rectangular box is 12 inches long, 9 inches wide, and 8 inches deep. How far apart are the lower, left, front corner and the upper, right, back corner?

Did you notice that all of the numbers in these problems were integers? That's not an accident. While there are certainly cases where "messy" numbers are appropriate, there are times when it's preferable for the numbers in the question and solution to "come out nice." In the article "Meta-Problems in

Mathematics," Al Cuoco wrote,

> *I have a conjecture: A great deal of classical mathematics was invented by teachers who wanted to make up problems that come out nice. Problems that come out nice allow students to concentrate on important ideas rather than messy calculations. They give students feedback that they are on the right track. They are easier to correct.* p. 373

Read more about it:
"Meta-Problems in Mathematics" appeared in the November 2000 issue of the College Mathematics Journal, *published by the Mathematical Association of America.*

But how do you construct problems that come out nice but aren't the ones the students have already seen? In section 4, you learned how to find all right triangles with integer sides and applied this knowledge to create triangles with all three sides and at least one altitude having integer length. In this section, you will apply your knowledge of Pythagorean triples to find other classroom cousins. Specifically, you will now address classroom cousins (or meta-problems), corresponding to the creation of problems 2–5 and the big questions below.

- How can you find right triangles so that all three sides and the altitude to the hypotenuse have integer lengths?

- How can you find triangles with integer coordinates and integer sides?

- How can you find triangles with integer sides and a 60° angle?

- How can we find rectangular boxes with integer-valued side lengths *and* diagonal?

Sides, altitudes, and vertices

> *How can you create right triangles so that the sides and the altitude to the hypotenuse are integer valued?*

> *How can you find triangles with integer coordinates and integer sides?*

Look back to see how the triangles in problems 2 and 4 were constructed. In problem 2, what's the relationship between the two subtriangles that are formed by the altitude? How does that guarantee that $\angle ACB$ will be a right angle? In problem 4, what's the length of the altitude to the edge with endpoints $(1, 2)$ and $(5, 2)$? What's special about the lengths of the pieces into which the altitude splits the segment?

6. Rewrite problem 2 so that $CD = 60$ and the resulting triangle has integer sides (you'll still need to specify AB).

PROBLEM

7. PYTHAGOREAN TRIANGLES WITH INTEGER ALTITUDES
Describe a method to create infinitely many Pythagorean triangles having altitudes with integer length.

8. Find 3 noncongruent triangles that have integer coordinates and sides. They don't have to be right triangles.

60° triples and triangles

How can you find triangles with integer sides and at least one 60° angle?

The following formula generates the so-called 60° triples (triangles with integer sides and at least one 60° angle). You can derive the formula in the *Further Exploration* materials.

A 60° TRIPLE FORMULA

$(2nd - d^2, n^2 - d^2, n^2 - nd + d^2)$ is a 60° triple whenever n and d are positive integers and $n > d$. Not only is every triple of this form a 60° triple; *every* 60° triple is similar to a triple of this form.

That is, (a, b, c) is a 60° triple if and only if there exist positive integers k, n, and d $(n > d)$ so that
$a = k(2nd - d^2)$,
$b = k(n^2 - d^2)$, and
$c = k(n^2 - nd + d^2)$ or
$a = k(n^2 - d^2)$,
$b = k(2nd - d^2)$, and
$c = k(n^2 - nd + d^2)$.

9. Show that all triangles with side lengths given by the above formula do, in fact, contain a 60° angle. Between which two sides is the angle?

10. Find 3 nonconguent triangles that have integer sides and exactly one 60° angle.

Three-dimensional cousins

We finish this section with one final meta-problem:

How can you find rectangular boxes with integer-valued side lengths and diagonal?

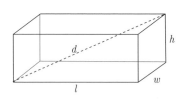

Problem 5: *A rectangular box is 12 inches long, 9 inches wide, and 8 inches deep. What's the furthest distance apart two points on the box can be from one another?*

You've already shown that if a rectangular box has length l, width w, and height h, then the length of its diagonal is $\sqrt{l^2 + w^2 + h^2}$. This is one of the many Pythagorean cousins we've met in this module. Thus, finding boxes with integer-valued sides and diagonal amounts to finding integer solutions to the equation $d^2 = l^2 + w^2 + h^2$. Go back over your solution to problem 5, which is repeated in the margin. Does this problem give you any ideas about how to generate more such examples?

Problem 5 worked out "nicely" because the diagonal of the *base* of the box had an integer length that was simultaneously the hypotenuse of one Pythagorean triangle and a leg (along with the height of the box) of another Pythagorean triangle. This property is significant, since it gives you something to work with when you try to construct more such boxes.

11. Find 3 other boxes with dimensions satisfying the property that the three dimensions and diagonal are integer-valued.

When you find counting numbers l, w, h, and d that satisfy $l^2 + w^2 + h^2 = d^2$, as you did in the previous problem, you're also finding counting numbers that are solutions to the equation $l^2 + w^2 = d^2 - h^2$, which leads to the final activity of this session— in fact, it's the last activity of the module.

Keep on the lookout for more Pythagorean cousins—there are some more in the Further Exploration *materials, but we've only scratched the surface. The Pythagorean family tree is a big one!*

PROBLEM

12. SUMS AND DIFFERENCES OF SQUARES
Which numbers can be expressed as the *sum* of the squares of two counting numbers and also as the *difference* of the squares of two counting numbers? Describe a method for generating infinitely many such numbers.

If you'd like to learn more about which numbers are the sum of two squares, see An Introduction to the Theory of Numbers, *5th ed., by Ivan Niven, Herbert Zuckerman, and Hugh Montgomery, John Wiley & Sons, 1991, or* Elementary Number Theory, *4th ed., by David M. Burton, WCB-McGraw Hill, 1998.*

Ways to think about it

THE DIFFERENCE OF TWO SQUARES *Which counting numbers can be expressed as the difference of the squares of two counting numbers?*

1. Start by making a list of the first 10 or so nonzero squares, then look at the differences of these squares. Alternatively, make a list of the counting numbers up to 20 and see which of these can be expressed as the difference of nonzero squares. Do you see any patterns in the list of counting numbers which are, or aren't, the difference of nonzero squares? Which even numbers are differences of squares? Which odd numbers? Enlarge your list, if necessary, to see the pattern.

   Once you have a conjecture, look carefully at how the list is structured—again, look at evens and odds separately. Pick a number just beyond your list and see if you can guess, from the preceding pattern, how to express it as a difference of two squares.

Problem: Determine the perimeter of right triangle ABC, given that $CD = 12$, and $AB = 25$.

2. Label the sides as shown below. What are the relationships between $x+y$, w, and z; between w, CD, and x; and between y, CD, and z (remember that $\triangle ABC$ is a special kind of triangle)? How are the three triangles related to one another? In particular, how are $\frac{w}{x}$ and $\frac{x+y}{w}$ related? What about $\frac{z}{y}$ and $\frac{x+y}{z}$? Solve for $x + y + w + z$ after determining the value of each variable first.

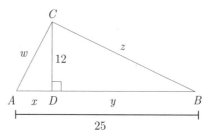

   It's also possible to solve for w and z by computing the area of $\triangle ABC$ in two different ways (one in terms of w and z).

Problem: Determine the perimeter of the triangle having vertices at the points $(1, 2)$, $(10, 14)$, and $(5, 2)$.

3. Of course, you need to determine the lengths of the segments created by these three points.

Problem: Compute the area of the triangle having side lengths 3, 7, and 8, given that one of its angles measures 60 degrees. Repeat the problem with the assumption that the side lengths are 7, 13, and 15 (and one of the angles is still 60 degrees).

4. Which angle measures 60°? Be careful, you can't assume the figure is drawn to scale. Which one of the angles (small, medium, large) must it be? Why? Then, drop a perpendicular from the vertex at the 60° angle and you'll have a nice 30-60-90 triangle to work with in order to determine the length of that altitude.

5. It will probably help to make a sketch of the box. Since we're claiming this is a Pythagorean cousin, there should be some right triangles you can work with. Where are they?

Problem: *A rectangular box is 12 inches long, 9 inches wide, and 8 inches deep. How far apart are the left, lower, front corner and the right, upper, back corner of the box?*

6. This problem is similar to problem 8 of the section 4 *Activities and Explorations*, but the resulting triangle is a right triangle here. What must the relationship be of the two subtriangles if $\angle ACB$ is to be a right angle? How are the two subtriangles in problem 2 related to one another? Can you find two similarly related triangles that share a leg of length 60?

Problem: *Rewrite problem 2 so that $CD = 60$ and the resulting right triangle still has integer sides (you'll need to specify AB).*

7. The general method should mirror your solution to the previous problem. If necessary, go back over the strategy you used and see how it can be generalized.

PYTHAGOREAN TRIANGLES WITH INTEGER ALTITUDES *Describe a method to create infinitely many Pythagorean triangles having altitudes with integer length.*

8. Look for similarities between the features of triangles from problems 2 and 3, and problems 3 and 8 in section 4. How can your work on these problems help you on this one?

Problem: *Find 3 noncongruent triangles that have integer coordinates and sides. They don't have to be right triangles.*

Problem: *Show that all triangles with side lengths given by the above formula do, in fact, contain a 60° angle. Between which two sides is the angle?*

9. What does the LAW OF COSINES say about triangles whose lengths come from the formula? Which angle (that is, between which sides) is the 60° angle? This is a difficult question, since n and d are not given. Compute, then factor, the three differences between side lengths. Why does the location of the angle depend on whether or not n is greater than, less than, or equal to $2d$? Be sure to be careful with your arithmetic.

10. Use the formula to find some 60° triples.

Problem: *Find 3 nonconguent triangles that have integer sides and exactly one 60° angle.*

11. This problem is related to problem 6, except here you need to match the *hypotenuse* of one triangle with a *leg* of another. One way to solve this problem is to look at the lists of triples you already have and hope for some "matches." If the necessary triples aren't in the table already, pick a length and determine whether it's possible to find one Pythagorean triangle with a hypotenuse of the specified value and another Pythagorean triangle with a leg of that length. The method

Problem: *Find 3 other boxes with dimensions satisfying the property that the three dimensions and diagonal are integer-valued.*

you used in problem 11 in section 4 (to find triples with one entry equal to 12) will be a good start. Use it to create more examples (with different lengths).

SUMS AND DIFFERENCES OF SQUARES *Which numbers can be expressed as the* sum *of the squares of two counting numbers and also as the* difference *of the squares of two different counting numbers? Describe a method for generating infinitely many such numbers.*

12. In problem 1, you characterized those numbers that can be expressed as the difference of squares of counting numbers (those that are either multiples of 4 greater than 4 or odd numbers greater than 1). You've also spent a significant amount of time investigating sums of squares, especially in section 4. While you haven't characterized all numbers that are the sum of the squares of counting numbers, you've found a lot of them. Remember, you don't have to find *all* numbers that are both the sum and difference of squares; you only need to describe a method for finding a lot of them.

So many cousins, so little time. We hope that we have piqued your interest to explore further.

Chapter V
Pascal's Revenge: Combinatorial Algebra

```
                              1
                           1     1
                        1     2     1
                     1     3     3     1
                  1     4     6     4     1
               1     5    10    10     5     1
            1     6    15    20    15     6     1
         1     7    21    35    35    21     7     1
      1     8    28    56    70    56    28     8     1
   1     9    36    84   126   126    84    36     9     1
1    10    45   120   210   252   210   120    55    10    1
 1    11    55   165   330   462   462   330   165    55    11    1
 1   12    66   220   495   792   924   792   495   220    66    12    1
1   13    78   286   715  1287  1716  1716  1287   715   286    78    13    1
1   14    91   364  1001  2002  3003  3432  3003  2002  1001   364    91    14    1
1   15   105   455  1365  3003  5005  6435  6435  5005  3003  1365   455   105    15    1
```

Introduction

These days, when you hear about "algebra across the grades" or "algebra for all," two things are often mentioned in the same breath:

- finding, describing, and explaining patterns;
- traditional algebra—using variables, transforming expressions, and solving equations.

"Using functions and graphs" is often added to the mix, too. Functions have become a major part of much of high school algebra.

What do these two things have to do with each other? Is it just that little kids do patterns and big kids write expressions, and expressions can sometimes be used to describe patterns? Does it make sense to call the pattern activities in elementary school "algebra"?

Paul Goldenberg once wrote a paper called "Algebra ≠ Functions ≠ Patterns."

This chapter will help you make connections between patterns and algebra. The patterns will arise from counting things (that's where the "combinatorial" part comes in). This context for looking at patterns is used for several reasons:

- Combinatorial thinking is difficult for many students.
- There are strikingly beautiful patterns that run through many combinatorial calculations (one is the ubiquitous Pascal triangle).
- The algebra involved in describing and explaining these patterns (things like exponentiation, recursion, sequences and series, and the binomial theorem) is right at the core of what secondary students need to know about algebra.

For a moment, suspend judgment about "what this is good for." The only context in this example is the algebra itself.

The patterns will show up in another situation as well: when using algebra and algebraic expressions to describe and explain the patterns that arise in counting things, you find yourself dealing with *patterns in the algebra itself*. For example, as every first-year algebra student learns, the pattern for factoring the difference of two squares is:

$$a^2 - b^2 = (a - b)(a + b)$$

This extends to a whole stream of factoring patterns:

$$a^2 - b^2 = (a - b)(a + b)$$
$$a^3 - b^3 = (a - b)(a^2 + ab + b^2)$$
$$a^4 - b^4 = (a - b)(a^3 + a^2b + ab^2 + b^3)$$
$$a^5 - b^5 = (a - b)(a^4 + a^3b + a^2b^2 + ab^3 + b^4)$$

$$\vdots \qquad \vdots$$

Describing and analyzing patterns like these is an important skill. These equations aren't expressing properties of numbers; they are expressing properties of *operations* (namely, addition, subtraction, and multiplication). Think, for example, about how you'd prove the $a^5 - b^5$ one. You might multiply everything in the long parenthesis by a, then by b, and subtract. What if you had to prove the $a^9 - b^9$ one? The $a^{20} - b^{20}$ one? Eventually, you'd start arguing *about* the calculation rather than explicitly carrying it out. You'd make implicit use of the properties of addition, subtraction, and multiplication, especially when talking about terms that cancel out. The a and b aren't important anymore—their meanings (if they ever had any) fade into the background, and you concentrate on what's between the as and bs in the expressions; that is, you concentrate on the *operations*. This reasoning about properties of operations to analyze patterns that arise in calculations is at the heart of contemporary algebra, and getting good at doing this is a skill all students need and can enjoy.

Think about how that skill might be developed in light of computer algebra systems. In this chapter, you will make use of CAS technology—think about its potential (and its potential pitfalls) in helping a broad range of students develop this knack for "calculating without calculating."

Why is it important? By the end of this chapter, you'll have some answers to that. Stay tuned . . . .

What is the $a^9 - b^9$ one?

Can you see why $a^{20} - b^{20}$ "works" without completely multiplying out the right-hand side?

Reasoning about calculations is an essential ingredient of algebraic thinking.

1. Trains of thought

In this activity, you'll be using Cuisenaire® rods of integer lengths to build "trains" that all share a common length. A "train of length 5" is a row of rods whose combined length is 5. Here are some examples:

1	2	2

2	1	2

1	3	1

1	4

5

This activity is adapted from "What Will Implementation Take?" by Ruth Parker in the September 1991 issue of the Mathematics Teacher. *We highly recommend you read the article for a nice description of how a version of this session played out in an eighth-grade class. Would the use of concrete materials work in a high school class? Would eighth-grade students be able to justify the conjectures that Parker presents?*

Notice that both the 1–2–2 train and the 2–1–2 train contain the same rods, but are listed separately. If you use identical rods in a different order, this counts as a separate train. Within a train you can repeat a length, and trains can contain different numbers of rods.

The usual mantras apply: Organize your work, make a table, look for patterns, eat an apple a day, look both ways before crossing the street, ...

1. Use a pile of rods to make *every* possible train with length 1, 2, 3, 4, and 5. Then compile a list of all such trains, using any notation that is meaningful to you. Be sure your group is thorough and does not miss any trains.

Reflect and Discuss

Project idea: Write a computer program that lists all the possible trains of any given length.

Note that you are not (yet) being asked for the number *of trains of a given length. You're being asked to provide instructions for listing all possible trains.*

2. Devise a set of directions that explains how to *list* all the trains of any given length. ▷

In order to do this, you'll need to think of a systematic procedure for constructing lists. See if someone else can use your directions (without any additional help) to list all trains of length 5. Don't forget to consult the *Ways to think about it* section (starting on page 159) if you get stuck on this—or any other—problem.

When you present your solution, either in writing or verbally, don't forget to mention the following:

- What methods did you use to create the lists?
- How did you make sure that you didn't miss any trains?
- How did you make sure that you didn't list any trains more than once?

Important questions when making a list (or counting): How do I know I listed them all? How do I know I listed each item only once?

Let's count 'em!

Now that you've come up with a way of listing them, the question you're probably asking yourself is, *How many trains of length* n *are there?* In most cases, you'll be able to adapt the method you developed above to count the trains of a given length. After all, if you can systematically list them, you can count them, right?

You may already have a conjecture. Let's test it.

PROBLEM

3. THE TRAIN PROBLEM:

Given any positive integer, n, derive a formula for the number of trains of length n. Explain your solution, the process you used to find it, and how you know it's correct *for all* n.

As a warm-up, you might first consider the following questions: How many trains of length 6 are there? of length 10? length 20? Can the process you used to justify your solution for specific lengths be used in the general case?

In order to list (or count) all the trains, it's helpful to come up with a systematic way to classify them. One way to classify the trains of a given length is by the number of cars they have.

The trains of a given length (5, say) can be further classified by the number of "cars" (that is, rods) they contain. So these trains:

There are a number of ways to classify or categorize trains of a given length. Besides the number of cars, what other classification schemes can you think of?

1	2	2

2	1	2

1	3	1

all have 3 cars, but this one:

1	2	1	1

has 4 cars. How many trains of length 4 have 1 car? 2 cars? 3 cars? 4 cars? Any number of cars? The information is readily

Do your students need charts like this? Many teachers think students need explicit instruction in how to organize data. Do you?

available in the form of the lists you compiled for problem 1, so let's reorganize the data with a chart:

Number of cars in the train → Total length of the train ↓	1	2	3	4	5	6
1						
2						
3						
4		3				
5						

To get you started, note that we placed a 3 in the box corresponding to length 4 and 2 cars. Do you agree with this? Refer to the list you compiled in problem 1.

4. Fill in the table above.

5. How many trains of length 12 have 3 cars?

PROBLEM

6. HOW MANY CARS PER TRAIN?

Mathematicians and computer scientists often use the term "algorithm" to denote a step-by-step process, especially one that can be implemented by a computer.

Describe a process for calculating the number of trains of length n that have exactly k cars.

Note: We're not necessarily looking for a formula—just a method for determining the answer (other than building all trains and counting those with 1 car, 2 cars, . . .). However, if you have a formula that you can justify, so much the better. Take some time to think about (and discuss) the problem, then feel free to consult the *Ways to think about it* section starting on page 159.

Reflect and Discuss

That explanation should not be based solely on evidence from specific values of n.

7. Find a formula for the sum of the entries of any row in the table above. Be sure to include an explanation of how you *know* the formula is correct.

Think about the following questions: What does the sum represent? That is, once you've totaled the row, what have you *counted*?

Ways to think about it

For your convenience, the problems are restated in the margin.

1. Half the battle here is to find a way of listing the trains (notation is always very important, as we'll discuss later). If you have enough rods, you might want to just build all of the trains of a given length. You could trace the rods, instead, but that's pretty time consuming. Think about what makes two different trains *different* and see if there's a way to categorize them systematically. Be sure that you get each train once *and only once*.

   Problem: Use a pile of rods to make every possible train with length $1, 2, 3, 4,$ and 5.

2. You can think about this problem in a variety of ways, but it is essential to be systematic in your listing. There are two possible classification schemes on which we will elaborate:

   Problem: Devise a set of directions that explains how to list all the trains of any given length.

   - Think constructively (systematically constructing trains of a given length);
   - Think recursively (build long trains from shorter ones).

   - *Think constructively:* Suppose you're interested in listing the trains of length 10. If your particular train is to have 3 cars, you can separate the train into 3 sections by putting separators on 2 of the 9 possible places for separators (see below).

   It will probably help to get out the rods again. Put 10 "singles" together, then separate them into sections to denote individual cars.

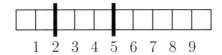

Now, in the train illustrated above, the first car has a length of 2, the second car has a length of 3, and the third car has a length of 5. The separators were put on places 2 and 5. Alternatively, we might insert a separator at place 5 and 9, giving us the 5–4–1 train.

What if you wanted your train to have 6 cars? You could create a train with cars of length 2, 3, 2, 1, 1, 1 by placing 5 separators in places 2, 5, 7, 8, and 9, as illustrated (or you could create a different train by placing the separators in different locations).

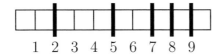

If you have a train of length n, how many locations for separators will you have?

Now, in order to create every possible train of length 10, you just insert from 0 to 9 separators in any of the possible places. To keep track of them, you'll probably need to further classify your trains (by the number of cars, for example). Does this specific example give you any ideas for the general case (trains of length n)?

- *Think recursively:* To get a handle on the recursive method, note that every train either has a caboose (final car) of length 1 or has a caboose of length greater than 1. If you take all the trains with a caboose of length 1 and remove the caboose, you get a train of length 4, right? Do you get *all* of the trains of length 4?

Hint: "reduce" the caboose

Now, given a train of length 5 with a caboose of length 2 or greater, how can you "shorten" it into a train of length 4? Does this give you an idea how to build the trains of length 5 *from* the trains of length 4? Will this method allow you to build trains of length 6 from trains of length 5? More importantly, does it give you a way to build all of the trains of length n from the trains of length $n-1$? ▷

Try it!

THE TRAIN PROBLEM:
Given any positive integer, n, find a formula for the number of trains of length n. Explain your solution, the process you used to find it, and how you know it's correct for all n.

3. From the lists you created in problem 1, you already know there is 1 train of length 1 and there are 2 trains of length 2, 4 trains of length 3, 8 trains of length 4, and 16 trains of length 5. You can also use the method you devised in problem 2 to list trains of several additional lengths to add to your nice collection of data. You have probably already *guessed* what the formula is, but how do you *know* your guess is correct? We'll consider each of the two suggested strategies for problem 2 in turn.

- *Think constructively:* If you used the separator idea, then you built each train of length 10, for example, by starting with 10 rods of length 1, then placing separators in some (or all) of their 9 possible locations. That is, when building a train of length 10, you either placed a separator at each possible separator location or you didn't. Then you had 9 decisions to make with two choices for each decision (whether or not to place the separator). And there are 2^9 ways to make those 9 decisions—do you see why?

Now, in the general case, how many separator locations will a train of length n have? What does that tell you about the number of trains of length n?

- *Think recursively:* One downside to thinking about a counting problem recursively is that you often don't get a nice formula without a lot of additional work. Fortunately, this case is an exception. Referring to the trains of length 5, how many have a caboose of length 1 and how many have a caboose of length greater than 1? Is the result (the relationship between these two numbers) a coincidence or is it generalizable? That is, does the same thing occur when you partition the trains of length 6 (or 4 or 3)? Can you convince yourself (and everyone else) that this always happens? If so, you're ready to provide a formula for the number of trains of length n, since you can "build up" from known information.

4. Use the lists you compiled in problem 1 to help you fill in the table. Alternatively, you can approach the problem from the perspective you used in problem 2. If you solved the problem recursively, think about how you can fill in one row of the table given the row above it. For example, how can you get a train of length 5 made up of 3 cars if you start with the trains of length 4? If you used the separator idea to solve problem 2, think about how to count the number of trains you could make using exactly 2 separators (when you're creating trains with 3 cars).

   Problem: *Fill in the table (showing the number of trains of length 1–5 consisting of 1–6 cars):*

5. You might recognize the entries in the table in problem 4 as coming from another familiar array of numbers (namely Pascal's triangle). Thus, if you believe that this pattern continues, you can find the corresponding entry in Pascal's triangle. Another approach is more constructive. In order to create trains consisting of 3 cars, you must place 2 separators within the 11 spaces for separators. How many ways are there to do this?

   Problem: *How many trains of length 12 have 3 cars?*

   Are you wondering whether the "Pascal" pattern is real or coincidental? We don't want to jump to any conclusions!

6. Try to generalize your method in problems 4 and 5. Before using the "fact" that our table is really Pascal's triangle in disguise, we must confirm that this is really a *fact*. Why must a given entry be the sum of the two entries "above" it? Think about what these entries represent and relate it to the recursive solution to problems 2 and 3. Taking the separator approach, how many ways are there to place $k-1$ separators in the $n-1$ possible spaces?

   Problem: *Describe a process for calculating the number of trains of length n that have exactly k cars.*

7. Translate this problem back into one involving train counting using the *meaning* of each table entry. In this context, what do you "get" when you add all the entries? That is, what does the total represent?

   Problem: *Find a formula for the sum of the entries of any row in the given table. Be sure to include an explanation of how you know the formula is correct.*

2. Getting there

The mathematics of counting is called Combinatorics.

In the first section, you derived methods for listing and counting all trains of a specified length as well as all trains of a given length having a specified number of cars. In this section, you will continue to develop ways of counting different things. While the contexts will be different, you'll recognize some friends along the way. Reflect on any connections you observe between this session and then last session (or other problems you've worked on in the past).

The following investigation has been part of progressive curricula for decades (going back, at least, to Jacobs' classic *Mathematics: A Human Endeavor*, published by W.H. Freeman & Company).

PROBLEM

Recall the two basic principles of counting:
- *Count everything once.*
- *Count nothing twice.*

1. MS. ANTON'S PATH PROBLEM

Ms. Anton insists on taking a different route to work every day. She will quit her job the day she has to repeat her route. The location of her home and work are pictured in the grid of streets below. If she never backtracks (she only travels north or east), how many days will she work at this job?

Note that two trips are different if they are not the same everywhere; they might overlap on some pieces though, like the two valid trips shown below.

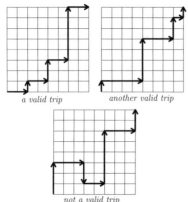

a valid trip   another valid trip

not a valid trip

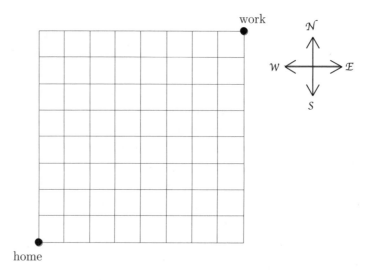

"Spelling out" a strategy

As you probably found when working on MS. ANTON'S PATH PROBLEM, there are many ways to count paths. One strategy is worth delving into more deeply: *Put the problem in a different, but approachable, context.* If you want to end up at, say, $(3, 2)$, you would have to travel 5 city blocks. Not any trip of five blocks will get you there, though. In order to get to $(3, 2)$, you have to end up going exactly three blocks east and two blocks north. In fact, if you start at $(0, 0)$, any arrangement of three Es and two Ns will get you to $(3, 2)$. So, you can encode the paths to $(3, 2)$ with strings like this:

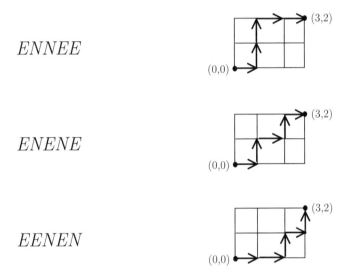

ENNEE

ENENE

EENEN

There are many other such paths, of course. Can you see how counting the paths from the origin to $(3, 2)$ is the same as counting five-letter "words" that are made up of three Es and two Ns? Can you figure out how many such words there are?

The problems of counting paths from the origin to $(3, 2)$ and of counting 5 letter words made of 3 Es and 2 Ns are said to be isomorphic, *a fancy way of saying they have the same inherent mathematical structure. Do you see how these two seemingly different problems are really the same?*

2. How many 5-letter "words" have 3 Es and 2 Ns?

3. How many "words" can you make from 2 Es and 3 Ns? From 4 Es and 1 N? From 1 E and 4 Ns? Can you predict two different "word problems" (for 5-letter words spelled with Es and Ns, only) that will have the same answer? Record your observations and justifications.

4. Translate the problem of getting from the origin to the point (a, b) into a "word problem." Can you derive a formula that solves both problems?

Pascal's Triangle

Pascal's Triangle has been referred to as the baking soda of mathematics—it's used for everything (and it helps keep your refrigerator smelling clean and fresh)!

Here's the fascinating number pattern commonly referred to as *Pascal's Triangle* (although it was discovered by many cultures long before the birth of its namesake, Blaise Pascal):

```
                              1
                           1     1
                        1     2     1
                     1     3     3     1
                  1     4     6     4     1
               1     5    10    10     5     1
            1     6    15    20    15     6     1
         1     7    21    35    35    21     7     1
      1     8    28    56    70    56    28     8     1
   1     9    36    84   126   126    84    36     9     1
1    10    45   120   210   252   210   120    55    10     1
1    11    55   165   330   462   462   330   165    55    11     1
1    12    66   220   495   792   924   792   495   220    66    12     1
1    13    78   286   715  1287  1716  1716  1287   715   286    78    13     1
1    14    91   364  1001  2002  3003  3432  3003  2002  1001   364    91    14     1
1    15   105   455  1365  3003  5005  6435  6435  5005  3003  1365   455   105    15     1
```

$$\therefore \qquad\qquad\qquad \vdots \qquad\qquad\qquad \vdots \qquad\qquad\qquad \ddots$$

5. Describe all patterns you can find in Pascal's Triangle, starting with the one implied by the figure below. ▷

This is often known as the "hockey stick" property, although some people refer to it as the "sock" property.

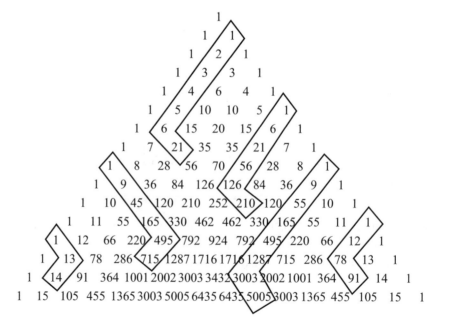

Which path will Pascal take to catch the train?

PROBLEM

6. THE TRAIN-PATH PROBLEM
Pascal's Triangle has shown up in two investigations so far: THE TRAIN PROBLEM and MS. ANTON'S PATH PROBLEM. Why? What do these two problems have to do with each other?

What underlying structure makes it possible to use Pascal's Triangle to solve both problems? Which specific train problem (how long and possibly how many cars?) corresponds to which path problem (from the origin to what point (a, b)?)? You will continue to consider these issues in section 3.

Ways to think about it

MS. ANTON'S PATH PROBLEM: *Ms. Anton insists on taking a different route to work every day. She will quit her job the day she has to repeat her route. Her work is exactly 8 blocks east and 8 blocks north of her home. If she never backtracks (she only travels north or east), how many days will she work at this job?*

1. If you simply draw paths—even using different colors, dashes, arrows, etc.—you are very likely to overlook something or to count something twice, even if you are very careful. (Trust us on this one—there are *a lot* more paths than you might first guess.) A better approach is to solve a few easier problems and look for patterns in those solutions. Specifically, pretend Ms. Anton's home and work are closer and solve the problem under this new assumption. But remember that if you want to use the pattern(s) you've found, you need to be sure that they apply to the case at hand. You may also choose to represent the problem in a new form, or couch the question in a different, yet familiar, context.

    There are several ways to think about this problem. In the following section, some contexts for thinking about the problem are provided, followed by some more specific suggestions.

    ## Coordinatize
    Suppose we think of Ms. Anton's grid as the first quadrant of the coordinate plane, and we assign coordinates in the usual way:

    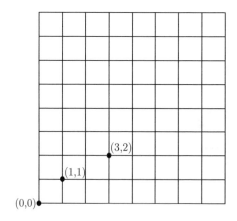

    Then MS. ANTON'S PATH PROBLEM becomes: *Determine the number of ways to get from the origin to the point* $(8, 8)$ *if you can only move 1 unit right or 1 unit up at a time.*

    ## Solve a simpler (but similar) problem
    Sometimes, solving a simpler problem uses strategies that can be successfully applied to the original problem:
    - How many ways are there to get to the point with coordinates $(3, 2)$? the point $(5, 4)$?

Solve a more general problem

Other times, it's useful to be *less* specific:

  – How many ways are there to get to the point with coordinates (a, b)?

Work recursively

Rather than start at the origin and move toward the terminal point, ask yourself how many points are adjacent to the terminal point (within the rules of the problem). To determine how many paths there are from the origin to these adjacent points, find *their* adjacent points, and so on. You can continue working backward from $(8, 8)$ or use this information to help you count from the origin out.

For example, $(7, 8)$ and $(8, 7)$ are the points which are adjacent to $(8, 8)$.

Hints with more details

The remaining suggestions go into a little more detail and provide more guidance than the previous ones.

- Suppose Ms. Anton lived much closer to her work (we'll work on a simpler, yet similar, problem first). How many possible paths are there for each of the following scenarios?

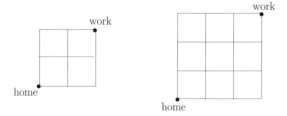

  Do the strategies you use to keep track of (and count) paths in these smaller cases generalize to Ms. ANTON'S PATH PROBLEM? Are there patterns that you *hope* will continue? Why *should* those patterns continue?

How can you make sure that you don't miss any paths? How can you be sure that you don't count a path twice?

- We could also use a recursive strategy. For Ms. Anton to get to work, she must get to either point A or point B on the diagram (see next page). So, to find the total number of paths, you can find the number of ways to A and the number of ways to B and add them. A little notation may be handy here: If we let $\#P$ be the number of ways to get from the origin to any point P, then

$$\# \text{ work} = \#A + \#B$$

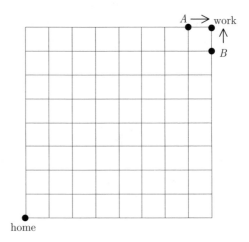

The additive formula: The number of ways to get to a specified point is the sum of the number of ways to get to its two "adjacent" points.

But how does this help? Go back to the starting point (the origin) and work toward the location of Ms. Anton's workplace, keeping track of how many ways there are to get to each point along the way. If you like, label each "corner" with the number of ways to get to it. How does each corner on the southern and western edges get labeled? You can then use the additive formula ▷ to determine the number of paths to each interior point.

• In order to get from home to work, Ms. Anton must go 8 blocks east and 8 blocks north, using any combination of 8 east and 8 north moves. That is, there are 16 decisions to be made (one at each corner along the way)—whether to proceed east or north. Now, at some corners there aren't any choices (which ones?). So counting paths is equivalent to arranging 8 easts and 8 norths.

Problem: How many 5-letter "words" have 3 Es and 2 Ns?

This should feel similar to using the separator strategy to count trains. Does knowing this help solve the problem?

2. How many ways are there to place 3 *E*s in a 5-letter word? Well, pick a location for the first *E*—there are 5 ways to do that. Then how many ways are there to choose the location of the second *E*? the third *E*? So how many ways are there to choose the three locations in order? How does the fact that any *E* is indistinguishable from any other affect the way you count possible words?

Problem: How many "words" can you make from 2 Es and 3 Ns? 4 Es and 1 N? 1 E and 4 Ns? Can you predict two different "word problems" that will have the same answer? Record your observations and justifications.

3. Determine the answers to these "word problems" using the method with which you solved the previous problem (or, just for the heck of it, try another strategy!), perhaps by comparing them to analogous train problems. Is it surprising that there are the same number of words with 3 *E*s and 2 *N*s as there are words with 3 *N*s and 2 *E*s? *Should* we be surprised? How can you explain this symmetry?

4. To get from $(0,0)$ to (a,b), how many total units east (right) and how many total units north (up) must one go? What type of "words" correspond to these paths? What methods have you already developed that will help you derive a formula?

5. Here are some ideas to get you started—the first of which is actually part of the *definition* of Pascal's Triangle, the second is about the "hockey stick" property.
   (a) How does a given entry in the triangle relate to the pair directly above it in the previous row?
   (b) How does the number on the "blade" relate to the numbers in the "handle"?
   (c) Investigate the "diagonals."
   (d) Are there rows all of whose entries seem to share a common divisor (greater than 1)?

6. This problem is intended to get you thinking about *what* the connections are and *why* they are connected in this way. After all, if two problems have similar solutions, there's probably a reason for it. One link the solutions share is the "additive property":

   The number of trains of length n having k cars is the number of trains of length $n-1$ having k cars *plus* the number of trains of length $n-1$ having $k-1$ cars (if n isn't 1).

   The number of (up/right) paths to the point (a, b) is the number of paths to $(a-1, b)$ *plus* the number of paths to $(a, b-1)$.

3. Trains and paths and triangles, oh my!

In the first two sections of this chapter, you solved several different counting problems—THE TRAIN PROBLEM, HOW MANY CARS PER TRAIN?, MS. ANTON'S PATH PROBLEM, and some variations on these themes—all of which shared a connection with Pascal's Triangle in one way or another. In addition, in the previous section, you explored Pascal's Triangle itself and made—or recalled—connections between Pascal's Triangle and the problems you solved (and hence between the problems, too).

```
              1
            1   1
          1   2   1
        1   3   3   1
      1   4   6   4   1
    1   5  10  10   5   1
  1   6  15  20  15   6   1
1   7  21  35  35  21   7   1
```

Reflect and Discuss

1. Try to recall or rederive the patterns you discovered in the previous two sections. Compare your list (and their justifications, if available) with others. Think *trains, paths,* and *Pascal.*

Pascal's Triangle is named for the French mathematician Blaise Pascal, but the triangle and its patterns were studied in ancient China and India, centuries before the birth of Pascal.

Pascal's Triangle has been around for a long time. Before continuing, there are some traditions of terminology and notation that are useful to be familiar with:

- It is standard to start numbering the rows with 0. So, row 2 is 1 2 1, row 5 is 1 5 10 10 5 1, and so on.

- It is also standard to start numbering the entries in any row with 0. Then, in row 5, entry 1 is 5, entry 2 is 10, and entry 0 is 1.

This is why it's helpful to avoid using labels like first and second—it might lead to a misunderstanding.

This may seem strange, but it turns out to be a useful convention. And, it's easy to remember what entry 1 in row n is. It's always n. But entry 1 in a row—and row 1 for that matter—doesn't really come *first*, which can be confusing, initially.

You may already be familiar with using the binomial coefficient $\binom{n}{k}$ to denote $Pas(n, k)$. The reason for using $Pas(n, k)$ should become clear to you as this section progresses. You'll learn the other notation in the next section.

- You're going to be working with the entries in Pascal's Triangle a lot in this section, so we'll introduce some (temporary) notation here. Let $Pas(n, k)$ denote entry k of row n of the triangle. Then, since row 6 of the triangle is 1 6 15 20 15 6 1, we know

$$Pas(6, 0) = 1, \ Pas(6, 1) = 6, \ Pas(6, 2) = 15,$$
$$Pas(6, 3) = 20, \ Pas(6, 4) = 15, \ Pas(6, 5) = 6,$$
$$\text{and} \ \ Pas(6, 6) = 1.$$

What do you know about binomials? Do you know any theorems?

- The entries in Pascal's Triangle are also called *binomial coefficients.* What's "binomial" about them? Stay tuned—the answer will be revealed in the next section.

Notation is only as good as what it buys you. The $Pas(n, k)$ notation buys you a lot, because it lets you say and think about properties of Pascal's Triangle in a particularly concise way. For example, one of the properties you found in problem 5 of section 2 was probably something like "each row starts and ends with 1, and any other entry is the sum of the two above it." This can be expressed by the following recursive rule that is usually used to *define* Pascal's Triangle:

DEFINITION

If n and k are integers such that $0 \leq k \leq n$, then $Pas(n, k)$ is defined by the rule:

$$Pas(n, k) = \begin{cases} 1 & \text{if } k = 0 \text{ or } n \\ Pas(n-1, k-1) + Pas(n-1, k) & \text{otherwise} \end{cases}$$

This is just a fancy mathematical way to say "each row starts and ends with 1, and any other entry is the sum of the two above it."

You can therefore use this definition to compute entries in Pascal's Triangle without writing out every preceding term. You just need to remember the additive property for interior entries and the fact that the "outside" entries (when $k = 0$ or n) are all equal to 1. For example,

$$\begin{aligned} Pas(4, 2) &= Pas(3, 1) + Pas(3, 2) \\ &= [Pas(2, 0) + Pas(2, 1)] + [Pas(2, 1) + Pas(2, 2)] \\ &= Pas(2, 0) + 2Pas(2, 1) + Pas(2, 2) \\ &= 1 + 2[Pas(1, 0) + Pas(1, 1)] + 1 \\ &= 1 + 2(1 + 1) + 1 = 6. \end{aligned}$$

The next three problems are designed to check your understanding of the new $Pas(n, k)$ notation. You'll be using it a lot, so it's important for everyone to be on the "same page."

2. Compute $Pas(6, 2)$ and $Pas(8, 5)$ using only the definition.

3. Use the $Pas(n, k)$ notation to express the fact that each row of Pascal's Triangle is a *palindrome* (that is, it reads the same forward and backward). More to the point, identify the other entry in row n of Pascal's Triangle that is equal to $Pas(n, k)$.

4. Express the hockey stick (or sock) property (investigated in problem 5 of section 2) in $Pas(n, k)$ notation.

Note that in problems 3 and 4, we're not looking for proofs of these properties; we just want you to get used to the meaning of the notation by translating the words into $Pas(n, k)$ notation.

The following problems are designed to connect the meaning and properties of $Pas(n,k)$ to familiar contexts:

Wouldn't it be nice to be able to compute any row of Pascal's Triangle without knowing the previous one? Do you think that's possible?

5. Take your algorithm for counting trains with a specified number of cars (from HOW MANY CARS PER TRAIN? in section 1) and write a formula for the number of trains of length n having k cars, using $Pas(n,k)$ notation.

Remember the word problems "isomorphic" to path problems?

6. Thinking of Ms. ANTON'S PATH PROBLEM (and its variations), use $Pas(n,k)$ notation to express the number of taxicab paths from the origin to (a,b) and the number of paths between points (a,b) and (c,d).

7. How many 12-letter "words" can you make from the letters E and N if you have to use exactly 8 Es? Express your answer using $Pas(n,k)$ notation.

In both problems 8 and 9, the intended formulas are relatively uncomplicated. Look at some examples and make a guess.

8. Use Pascal's Triangle to help you conjecture a formula for $\sum\limits_{k=0}^{n} Pas(n,k)$.

9. Conjecture a formula for $\sum\limits_{k=0}^{n} (-1)^k Pas(n,k)$.

Eerie connections

This is not very precise, but it turns out that many counting problems lead to the same recursion as the one used to generate Pascal's Triangle in the definition on page 171.

It really is true that Pascal's Triangle shows up in the strangest places. The reason it shows up so often isn't strange, though. The simple fact is that many phenomena have the recursive property that *any number is the sum of the two above it.*

Eerie connection #1

For example, suppose you wanted to find the number of 3-element subsets that you could make from the letters in

$$\{A, B, C, D, E, F, G\}$$

Of course, the order in which elements are listed doesn't matter, since $\{A,B,C\}$ and $\{B,C,A\}$ are the same set.

You might want to start with the smaller sets first!

10. Try it! List all the subsets of the set $\{A, B, C, D, E, F, G\}$, all the subsets of $\{A, B, C, D, E, F\}$, all the subsets of $\{A, B, C, D, E\}$, all subsets of $\{A, B, C, D\}$, all subsets of $\{A, B, C\}$, all subsets of $\{A, B\}$, and all subsets of $\{A\}$.

11. Use the results of problem 10 to determine the number of k element subsets in n element sets, where $0 \leq k \leq n \leq 7$.

You've probably already guessed what the next problem is:

12. Make a conjecture about the number of k-element subsets in a set with n elements, where k ranges from 0 to n.

Of course, you're going to be asked to justify your conjecture in a few moments. To get started, recall that it's often helpful to invent some shorthand notation for what you're looking at. Fortunately, someone has already invented a notation for us. Let $_7C_3$ stand for the number of 3-element subsets in a 7-element set. More generally, let $_nC_k$ stand for the number of k-element subsets in a n-element set.

Another common notation for this is $C(7,3)$.

*We're starting with 7 elements and **C**hoose 3 of them to form a subset.*

Your conjecture was probably something like

$$_nC_k = Pas(n, k).$$

Thus, to confirm the conjecture, you need to prove that
- $_nC_0 = {}_nC_n = 1$;
- If $0 < k < n$, then $_nC_k = {}_{n-1}C_{k-1} + {}_{n-1}C_k$.

In order to prove the first piece (that the outside entries of the $_nC_k$ "triangle" equal 1, just like in Pascal's Triangle), think about what it *means* to choose *all* or *none* of the elements of your set in order to make a subset.

13. Provide a convincing argument for the statement:
$$_nC_0 = 1 = {}_nC_n \text{ for } \textit{all} \text{ positive integers, } n.$$

PROBLEM

14. PASCAL'S SUBSET THEOREM
Continue this line of reasoning to prove that if $0 < k < n$, then $_nC_k = {}_{n-1}C_{k-1} + {}_{n-1}C_k$, confirming that
$$Pas(n, k) = {}_nC_k \text{ if } 0 \le k \le n.$$

Eerie connection #2

You've probably worked with factorials before. Recall that if n is a positive integer, then $n!$ (read "n factorial") is defined by

$$n! = 1 \cdot 2 \cdot 3 \cdot 4 \cdot \ldots \cdot n,$$

while 0! is defined to be 1. ◁

Using upper case π to denote product (just as we use $\sum$ to denote sum), this is often abbreviated $n! = \prod_{k=1}^{n} n$

Why is it reasonable to define 0! to equal 1?

PROBLEM

15. PASCAL'S FACTORIAL THEOREM

Use the method for proving PASCAL'S SUBSET THEOREM to prove that

$$Pas(n,k) = \frac{n!}{k!\,(n-k)!} \text{ if } 0 \le k \le n.$$

Alternatively, since you now know that $Pas(n,k) = {}_nC_k$, you can use a counting argument to show that ${}_nC_k = \frac{n!}{k!\,(n-k)!}$.

Summing up

Tying the work of this section together into a nice big bow, you have found three very different looking representations for the same quantity:

$$\boxed{{}_nC_k = Pas(n,k) = \frac{n!}{k!\,(n-k)!}}$$

This turns out to be very convenient. You can use Pascal's Triangle to solve many counting problems *and* you can use the factorial formula to fill in the entries of Pascal's Triangle. For, example, if you need to find $Pas(12,3)$, you don't have to write out 13 rows (starting with row 0) of the triangle. Instead, you can just compute $\frac{12!}{3!9!}$ and get on with your life!

That's an exclamation point; We have no idea what life factorial equals.

In the *Further Exploration* materials, you'll be asked to explore this formula further and to use it to more efficiently solve problems from previous sections. In a later section, you'll use it to determine which event is more likely: winning the lottery or guessing the license plate of the next car that drives by!

Ways to think about it

1. Here are some questions to jog your memory.
   - What is the total number of trains of length n, and what is the number of trains of length n with k cars?
   - What is the number of taxicab paths Ms. Anton can take to her work? How many paths are there from the point (a, b) to the point (c, d)?
   - What is the rule that defines the entries in Pascal's Triangle?
   - What is the "hockey stick" (or sock) property of Pascal's Triangle? (See problem 4, below.)

   Problem: Try to recall or rederive the patterns you discovered in the previous two sections. Compare your list (and their justifications, if available) with others.

2. Think about the meaning of $Pas(n, k)$ in terms of both Pascal's Triangle and its additive property. Review the previous example, if necessary.

   Problem: Compute $Pas(6, 2)$ and $Pas(8, 5)$ using only the definition.

3. Observe the symmetry in each row of Pascal's Triangle. How can you express that symmetry using the "Pas" notation?

   Problem: Use the $Pas(n, k)$ notation to express the fact that each row of Pascal's Triangle is a palindrome.

4. Translate the property illustrated by the figure below into $Pas(n, k)$ notation.

   Problem: Express the hockey stick (or sock) property (mentioned in problem 5 of section 2) in "Pas" notation.

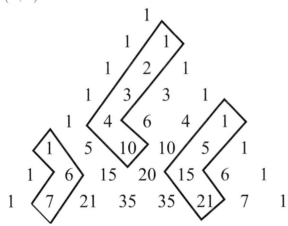

5. Recall that each row of the table (in section 2 on page 158) showing the number of trains of a given length, arranged by the number of cars they had, was a row of Pascal's Triangle. Which row was it, though? To remind yourself, think about THE TRAIN PROBLEM again.

   Problem: Write a formula for the number of trains of length n with k cars, using $Pas(n, k)$ notation.

6. What connection did you find between Ms. ANTON'S PATH PROBLEM and Pascal's Triangle?

   Problem: Use "Pas" notation to express the number of taxicab paths from the origin to (a, b) and the number of paths between points (a, b) and (c, d).

Problem: How many 12-letter words can you make from the letters E and N if you have to use exactly 8 Es?

Problem: Use Pascal's Triangle to help you conjecture a "simple" formula for $\sum_{k=0}^{n} Pas(n,k)$.

Problem: Conjecture a simple formula for
$$\sum_{k=0}^{n} (-1)^k Pas(n,k).$$

Problem: List all the subsets of each of the following sets: $\{A,B,C,D,E,F,G\}$, $\{A,B,C,D,E,F\}$, $\{A,B,C,D,E\}$, $\{A,B,C,D\}$, $\{A,B,C\}$, $\{A,B\}$, and $\{A\}$.

Problem: Use the results of problem 10 to determine the number of k-element subsets in n-element sets, where $0 \le k \le n \le 7$.

Problem: Make a conjecture about the number of k-element subsets in a set with n elements, where k ranges from 0 to n.

Problem: Provide a convincing argument for the statement: $_nC_0 = 1 = {_nC_n}$ for all positive integers, n.

PASCAL'S SUBSET THEOREM: *Prove that if $0 < k < n$, then $_nC_k = {_{n-1}C_{k-1}} + {_{n-1}C_k}$, confirming that $Pas(n,k) = {_nC_k}$ if $0 \le k \le n$. You can pick any element to be distinguished.*

Be sure you agree that this argument shows that $_7C_3 = {_6C_2} + {_6C_3}$.

7. Recall the connection between "word problems" and "path problems."

8. First, translate the formal summation notation into more informal language (to be sure you know what you're looking at). Then, make a table for several values of n.

9. You can approach this problem in much the same way as you did the previous one. Take care to keep track of when you should be adding and when you should be subtracting (depending on the sign of $(-1)^k$).

10. As in previous sections, recall the important rules for listing: *Don't miss anything* and *Don't list anything twice*. To ensure the rules are followed, devise a systematic listing method, further categorizing the subsets according to the number of elements in each.

11. Make a table based on the work you did in problem 10. What numerical properties are shared by the table entries? Do you recognize a pattern?

12. Compare the numbers you got in problem 11 to something familiar. You can also think about the problem more abstractly, if you prefer. How many ways are there to choose k elements from a set of n elements?

13. What do $_nC_0$ and $_nC_n$ mean? That is, what does the *definition* say about the symbols $_nC_0$ and $_nC_n$? How many 0-element subsets will a set have? How many n-element subsets (if the set has n elements to start with)?

14. Remember that $_nC_k$ stands for the number of k-element subsets in an n-element set. Consider the following example, which uses a very useful strategy: the "distinguished element" method.

   - Let's think back to the set $S = \{A,B,C,D,E,F,G\}$ and suppose that $k = 3$. Pick one of the seven elements to be special. We'll pick G as the "distinguished element." The key fact to keep in mind is that each subset of S either contains G or it doesn't. So, the number of 3-element subsets of S is the number of 3-element subsets of S that *do not* contain G *plus* the number of

3-element subsets that *do* contain G. But a 3-element subset of S that *doesn't* contain G is just a subset of $\{A, B, C, D, E, F\}$, a set with 6 elements (1 fewer than S). Similarly, a 3-element subset of S that *does* contain G is a 2-element subset of $\{A, B, C, D, E, F\}$ with G "added." Thus, $_7C_3 = {_6C_2} + {_6C_3}$.

How does the specific case ($n = 7$, $k = 3$) generalize to the general case? Was the choice of 7 and 3 essential in the discussion?

15. There are a number of ways to think about solving this problem:

    - Argue as above by showing that $\frac{n!}{k!(n-k)!}$ satisfies the additive property of Pascal's Triangle. That is, show that $\frac{n!}{k!(n-k)!} = 1$ when $k = 0$ or n (which is immediate from the definition), and that when $0 < k < n$, we have

      $$\frac{n!}{k!(n-k)!} = \frac{(n-1)!}{(k-1)![(n-1)-(k-1)]!} + \frac{(n-1)!}{k!(n-1-k)!}$$

    - You can also derive the connection directly by attempting to count the number of ways to choose a k-element subset from a set with n elements and arrive at $\frac{n!}{k!(n-k)!}$. To that end, how many ways *are there* to do this? Imagine that you've got the n different elements sitting on the table in front of you. In how many ways can you choose k of them? Well, let's start small—how many ways are there to pick the *first* element? Obviously n, right? After all, it can be any of the n elements in the set. OK, then since there are $n - 1$ elements left to choose from, there are $n-1$ ways to choose the second element. Similarly, there are $n-2$ ways to choose the third element, ... Finally, there are $n - (k - 1) = n - k + 1$ ways to choose the kth element, assuming the first $k - 1$ have already been chosen. Putting all of this information together, there are $n(n - 1)$ ways to choose the first 2 elements of my subset, $n(n - 1)(n - 2)$ ways to choose the first 3 elements, ... Therefore, there are $n(n - 1)(n - 2) \cdots (n - k + 1)$ ways to choose all k elements of my subset *if I choose them in a specified order.* "Aha!," you say, "but you can't choose them in order because the order of the elements doesn't matter in a subset!" Right you are! We just painstakingly counted the number of ways to choose k elements *in order* from a set of n elements. So, how can we "unorder" them? We

---

Sidebar:

PASCAL'S FACTORIAL THEOREM *Prove that $Pas(n,k) = \frac{n!}{k!(n-k)!}$ if $0 \le k \le n$.*

This is also called Pascal's Law and turns out to be an exercise in very careful algebraic manipulation.

You're right if you said, "Wait a minute, there's no such thing as a first element in a set!" Bear with us and we'll deal with that important issue soon.

merely need to decide how many times we "overcounted" each k-element subset using our algorithm. That's actually not too hard, because we need only determine the number of ways to rearrange k elements (that is, choose k elements *in order* from a set of k elements), and we know how to do that! There are $k!$ ways to rearrange k elements. **Make sure you see why that's true before going on.**

Now, putting all of this together, we've shown that

$$_nC_k = \frac{n(n-1)(n-2)\cdots(n-k+1)}{k!}.$$

This book will not *self-destruct in 10 seconds.*

Your job, if you choose to accept it, is to show algebraically that this equals $\frac{n!}{k!(n-k)!}$.

4. Binomial theorem connection

In sections 1–3, you uncovered connections between Pascal's Triangle and a variety of disparate problem contexts—paths from one point to another in taxicab geometry, trains of a given length made of a specified number of cars, subsets of a certain size, choosing k things from among n—although each problem required counting in one way or another.

You also learned several different ways of determining or defining the entries in Pascal's Triangle. In this section, you will continue to explore Pascal's ubiquitous triangle and find another context in which it makes a surprising appearance.

Don't worry—you'll be reminded of these shortly.

The Binomial Theorem is a theorem about binomials—now there's a surprise! More specifically, it's about *positive integer* powers of the binomial expression $a + b$. You'll be asked to conjecture a formula for $(a + b)^n$ soon, but first consider a few special cases. You should expand the first cases by hand in order to see how the result is put together. Then, you can use a Computer Algebra System—perhaps computer software like *Maple*, *Mathematica*, or *DERIVE*, or a hand-held calculator with *CAS* capabilities like the *TI*–92 (or 89), the *Casio CFX*–9970G (or *FX*–2.0), or the *HP*–48G (or GX)—to expand the larger cases.

The word "binomial" means two terms (and "polynomial" means many terms).

If you don't have a CAS available, don't worry. Your facilitator will have some ideas about what to do!

1.   Expand the following binomial powers by hand:

$$(a + b)^2$$
$$(a + b)^3$$
$$(a + b)^4$$
$$(a + b)^5$$

Multiplying everything out by hand provides some useful connections (for instance, how to expand one power from an earlier power) which are lost when using a CAS. This is a case where the symbolic manipulation is teaching more than what the answer is.

2.   (a) Use your CAS to expand $(a + b)^{10}$.
   (b) Use the expansion of $(a + b)^{10}$ in part (a) to expand $(a + b)^{11}$ *without* using a CAS. Explain what you did.
   (c) Explain how to find the expansion of $(a + b)^{n+1}$ using the expansion of $(a + b)^n$.

Brief instructions for using the TI-89 calculator are provided in the Ways to think about it *section on page 184.*

On to the main result of this section, the Binomial Theorem. Complete the statement of the theorem, then be sure to *prove* the statement.

PROBLEM

If you don't recall the result and/or proof immediately, use the standard problem solving techniques: look at some specific examples, make a conjecture, etc.

3.   THE BINOMIAL THEOREM

Complete the statement of, and then prove, the Binomial Theorem:

If a and b are real (or complex) numbers and n is a non-negative integer, then

$$(a+b)^n = \sum_{k=0}^{n} \underline{\hspace{5cm}}$$

Check Your Understanding

Now that you've stated and proven the Binomial Theorem, you should apply it!

Of course, you can (and should) use the Binomial Theorem.

4.   (a) Expand $(x+y)^7$ by hand.
(b) Expand $(x+2y)^5$ by hand.

5.   What is the coefficient of $a^5 b^2$ in $(a+b)^7$? What other term has the same coefficient?

Pascal connections

One way to state THE BINOMIAL THEOREM is

$$(x+y)^n = \sum_{k=0}^{n} \binom{n}{k} x^k y^{n-k},$$

where $\binom{n}{k}$ is called a *binomial coefficient*. Using the $Pas(n,k)$ notation, the theorem can also be expressed as

$$(x+y)^n = \sum_{k=0}^{n} Pas(n,k) x^k y^{n-k},$$

where $Pas(n,k)$ is entry k in row n of Pascal's Triangle. Your proof of the Binomial Theorem should imply that $Pas(n,k) = \binom{n}{k}$, and when you combine this with what you learned in the previous section, you have the following:

$$\boxed{\binom{n}{k} = Pas(n,k) = {}_nC_k = \frac{n!}{k!(n-k)!}}$$

You now have *at least* four ways to think about $\binom{n}{k}$.

P. *The pattern perspective:* $\binom{n}{k}$ is entry k in row n of Pascal's Triangle. Thus, when $0 < k < n$,

$$\binom{n}{k} = \binom{n-1}{k-1} + \binom{n-1}{k}.$$

C. *The combinatorial perspective:* $\binom{n}{k}$ is equal to the number of k-element subsets of an n-element set.

Ar. *The arithmetic perspective:* $\binom{n}{k} = \frac{n!}{k!(n-k)!}$.

We will no longer include the phrase "when $0 \le k \le n$," although it is assumed, since other choices of k and n don't make sense.

Al. *The algebraic perspective:* $\binom{n}{k}$ is the coefficient of $a^k b^{n-k}$ (and $a^{n-k} b^k$) in the expansion of $(a+b)^n$.

Finally, we see why they call $\binom{n}{k}$ a binomial coefficient.

You might remember the next three problems from section 3. Solve them again, using one (or more) of the various perspectives discussed above.

6. Pick at least two of the above perspectives and show why each can be used to explain the fact that the sum of the entries in row n of Pascal's Triangle is 2^n.

7. Show that $\binom{n}{k} = \binom{n}{n-k}$, using as many perspectives as you can.

8. The alternating sum of the entries in row 5 of Pascal's Triangle is

$$\binom{5}{0} - \binom{5}{1} + \binom{5}{2} - \binom{5}{3} + \binom{5}{4} - \binom{5}{5},$$

which equals 0. What can you say about the alternating sum of the entries from *every* row of Pascal's Triangle?

Explain your statements. What perspective are you using?

9. State another property that you know about binomial coefficients that can be understood from more than one of these perspectives.

Think back over the previous sections if you have trouble remembering any more properties.

PROBLEM

10. HAN AND MARVIN'S PROOF:
In the dialogue that follows, Han and Marvin are discussing a *combinatorial* proof of the Binomial Theorem. Finish the discussion and proof for them. Be sure to provide a proof of the general result, not just the $n = 5$ case.

Han:	I have another proof of the Binomial Theorem.
Marvin:	How's it go?
Han:	Well, look at $(a + b)^5$. It's really just

$$(a + b)(a + b)(a + b)(a + b)(a + b), \text{ right?}$$

Marvin:	And you want to *do* that?
Han:	I want to *imagine* doing it. If I multiplied all this out, I'd get a sum of terms, each of which is a sum of some as multiplied by some bs. I get each term by taking a letter from each set of parentheses, then multiplying them together. For example, I could take a from parentheses 1, 2, and 4 and b from parentheses 3 and 5. That would give me an a^3b^2.
Marvin:	But you could also get an a^3b^2 by taking a from parentheses 1, 2, and 3 and b from parentheses 4 and 5.
Han:	Right, so the *coefficient* of a^3b^2 will be the number of ways I can pick 3 as and 2 bs from the 5 parentheses.
Marvin:	And *that* is just the number of ways you can pick three things (the as) from each of the five parentheses. So it's $\binom{5}{3}$.
Han:	Or, think of it as the number of ways you can pick two things (two bs) from the five parentheses. That's $\binom{5}{2}$, which is the *same* as $\binom{5}{3}$.
Marvin:	OK, call it $\binom{5}{2}$ if you want. So, we have one part of $(a + b)^5$. It's $\binom{5}{2}a^3b^2$.
Han:	And the same idea applies to other terms. You can pick no as and five bs, one a and four bs, ...

Reflect and Discuss

The Binomial Theorem is a popular tool for solving many problems in mathematical contests. In fact, whenever you see a sum involving binomial coefficients, the first thing you should think of is the Binomial Theorem. Here are some additional problems which you can solve by applying the Binomial Theorem in just the right way. You'll probably recognize the first two.

11. Compute each of the following sums for every choice of positive integer, n. (More precisely, conjecture a more *succinct* formula, then *prove* that your conjecture is correct.)

For example, in the previous section, you conjectured that $\sum_{k=0}^{n} \binom{n}{k} = 2^n$ and $\sum_{k=0}^{n} (-1)^k \binom{n}{k} = 0.$

(a) $\displaystyle\sum_{k=0}^{n} \binom{n}{k} 2^k$

(b) $\displaystyle\sum_{k=0}^{n} \binom{n}{k} r^k$, where r is a specific real number.

(c) $\displaystyle\sum_{k=0}^{n} \binom{n}{k} (-1)^k 2^{n-k}$

(d) $\displaystyle\sum_{k=0}^{n} \frac{\binom{n}{k} 3^{n-k}}{4^k}$

Here's one last puzzler to consider:

12. Define E to be the sum of the binomial coefficients, $\binom{n}{k}$, where k is even:

$$E = \binom{n}{0} + \binom{n}{2} + \cdots = \sum_{k \text{ even}} \binom{n}{k}.$$

Also, let O be the sum of the $\binom{n}{k}$ for which k is odd.

$$O = \binom{n}{1} + \binom{n}{3} + \cdots = \sum_{k \text{ odd}} \binom{n}{k}.$$

How do E and O compare?

Ways to think about it

Problem: *Expand the following binomial powers:* $(a+b)^2$, $(a+b)^3$, $(a+b)^4$, $(a+b)^5$.

Problem: *(a) Use a CAS to expand $(a+b)^{10}$.*
(b) Use the expansion of $(a+b)^{10}$ to expand $(a+b)^{11}$ without using a CAS.
(c) Explain how to find the expansion of $(a+b)^{n+1}$ using the expansion of $(a+b)^n$.

With Maple, you can also evaluate `expand((a+b)^5);`

Space issues preclude us from providing directions for every calculator and software type. If you have another calculator or software, consult its manual—or better yet, work with a neighbor to figure it out

THE BINOMIAL THEOREM: *State and prove the Binomial Theorem.*

1. Look for patterns and timesaving techniques that allow you to more quickly arrive at your solution. For example, you can use the fact that $(a+b)^{n+1} = (a+b)(a+b)^n$. Be careful to avoid arithmetic errors—you'll be using your results in subsequent problems.

2. (a) With a TI-89 or TI-92, this is how you could expand $(a+b)^5$:

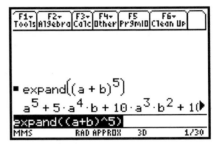

You can use the **alpha** key to spell out the word **expand** or you can use the **F2 Algebra** key and choose **3:expand(**. "Arrowing up" to the output line on the screen and then arrowing over to the right will allow you to see the complete expansion.

(b), (c) In order to expand $(a+b)^{n+1}$ from $(a+b)^n$, use the fact that $(a+b)^{n+1} = (a+b)(a+b)^n$. First consider smaller cases. For example, consider the task of getting $(a+b)^4$ from $(a+b)^3$, which equals $a^3 + 3a^2b + 3ab^2 + b^3$:

$$
\begin{array}{ccccccccc}
a^3 & + & 3a^2b & + & 3ab^2 & + & b^3 \\
{}_{\times a}\diagup\diagdown{}^{\times b} & & {}_{\times a}\diagup\diagdown{}^{\times b} & & {}_{\times a}\diagup\diagdown{}^{\times b} & & {}_{\times a}\diagup\diagdown{}^{\times b} \\
a^4 \quad + & & 4a^3b \quad + & & 6a^2b^2 \quad + & & 4ab^3 \quad + & & b^4
\end{array}
$$

3. To make a conjecture, look back at problems 1 and 2, then generalize the pattern you see in the coefficients of the polynomials.

Now, for the proof of the conjecture. You may have recognized the coefficients of the polynomials in this problem as entries in Pascal's Triangle:

$$
\begin{array}{l|c}
(a+b)^0 = 1 & 1 \\
(a+b)^1 = a+b & 1\quad 1 \\
(a+b)^2 = a^2 + 2ab + b^2 & 1\quad 2\quad 1 \\
(a+b)^3 = a^3 + 3a^2b + 3ab^2 + b^3 & 1\quad 3\quad 3\quad 1
\end{array}
$$

So how can you approach the *general* proof? How does your reasoning in problem 2 help? Does knowing your conjecture is correct for $(a+b)^{n-1}$ help you prove it's correct for $(a+b)^n$? If so, you can use induction.

4 – 5. Remember, $\binom{n}{k}$ is entry k in row n. Also remember that rows and entries start "counting" at 0, not 1. Express your answer *first* in terms of binomial coefficients, *then* as integers (i.e. first $\binom{5}{2}$, then 10). Breaking the arithmetic up into two pieces will help minimize errors.

6 – 8. Recast the statements of the results in terms of the different perspectives, then try to justify them. Why should entries in Pascal's Triangle (or coefficients in the expansion of $(a+b)^n$, the number of subsets of a given size, or $\frac{n!}{k!(n-k)!}$) "act" this way? In problem 7, in order to use the algebraic perspective, you need to see what choice of a and b will give you $(a+b)^n = \sum_{k=0}^{n} \binom{n}{k}$.

9. Look for more patterns in Pascal's Triangle. For instance,
- $\binom{n}{k} + \binom{n}{k+1} = ?$
- $\binom{n}{n} = ?$
- $\binom{n}{1} = ?$
- The hockey stick theorem.

10. We know $(a + b)^n = (a + b)(a + b) \cdots (a + b)$. How many times does $a^k b^{n-k}$ "appear" in the expansion? How many ways are there to choose k as from n parentheses?

11. Try to make each expression look like the "answer" to a Binomial Theorem "question." That is, rewrite the expression so that it looks like

$$\sum_{k=0}^{n} \binom{n}{k} a^k b^{n-k}.$$

Then, your sum must equal $(a+b)^n$. You can use the "guess, check, revise" method. Try various choices for a and b and check to see if your guess is correct. If not, analyze what's wrong and "fix" the guess.

(a)–(b) You've seen the answers, now prove they're right. If it's been a while since you completed the previous

Problem: Expand $(x + y)^7$ and $(x + 2y)^5$ by hand (using the Binomial Theorem).

Problem: What is the coefficient of $a^5 b^2$ in $(a + b)^7$? What other term has the same coefficient?

Problem: Pick at least two of the above perspectives and show why each can be used to explain the fact that the sum of the entries in the nth row of Pascal's Triangle is 2^n.

Problem: Show that $\binom{n}{k} = \binom{n}{n-k}$, using as many perspectives as you can.

Problem: What can you say about "alternating sum" of the entries in every row of Pascal's Triangle?

Problem: State another property of binomial coefficients that can be understood from more than one of these perspectives.

HAN AND MARVIN'S PROOF: *Use Han and Marvin's method to prove the Binomial Theorem.*

Problem: Compute each of the following sums for every choice of positive integer n (more precisely, conjecture a more succinct formula, then prove that you're correct).

(a) $\sum_{k=0}^{n} \binom{n}{k} 2^k$

(b) $\sum_{k=0}^{n} \binom{n}{k} r^k$, *where r is a specific real number.*

(c) $\sum_{k=0}^{n} \binom{n}{k}(-1)^k 2^{n-k}$

(d) $\sum_{k=0}^{n} \frac{\binom{n}{k} 3^{n-k}}{4^k}$

section, take a few minutes to look at some special cases for n, then make and prove your conjecture.

(c) After looking at a few examples, you can come up with a conjecture. By carefully choosing particular values for a and b in the Binomial Theorem, you can prove your conjecture.

(d) It will help to recognize that $\frac{1}{4^k} = \left(\frac{1}{4}\right)^k$.

Problem: *Let* $E = \sum\limits_{k \text{ even}} \binom{n}{k}$ *and* $O = \sum\limits_{k \text{ odd}} \binom{n}{k}$. *How do E and O compare?*

12. Look at a few examples in order to give yourself enough information to formulate a conjecture. What can you say about $E - O$? If you rearrange the terms in $E - O$, you might recognize what you get.

5. Supercalifragilisticgeneratingfunctionology

Rolling the dice

Many elementary and middle school curricula ask students to experiment with probability. One of the most popular experiments has to do with throwing dice. For example, one could ask students the following kinds of questions. *Take a few minutes to work on these alone or with a partner.*

1. When tossing a single die, how many different numbers can show up? What is the most likely number?

2. When tossing two dice, how many different *pairs* can show up? How many different *sums* can show up? What is the most likely sum?

3. When tossing three dice, how many different triples can show up? How many different sums can show up? What do you think is the most likely sum?

Note that you are not being asked to determine the distribution of these sums, yet.

Reflect and Discuss

4. When tossing n dice, how many different n-tuples can show up? How many different sums can show up? What do you think is the most likely sum?

An n-tuple is an ordered list of n elements; for example, $(a_1, a_2, \ldots, a_n)$. Thus, "two-tuples" and "three-tuples" are ordered pairs and triples.

There are at least two different, yet related, approaches to counting the dice sums mentioned in these problems, which could be summarized as *listing them* and *imagine listing them*. Literally listing all of the possible dice rolls is not a very efficient method for determining the possible sums when ten dice are rolled, but it works very well when dealing with two dice. If you make a table that takes each of the two dice rolls into account, you see that there are 36 possibilities, resulting in a total of 11 sums:

Perhaps your group made such a table when solving problem 2.

Die 2→ Die 1↓	1	2	3	4	5	6
1	2	3	4	5	6	7
2	3	4	5	6	7	8
3	4	5	6	7	8	9
4	5	6	7	8	9	10
5	6	7	8	9	10	11
6	7	8	9	10	11	12

As you no doubt noticed, it's possible to determine the possible sums—but not their frequency—without listing all possible dice rolls. Since the integers 1–6 are the possibilities for a single roll, the smallest possible sum is 2, the largest possible sum is 12, and all intermediate sums can be shown to be possible, as well. When ten dice are rolled, it's still possible—but it requires a little bit of work—to show that the possible sums are the integers between (and including) 10 and 60. So, it's possible to determine the range of sums without listing them all, but it's not clear how you could determine the *most likely sum* without making a list of all possible rolls and recording the resulting sum. The two-dice table not only tells you that 7 is the most likely sum, it also tells you how the other sums are *distributed*:

Of course, all this is idealized. It says nothing about any particular actual game of dice. You can ask students to throw two dice many times and tally the sums. That's a nice experiment—especially for a Friday afternoon—and the results often closely approximate the idealization presented here. But be careful: Experiment alone is not mathematics.

Sum	Number of occurrences
2	1
3	2
4	3
5	4
6	5
7	6
8	5
9	4
10	3
11	2
12	1

Now, you're probably asking yourself:

If you weren't asking yourself this, please do so now!

> *When n dice are thrown, how are the possible sums distributed? Can we determine the distribution as we did in the case n = 2?*

First consider the case $n = 3$.

Determining the distribution table for 3 dice is much easier if you use the "2 dice" table above. Similarly, when completing the "n dice" table, use the "n − 1 dice" table.

5. Make a table that reports the number of occurrences of each possible sum when *three* dice are thrown. If there's time, construct similar tables for more dice (4 or 5, say).

You may have noticed that the distribution tables for 2 and 3 dice (and for n dice, in fact) are symmetric. Think about how to predict which sums have equal distribution and why these sums should occur with equal frequency.

6. Describe and explain the symmetry in the sum distribution table for 1, 2, and 3 dice. Use your results to fill in the blank in the following sentence:

> *When n dice are thrown, the number of ways to get a sum of S is equal to the number of ways of getting a sum of _____.*

Therefore, these two sums are equally likely.

Be sure to prove that your conjecture is correct.

Abstract clotheslines

Here's a seemingly cockeyed idea: Take the distribution of sums for two dice and hang it out on a "clothesline" of powers of x:

$$x^2 + 2x^3 + 3x^4 + 4x^5 + 5x^6 + 6x^7 + 5x^8 + 4x^9 + 3x^{10} + 2x^{11} + x^{12}$$

This image of an expression as a clothesline is due to Herbert Wilf and is taken from his beautiful book, Generatingfunctionology *(Academic Press, 1993).*

Note that the general term here is

$$\{\text{number of ways you can get } s \text{ as a sum}\} \times x^s$$

Why would you do such a thing? Well, it's just another code—another representation, if you will—of the information in the above table. It may even be easier to write down. It certainly takes less space. And, if you want to, you can "do algebra" with this expression. For example, do you have the urge to factor it?

7. Using a *CAS* or paper and pencil, completely factor the 2-dice distribution polynomial:

$$x^2 + 2x^3 + 3x^4 + 4x^5 + 5x^6 + 6x^7 + 5x^8 + 4x^9 + 3x^{10} + 2x^{11} + x^{12}.$$

One way or another, you should have found that the polynomial is equal to

$$x^2(x+1)^2(x^2+x+1)^2(x^2-x+1)^2.$$

Try factoring it by hand and see how far you get. Don't be shy about using a CAS to finish off the job. In any case, check the result by hand. If not, take a few minutes to confirm this claim.

Now dig a little deeper into this factorization. It can't come out so nice without something going on, some hidden meaning, behind the scenes. Here's just one possible interpretation of the factorization:

Notice that each factor is a square. That is, our original distribution polynomial factors as

$$\left[x(x+1)(x^2+x+1)(x^2-x+1)\right]^2.$$

One thing formal algebraists do is hunt for hidden meanings that emerge from algebraic calculations. Could the power of 2 in the factorization have anything to do with the fact that we rolled 2 dice?

The insides may be too complicated to think about, so expand this product (without the square):

$$x(x+1)(x^2+x+1)(x^2-x+1) = x + x^2 + x^3 + x^4 + x^5 + x^6.$$

Check for yourself (by hand or with the help of a CAS) that this is true.

Well, isn't that interesting? We've just shown that

$$x^2 + 2x^3 + 3x^4 + 4x^5 + 5x^6 + 6x^7 + 5x^8 + 4x^9 + 3x^{10} + 2x^{11} + x^{12}$$

$$\text{equals} \qquad \left(x + x^2 + x^3 + x^4 + x^5 + x^6\right)^2.$$

Do you agree that $x + x^2 + x^3 + x^4 + x^5 + x^6$ is the distribution polynomial for the rolls of 1 die?

Among other things, this says that the distribution polynomial for two dice is the square of the distribution polynomial for one die. You're now going to figure out why this *should* be the case. With any luck, it will provide insight into the general situation (with n dice).

8. Explain, as if you were working with a student, how you'd expand expression $\left(x + x^2 + x^3 + x^4 + x^5 + x^6\right)^2$.

How, for example, would you get the coefficient of x^6 in the product? How would you get the coefficient of x^{10} in the product? How would you get the coefficient of x^k in the product?

9. Use your solution to problem 8 to explain why the expansion of $\left(x + x^2 + x^3 + x^4 + x^5 + x^6\right)^2$ should give you the distribution polynomial for the sums that show up when rolling two dice.

PROBLEM

10. THE DICE SUM PROBLEM
Conjecture the value of the distribution polynomial for the possible sums when you throw n dice. Prove that your conjecture is correct.

Let's stop using *distribution polynomial* and convert to the more standard term *generating function*. Given a sequence of numbers $\{a_k\}$ (finite or infinite), a generating function for the sequence is of the form $\sum a_k x^k$. That is, the generating function is a polynomial (or power series) for which the coefficient of x^k is a_k for each k.

For example, a generating function for the Fibonacci sequence is $1 + x + 2x^2 + 3x^3 + 5x^4 + 8x^5 + \ldots$.

The next two problems require you to use the generating function you found in problem 10 to answer some questions about a various number of dice rolls.

Check Your Understanding

11. Determine the sum of the coefficients of the generating functions for the 2-, 3-, and 4-dice sum problems. State and prove a conjecture about the sum of the coefficients in the generating function for the n-dice sum problem.

12. Determine the most *likely* sums, as well as their frequency, when 4, 5, and 6 dice are thrown. Do the answers match your conjecture from problem 4? If not, make a new conjecture for the sum that is most likely when n dice are thrown.

What does this have to do with Pascal's Triangle?

Since each row of Pascal's Triangle is a sequence of numbers, you can create a generating function for each row.

13. Find a generating function for row n of Pascal's Triangle.

14. Find a *two-variable* generating function that gives you the distribution of heads and tails when you toss n coins. Carefully demonstrate and explain how to use the function to, for example, determine the number of ways to get 3 heads and 2 tails when you flip a coin 5 times (or when you flip 5 coins).

You probably knew Pascal's Triangle would show up again, didn't you?

Do you remember working with a polynomial for which the coefficient of x^k is equal to $\binom{n}{k}$?

Reflect and Discuss

15. Did you notice that the function you found in problem 14 is also a generating function for row n of Pascal's Triangle? Make sense of this connection by examining the two problems more closely. What do these contexts have in common?

You've just scratched the surface of the power of generating functions, not to mention the utility of—and connections among—combinatorial algebra, Pascal's Triangle, the Binomial Theorem, and generating functions. For more information and problems concerning generating functions, please consult the *Further Exploration* materials or your local (mathematics) library.

Ways to think about it

Problem: 1. *When tossing a single die, how many different numbers can show up? What is the most likely number?*
2. *When tossing two dice, how many different pairs can show up? How many different sums can show up? What is the most likely sum?*
3. *With three dice, how many different triples can show up? How many different sums? What do you think is the most likely sum?*

1–3. Try it (or at least imagine it)! Using what you know about 1 die will help you determine the possibilities for 2 (or more) dice. What are the smallest and largest possible sums? Do all of the *intermediate* sums also occur? With two or three dice, it's possible to list all of the possible pairs (or triples) and use that information to determine the frequency of each possible sum. Note that in problem 3, you are not asked to determine the most likely sum, you are asked to guess what the sum might be, so you don't have to list all of the possibilities in that case. Is there a way to answer these questions without listing all the possibilities?

Problem: *When tossing n dice, how many different n-tuples can show up? How many different sums can show up? What do you think is the most likely sum?*

4. This one's obviously harder to *try*. Search for patterns in the previous solutions, but also be able to explain how you know the pattern continues and how you know your general solution is correct. You can quickly determine the smallest and largest sums, but how do you know you also get all of the sums "in between"?

Problem: *Make a table which reports the number of occurrences of each possible sum when three dice are thrown.*

5. Use the table for 2 dice to build your "3-dice table." For example, in order to roll a sum of 10 with 3 dice, what are the possible "partial sums" you could have had if you just added the first 2 dice? Be careful about jumping to conclusions about "patterns" here. Watch out for a red herring as you consider sums that are close to the "middle."

Problem: *When n dice are thrown, the number of ways to get a sum of S is equal to the number of ways of getting a sum of _____.*

6. Imagine throwing standard dice on a clear glass table with one person looking down on the dice and another looking up at the dice from below the table. If one die is thrown and the person above the table sees a 5, what does the person below the table see? Now, consider what happens with 2 dice. If the person above the table sees a sum of 10, what sum does the person below the table see? What about the $n = 3$ case? The general case?

Note that if the dice (or number cubes) you are using aren't set up so that opposite sides sum to 7, you can always renumber them so that this property is satisfied.

Problem: *Using a CAS or paper and pencil, completely factor the "distribution polynomial" $x^2 + 2x^3 + 3x^4 + 4x^5 + 5x^6 + 6x^7 + 5x^8 + 4x^9 + 3x^{10} + 2x^{11} + x^{12}$.*

7. As always, be very careful to correctly enter values into the CAS and to try to avoid any arithmetic errors in your calculations. It wouldn't hurt to recheck your calculations or compare your work with a partner (or both).

8. How would Han and Marvin (the kids from section 4 who came up with a proof of the binomial theorem by imagining how the expansion of powers of a polynomial works) solve this problem? Remember, you want to explain as if you were talking to a student. Which powers of x—from each set of parentheses—will combine to give you x^6? x^{10}? x^k?

Problem: *Explain how you'd multiply out* $\left(x + x^2 + x^3 + x^4 + x^5 + x^6\right)^2$. *How would you get the coefficient of x^k in the product?*

9. Translate your explanation in problem 8 to this situation. Of course, first you have to see how the two questions are related.

Problem: *Explain why the expansion of* $\left(x + x^2 + x^3 + x^4 + x^5 + x^6\right)^2$ *should give the distribution for the sums that show up when rolling two dice.*

10. Based on the data collected, you've probably guessed that the distribution polynomial (for the sums that occur when n dice are rolled) is $(x + x^2 + x^3 + x^4 + x^5 + x^6)^n$. How can you adapt your explanation in problems 8 and 9 to the general case? How is the coefficient of x^k in the expansion of this polynomial related to the number of ways to get a sum of k when n-dice are rolled?

THE DICE SUM PROBLEM: *Conjecture the value of the distribution polynomial for the possible sums when you throw n dice. Prove that your conjecture is correct.*

11. First, determine the generating function for 2, 3, and 4 dice and compute the sum of their coefficients. In what context have these numbers come up before (earlier in the section)? What do you think will happen when n dice are rolled. To prove the conjecture, it will help to think of another way to determine the sum of the coefficients in these polynomials. What value of x can you substitute in order to add up the coefficients? You did something similar to this in the previous section when working with the Binomial Theorem. What do the individual coefficients represent?

Problem: *Determine the sum of the coefficients of the generating functions for the 2-, 3-, and 4-dice sum problems. State and prove a conjecture about the sum of the coefficients in the generating function for the n dice sum problem.*

12. Use your *CAS* (if you have one) to expand the generating function for the specified number of dice. Note that with some values of n, two sums are tied for most likely, while other values of n correspond to a single most likely sum. Which is which? The most likely sum seems to occur near the middle of the range of possible sums. Try to be a little more specific in your response. For a given number of dice (say, n), which sum or sums are more likely?

Problem: *Determine the most likely sums, as well as their frequency, when 4, 5, and 6 dice are thrown. Do the answers match your conjecture from problem 4? If not, make a new conjecture for the sum that is most likely when n dice are thrown.*

13. We've got two words for you: Section 4 (OK, that's really *one* word and *one* numeral). For those of you who'd prefer more words, there are a couple of ways to think about it: In order for our generating function to "generate" the en-

Problem: *Find a generating function that gives you the row n of Pascal's Triangle.*

tries in row n of Pascal's Triangle, you need the coefficient of x^k to be $\binom{n}{k}$. If that doesn't help, create the generating functions for several different rows of the triangle and factor them like you did with the dice problem generating function before.

Problem: *What's a (two-variable) generating function that gives you the distribution of heads and tails when you toss n coins? Carefully demonstrate and explain how to use the function to, for example, determine the number of ways to get 3 heads and 2 tails when you flip a coin 5 times (or when you flip 5 coins).*

14. Let's call our two variables H and T (although their choice is irrelevant, it's nice to choose meaningful symbols when possible)! Since on each coin toss, the only possibilities are H or T, what should the distribution polynomial for one coin toss look like? When you square the polynomial, do you get the distribution polynomial corresponding to two coin tosses? Should you? Why?

Problem: *The function you found in problem 14 is a generating function for row n of Pascal's Triangle. Make sense of this connection by examining the two problems more closely. What do these contexts have in common?*

15. Pick a *perspective, any* perspective. (See section 4.) How can you view the coin-tossing problem from these perspectives?

Chapter VI

Problems for the Classroom

What is Mathematical Investigation?

The following problems were adapted from *Problems with a Point*, a collection of focused problem sets for students in grades 6-12 developed at Education Development Center, Inc.

First to 50

First to 50 is a two-player number game. Here is how the game is played:

- Player 1 starts by picking a number from 1 to 9.
- Player 2 does the same thing, then adds that number to the one chosen by Player 1.
- The game continues with the players taking turns picking a digit and adding it to the total.
- The player whose number brings the total to 50 wins.

Play *First to 50* several times with a partner, then answer the following questions. Justify your responses.

1. There is a strategy that one of the players can use to win *every* game.
    (a) What is the strategy, and which player (Player 1 or 2) is guaranteed to win if he or she uses the strategy?
    (b) If your opponent doesn't know about this strategy, explain how you can still win most of the time, whether you are Player 1 or 2.

In First to 100 *and* First to 75, *the rules are the same as in* First to 50, *except the winner is the first to 100 (or 75).*

2. How, if at all, does your strategy change if you play *First to 100* instead?

3. How, if at all, does your strategy change if you play *First to 75* instead?

4. **Challenge:** Now, change the rules of *First to 100*. Pick a number less than 100—call it n—and let that be the largest number a player can choose on each turn (in the original game, n was 9). If the goal is still to be the player who makes the total equal 100, come up with a winning strategy for this new game that depends on the n that is chosen.

Fibonacci's rabbits

Leonardo Pisano,better known as Fibonacci, is probably best known for a problem he posed in *Liber Abaci*, a compendium of the arithmetic and algebra knowledge he had obtained during his travels in North Africa. Here's a version of the "rabbit problem":

> Suppose you go to an uninhabited island with a pair of newborn rabbits (one male and one female) who mature at the age of one month, have two offspring (one male and one female) each month after that, and live forever. Each pair of rabbits matures in one month and then produces a pair of newborns at the beginning of every following month. How many pairs of rabbits will there be in a year?

At the beginning of the first month, there are just the original, newborn pair of rabbits. At the beginning of the second month, those rabbits are now mature and will produce a pair of rabbits at the beginning of the next month. The following table then shows the number of pairs of rabbits at the beginning of the first three months:

month	1	2	3
pairs of rabbits	1	1	2

The original rabbits will produce another pair of rabbits at the beginning of the fourth month, but the pair of rabbits that was born at the beginning of the third month has just matured, so those rabbits won't produce a pair of rabbits until the beginning of the fifth month.

5. (a) How many pairs of *newborn* rabbits will arrive at the beginning of month 4?
   (b) How many pairs of rabbits (of all ages) will there be at the beginning of month 4?

6. (a) How many pairs of *newborn* rabbits will arrive at the beginning of month 5?
   (b) How many pairs of rabbits (of all ages) will there be at the beginning of month 5?

7. (a) How many pairs of *newborn* rabbits will arrive at the beginning of month 6?
   (b) How many pairs of rabbits (of all ages) will there be at the beginning of month 6?

8. (a) How many pairs of *newborn* rabbits will arrive at the

beginning of month n? Express your answer in terms of the number of pairs of rabbits which were alive in previous months.

(b) How many pairs of rabbits (of all ages) will there be at the beginning of month n? Express your answer in terms of the number of pairs of rabbits which were alive in previous months.

9. (a) Fill in the blanks in the table below.

month	1	2	3	4	5	6	7	8	9	10	11	12	13
pairs of rabbits	1	1	2										

How many pairs of rabbits will there be in a year?

(b) Solve Fibonacci's rabbit problem, as stated on page 1.

The sequence generated by the rabbit problem (the number of pairs of rabbits alive at the beginning of a given month) is called the *Fibonacci sequence*. The symbol F_n is used to represent the nth number in the Fibonacci sequence. Using your solution to the previous problems, you know that $F_1 = F_2 = 1$, $F_3 = 2$, $F_4 = 3$, and so on.

F_n is sometimes called the nth Fibonacci number.

10. (a) What is F_{12}?
     (b) What is F_{15}?

11. Express F_n as a function of the previous terms of the sequence for all $n \geq 3$.

12. **Investigation:** List the first 30 Fibonacci numbers and look for patterns in the terms. Specifically,
     (a) Which terms are even?
     (b) Which terms are multiples of 3?
     (c) Which terms are multiples of 5?
     (d) What other patterns do you notice?
     (e) Must the patterns you observed continue forever?

You could also use a spreadsheet program to generate as long a list as you want.

13. **Challenge:** Write a calculator or computer program that will compute any term in the Fibonacci sequence.

Solutions

First to 50

1. (a) In *First to 50*, the worst total to have just before your turn is 40, since there's no way to add a positive digit to get from 40 to 50 *and* whatever digit you choose, your opponent will get to 50 (and win) by choosing 10 minus your number. But if the total before your turn is greater than 30 and less than 40, the total is from

1 to 9 away from 40, so you can choose the digit that will make the total equal to 40 and then you can win on your next turn.

This means, of course, that you want the total to be 40 on your opponent's last turn. How can you make this happen? For exactly the same reason that 40 is a bad number (if it's your turn), so is 30. This is because if the total is 30, then no matter what digit you choose on your turn, your opponent can choose 10 minus your number and make the total 40 on your next turn, which we've already found is a bad total. For the same reason, 20 is a bad total and so is 10. But then 0 is a bad total, too, so it's better to be Player 2 than Player 1. If you go second and use the "10 minus Player 1's number" strategy, you'll win every game.

(b) Player 2 can always win by following the "10 minus Player 1's number" strategy. Player 1's best (and only) hope is that Player 2 does not know the "10 minus" strategy. If Player 2 ever fails to follow that strategy, then Player 1 *can* win the game. If the total is *not* a multiple of 10 when it's Player 1's turn, Player 1 can make the total a multiple of 10 (since the total will be between 1 and 9 away from the next multiple of 10). Then, following the "10 minus" strategy will guarantee victory.

2. Since 100 is also a multiple of 10 (like 50), you want to be Player 2 and use the "10 minus" strategy. As in *First to 50*, if you are Player 1, you can only hope that Player 1 doesn't know the strategy, then force the total to be a multiple of 10 as soon as you can.

3. Since 75 is not a multiple of 10, the strategy has to change for *First to 75*. Now, the bad totals to have at the start of your turn are 65, 55, 45, 35, 25, 15, and 5. Therefore, it's best to be Player 1, since you can pick 5 on your turn, then use the "10 minus" strategy to force the totals to be 5 more than a multiple of 10 at the end of each of your turns. If you are Player 2, you can still win if Player 1 doesn't choose 5 on his or her first turn or if the total at the beginning of your turn is ever something other than 5, 15, 25, 35, 45, 55, or 65. If this happens, the total will have to be between 1 and 9 from one of the "bad" numbers. That means that you can choose a positive digit that will make the total at the end of your turn be 5 more than a

multiple of 10 and you will win if you use the "10 minus" strategy.

4. Given a number between 1 and n, it's always possible to choose a number in the same range so that the two numbers add up to $n + 1$, and it is *impossible* to get $n + 1$ in a single turn. Therefore, the bad numbers are those that are a multiple of $n + 1$ less than 100: $100 - (n + 1)$, $100 - 2(n + 1)$, and so on. At the beginning of your opponent's turn, if the total is bad, you can keep it that way by choosing the number that is $n + 1$ minus the number your opponent chose. The totals for your opponent will always be a multiple of $n + 1$ less than 100, so you'll keep him or her from winning, as long as you don't make any arithmetic errors!

As in the original games, the winning strategy depends on whether 100 is a multiple of $n + 1$:

- If 100 is *not* a multiple of $n + 1$, you want to go first and start by choosing the number that makes the total a multiple of $n + 1$ less than 100. Since a number is 100 minus a multiple of $n + 1$ exactly when 100 minus that number is a multiple of $n + 1$, your first number should be chosen so that 100 minus your number is a multiple of $n + 1$. (This is always possible, since if 100 is not a multiple of $n + 1$, its remainder when divided by $n + 1$ will be a number from 1 to n.) Now that you've forced your opponent to a bad total, you continue with choosing $n + 1$ minus his or her choice on your remaining turns.

Using algebraic notation, if 100 is not a multiple of $n + 1$, you want to go first and choose the number f, where $100 - f$ is a multiple of $n + 1$.

- If 100 *is* a multiple of $n + 1$, you want to go second and follow the strategy of choosing $n + 1$ minus the number your opponent chooses at each turn.

Fibonacci's rabbits

5. (a) At the beginning of the fourth month, the original pair of rabbits will produce another pair of rabbits, but the other pair will not produce a pair of rabbits until the beginning of the next month. Therefore, 1 new pair of rabbits will be produced.

   (b) Combining the newborn pair with the two pairs of rabbits that were already there gives us a total of 3 pairs of rabbits at the beginning of the fourth month. Two pairs of these rabbits will each produce a pair of newborns in the next month.

6. (a) Since it takes two months for a pair of rabbits to mature and then have a pair of rabbits themselves (from then on, they'll produce a pair of rabbits at the beginning of every month), the number of new pairs born at the beginning of the fifth month will be the number of pairs that were alive at the beginning of the third month. That is, there will be 2 newborn pairs of rabbits at the beginning of the fifth month.

    (b) Combining the 2 newborn pairs with the 3 pairs that were already alive the previous month gives a total of 5 pairs of rabbits at the beginning of the fifth month.

7. (a) Using the same strategy as the previous problem, the number of pairs of newborns at the beginning of the sixth month is the number pairs that were alive at the beginning of the fourth month, which is 3.

    (b) There will be 5 pairs of rabbits alive during the fifth month and 3 pairs born at the beginning of the sixth month, so there will be a total of 8 pairs of rabbits at the beginning of the sixth month.

8. (a) Again, using the strategy developed in part (a) of problems 1–3, the number of pairs of rabbits born at the beginning of month n will be the number of rabbits that were alive at the beginning of month $n - 2$.

    (b) We need to add the number of newborn pairs to the number of pairs that were alive the previous month. That's the sum of the number of rabbits alive at the beginning of month $n - 2$ and the number of rabbits alive at the beginning of month $n - 1$. Stated a little more succinctly, at the beginning of any month, starting with the third month, the number of pairs of rabbits will be the sum of the number of pairs of rabbits there were in the previous two months.

9. (a) The entries for months 4–6 are the solutions to part (b) of questions 1–3. Using the fact that the number of pairs of rabbits at the beginning of any month (after the second month, at least) is the sum of the number of pairs of rabbits present the previous two months, the number of pairs of rabbits at the beginning of the seventh month is $5+8$, or 13. Similarly, there are $8+13$ (or 21) pairs of rabbits at the beginning of the eighth month, $13+21$ (or 34) pairs of rabbits at the beginning of the ninth month, $21 + 34$ (or 55) pairs of rabbits at the beginning of the tenth month, $55+34$ (or 89) pairs

of rabbits at the beginning of the eleventh month, and $55 + 89$ (or 144) pairs of rabbits at the beginning of the twelfth month. The completed table is shown in the answer to this problem.

(b)   Twelve months after the beginning of the first month is the beginning of the thirteenth month, so there are 233 pairs of rabbits alive after a year has passed.

10.   (a) F_{12} is the number of pairs of rabbits alive at the beginning of the twelfth month, which the table shows us is 144.

(b)   We know that F_{14} is the sum of F_{12} and F_{13}, which equals 377. Similarly, F_{15} is the sum of F_{13} and F_{14}, which is 610.

11.   As problems 1–6 show us, as long as $n \geq 3$, F_n will be the sum of F_{n-2} and F_{n-1}. That is, $F_n = F_{n-2} + F_{n-1}$.

12.   (a)   If n is a multiple of 3, then F_n is even.
(b)   If n is a multiple of 4, then F_n is a multiple of 3.
(c)   If n is a multiple of 5, then F_n is a multiple of 5.
(d)   In general, if n is a multiple of m, then F_n is a multiple of F_m.
(e)   These patterns *do* continue forever. To see why the pattern in part (a) continues, observe that the sequence of terms alternates in the patter odd, odd, even, odd, odd, even, ... The reason this has to continue comes from the way the Fibonacci numbers are defined (any entry starting with the third is the sum of the previous two entries). If the previous two entries are odd, the next entry (the sum of the previous 2) must be even, the next term must be odd (sum of odd and even), as must the next term (even plus odd), the next term is even (odd plus odd), and so on. You can also see this symbolically, using the principle of mathematical induction. We know that F_3, F_6, and F_9 are all even, since they equal 2, 8, and 34, respectively. Now, suppose you know that F_{3m} is even for some positive integer m. Then

$$
\begin{aligned}
F_{3(m+1)} &= F_{3m+3} \\
&= F_{3m+1} + F_{3m+2} \\
&= F_{3m+1} + (F_{3m} + F_{3m+1}) = F_{3m} + 2F_{3m+1},
\end{aligned}
$$

which is even, since F_{3m} was assumed to be even and $2F_{3m+1}$ is even, too. Therefore, F_{3n} is even for all positive integers n, as conjectured.

To see that the pattern in part (b) holds, use mathematical induction, and the fact that

$$F_{4m+4} = 3F_{4m+1} + 2F_{4m}$$

(be sure to show this is true).

To see that the pattern in part (c) holds, use mathematical induction, and the fact that

$$F_{5m+5} = 5F_{5m+1} + 3F_{5m}$$

(be sure to show this is true).

In general, $F_{km+k} = F_k \cdot F_{km+1} + F_{k-1} \cdot F_{km}$, which is also possible to prove using induction.

13. The program will probably mimic the procedure used to fill in the table for problem 5. There are many ways to do this (see the program in the answer, for example), but the main idea of any program is to incorporate the fact that $F_n = F_{n-2} + F_{n-1}$ when $n \geq 3$.

Dissections and Area

Many kids are very interested in why things work the way they do, and acknowledging the justification side of mathematics is important. However, figuring out the answer is usually a lot more fun than carefully making sure you're right. Here are some other problems along these lines.

1. You might recognize the seven pieces below as tangrams.
    (a) Cut out the shapes (or use a set of tangrams from your classroom) and rearrange them into one big square.
    (b) Given that the small square has an area of one unit, find the area of the square constructed from all seven shapes.

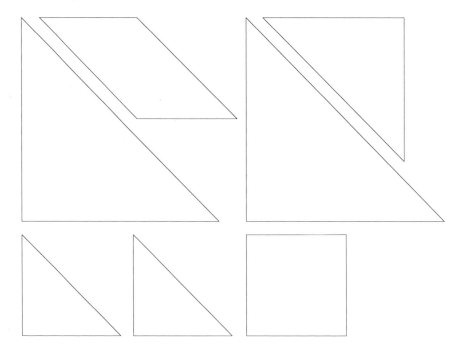

2. Now use the 2 big triangles to make a triangle, a square, and a parallelogram. What are each of the new figures' areas?

3. Use the tangram pieces to make the horse shown in the margin (not to scale). What is its area?

4. Make some other interesting shapes, trace them, and challenge your classmates to create them with the tangram pieces.

Pattern blocks are manipulatives often used in elementary schools and it's possible that you have some in your school, if not in your classroom. The blocks come in 6 shapes: green equilateral triangle, orange square, yellow regular hexagon, a red isosceles trapezoid that is half the hexagon, a blue rhombus with an angle of 60°, and a beige rhombus with an angle of 30°. Each edge length (except for the long side of the trapezoid, which is half a hexagon) is one inch, which makes the blocks fit together nicely.

The pattern blocks

The blocks are good for teaching elementary ideas about area, and as an area model of some simple fractions. For example, you could decree that the triangle has area 1, and find the areas of the other pattern blocks, or shapes made with several pieces. Or you could decree that the hexagon is the unit of area, and ask about the areas of the other pieces.

5. Find the areas of all the pattern blocks in triangular inches (that is, assuming that the area of the equilateral triangle is 1). Note that the square may not have area 1, since area is not being measured in square inches.

6. Now, instead, assume that the area of the square is 1, and find the areas of all the pattern blocks.

Solutions

1. (a) Here's one solution to forming a square:

(b) As shown in problem 1 of section 1, the area of the square is 8 square units.

2. The figures are created below:

 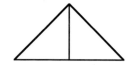 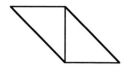

The area of each of the figures is 4 (observe that the legs of each triangle have length 2, so each of their areas is 2).

3. The horse is arranged as below (since all pieces are used, its area is 8):

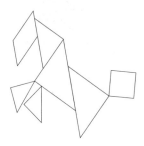

4. There are lots of possible figures (and many books and websites with examples).

5. The (blue) rhombus can be created (as a tangram) with two (green) triangles, the trapezoid is equivalent to three triangles, and the hexagon is made up of six triangles, so the area of the rhombus, in triangular inches, is 2, the area of the trapezoid is 3, and the area of the hexagon is 6 (of course, the area of the triangle is 1). The (orange) square's area is more difficult to determine in triangular inches. Since the equilateral triangle with side length 1 has area (measured in square units) $\frac{\sqrt{3}}{4}$ (it has height $\frac{\sqrt{3}}{2}$ and base 1), one triangular inch is $\frac{\sqrt{3}}{4}$ square inches. Then a 1×1 square has triangular area $\frac{4}{\sqrt{3}} = \frac{4\sqrt{3}}{3}$.

6. If the area of the square is 1, then the area of the triangle is $\frac{\sqrt{3}}{4}$ (as explained above). But then the area of the rhombus is twice that (or $\frac{\sqrt{3}}{2}$), the area of the trapezoid is $\frac{3\sqrt{3}}{4}$, and the area of the hexagon is $\frac{3\sqrt{3}}{2}$.

Linearity and Proportional Reasoning

The following additional problems require students to use proportional reasoning. Although algebra could be used for each, all can be solved without it, also.

1. In Ms. Anton's class, $\frac{4}{7}$ of the students were girls. After midyear, some students left and others came in. The new class had the same number of girls, but 3 more boys, which made the class half boys and half girls. How many students are in the new class?

2. Ramp City's public library had four different entrances, each with a ramp for people in wheelchairs and parents with strollers. The horizontal lengths and heights of the ramps are given in the following table. Put the ramps in order from least steep to steepest.

Entrance	Length	Height
North	96 inches	6 inches
East	180 inches	10 inches
South	160 inches	8 inches
West	72 inches	4 inches

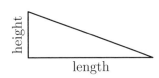

3. Here are U.S. Census population data for Tennessee during the years from 1800 to 2000. (Numbers for 1800 and 1810 are approximate.)

Year	Population	Year	Population
1800	106,000	1910	2,184,789
1810	262,000	1920	2,337,885
1820	422,823	1930	2,616,556
1830	681,904	1940	2,915,841
1840	829,210	1950	3,291,718
1850	1,002,717	1960	3,567,089
1860	1,109,801	1970	3,926,018
1870	1,258,520	1980	4,591,023
1880	1,542,359	1990	4,877,203
1890	1,767,518	2000	5,689,283
1900	2,020,616		

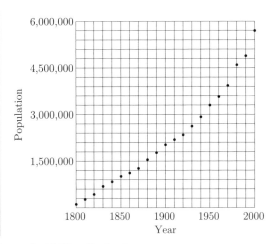

(a) From the census figures of 1940 and 1980, find the equation of a straight line for estimating the population at any time between 1940 and 1980.

(b) If you were to use your equation to estimate the population in 1950, 1960, and 1970, would your estimates be too low or too high? How do you know?

(c) Find the estimates and compare them to the actual data in the table.

(d) Find equations for estimating the population any time between
   (i) 1940 and 1950
   (ii) 1950 and 1960
   (iii) 1960 and 1970
   (iv) 1970 and 1980

(e) Compare the slopes and write a summary of your conclusions.

4. The following seems to prove that $0 = 2$ or $0 = -2$. What went wrong?

$$
\begin{aligned}
4 &= 2^2 \\
4 &= (1+1)^2 \\
4 &= 1^2 + 1^2 \\
4 &= 1+1 \\
4 &= 2
\end{aligned}
$$

5. Here's another proof gone wrong. Explain what happened.

$$
\begin{aligned}
1 &= 1^1 \\
1 &= 1^{3-2} \\
1 &= 1^3 - 1^2 \\
1 &= 1-1 \\
1 &= 0
\end{aligned}
$$

6. What do the "proofs" in problems 4 and 5 have in common?

7. Can you use a similar idea and each of the following starts to write a false proof? If so, do it. If not, why not?
   (a) $2 = 2 \cdot 1$
        $2 = 2(3-2)$
   (b) $2 = 2 \cdot 1$
        $2 = 2(1 \cdot 1)$

Multi-variable functions are no longer the province of Algebra 2 and higher classes. As you saw earlier in the text, some middle school textbooks present them in a manner appropriate to the skills of pre-algebra and beginning algebra students.

8. Tricycles (with three wheels) and bicycles (with two wheels) are crowded into the storeroom of a bicycle shop. Sophie has been assigned to do an inventory, but she can't distinguish the tricycles and bicycles in the crowded room, since all of the wheels are the same size. She can count exactly 17 seats and 40 wheels in the storeroom. How many tricycles and how many bicycles are there?

9. A few years later, the tricycles have gone out of style and two-seat bicycles are in. During inventory, Sophie counts 40 wheels but 27 seats. How many one-seat and two-seat bicycles are there?

10. The *Mathematics Hall of Fame* has recently opened. General admission tickets cost $6, senior citizen tickets cost $5, and student tickets cost $4, but all tickets look alike. In the first hour, 20 people bought tickets, spending a total of $100. Can you determine how many of each type of ticket was sold? Is there only *one* possibility?

11. The post office in Oops City is running low on its stamp supply. Only 3 cent and 7 cent stamps are available.
    (a) A customer wants to buy stamps to send a letter, but the postage is 55 cents. Is there a combination of stamps that will work? If so, what is it?
    (b) A customer walks in with an envelope that is partially stamped. She needs another 5 cents worth of stamps to have proper postage. Can she get that exact amount from the available stamps?
    (c) What values from 1 to 12 can be created using only 3 and 7 cent stamps? What values greater than 12 can be created?

12. The Oops City post office workers had a great time figuring out what postages they could create with 3 and 7 cent stamps. When the city officials heard, they decided to change their money system—only 3 and 7 dollar bills can be used!
    (a) From your answer to problem 11c, what prices can be paid for exactly using 3 and 7 dollar bills?
    (b) Of course, stores will be able to give change. For example, to pay for a $13 item, you could give four 7s and get five 3s in change: $28 - 15 = 13$. Of the values in problem 11c that were *not* possible with the stamps, which can be created by giving change?

13. Try to generalize your results in problems 11 and 12.
   (a) If the available stamps are a and b cents, what postages are possible?
   (b) Suppose for some value n you can get every greater value using the two types of stamps. What do you know about a and b? **Challenge:** What's the smallest n possible, in terms of a and b? That is, what's the largest value that *can't* be created using the two types of stamps?
   (c) If the available bills are a and b dollars, can you create any price possible (allowing change)? If so, explain. If not, what values of a and b will allow you to create any price possible?

Solutions

1. Suppose the rectangles below represent Ms. Anton's original class, and the shaded portion represents the girls. For this to be half boys and half girls, without changing the number of girls, an additional unshaded rectangle should be added. Since 3 boys joined the class, each rectangle must represent 3 students. The final class has 8 rectangles, so there are 24 students in the new class.

For an algebraic answer, you might let the number of students in the old class be x. Then $\frac{4}{7}x$ are girls and $\frac{3}{7}x$ are boys. Three boys join the class, making the number of boys $\frac{3}{7}x + 3$. Since the class is half boys and half girls, you have the following:

$$\frac{4}{7}x = \frac{3}{7}x + 3$$
$$4x = 3x + 21$$
$$x = 21$$

So there were 21 students in the old class and 24 students in the new class.

2. One way to think about this is to use the idea that slope is the steepness, and then use coordinates for each ramp. Another way is to write ratios:

Entrance	Length	Height	$\frac{\text{length}}{\text{height}}$	$\frac{\text{length}}{\text{total}}$
North	96 in.	6 in.	$\frac{96}{6} = 16$	$\frac{96}{102} = \frac{16}{17}$
East	180 in.	10 in.	$\frac{180}{10} = 18$	$\frac{180}{190} = \frac{18}{19}$
South	160 in.	8 in.	$\frac{160}{8} = 20$	$\frac{160}{168} = \frac{20}{21}$
West	72 in.	4 in.	$\frac{72}{4} = 18$	$\frac{72}{76} = \frac{18}{19}$

The relative steepness is more obvious from the $\frac{\text{length}}{\text{height}}$ ratio, but from either you can get the ranking (least steep to steepest): North, East tied with West, and South.

3. (a) Between 1940 and 1980, the slope $= \frac{4591023 - 2915841}{40} = 41879.55$, and the equation of the line is $y = 41879.55x - 78330486$.

   (b) The estimates from the line should be too high. If you draw a line connecting the data points for 1940 and 1980, it is above the actual values in between.

   (c) The estimates are indeed too high, as shown here:

	Estimate	Actual
1950:	3334636	3291718
1960:	3753432	3567089
1970:	4172227	3926018

   (d)

   $$1940 - 1950y = 37587.7x - 70004297$$
   $$1950 - 1960y = 27537.1x - 50405627$$
   $$1960 - 1970y = 35892.9x - 66782995$$
   $$1970 - 1980y = 66500.5x - 127079967$$

   (e) The slopes show that the population of Tennessee was increasing fastest between 1970 and 1980, at about 66,500 people per year.

4. The proof incorrectly used the additive homomorphism property: $(1 + 1)^2 = 1^2 + 1^2$ is not true.

5. The proof incorrectly used the additive homomorphism property: $1^{3-2} = 1^3 - 1^2$ is not true.

6. Both proofs used an additive homomorphism property with a mathematical operation that doesn't have that property.

7. (a) You cannot continue to write a false proof (in the same way) in this case, because there is no subtly false state-

ment to replace $2(3 - 2)$. Here, the additive homomorphism property would apply correctly.

(b) You can complete this with a false proof:

$$
\begin{aligned}
2 &= 2 \cdot 1 \\
2 &= 2(1 \cdot 1) \\
2 &= 2(1) \cdot 2(1) \\
2 &= 4
\end{aligned}
$$

8. Let T be the number of tricycles and B the number of bicycles. From the given information, $T + B = 17$ and $3T + 2B = 40$. You can use these equations to find that there are 6 tricycles and 11 bicycles.

$$
\begin{aligned}
3T + 2(17 - T) &= 40 \\
3T + 34 - 2T &= 40 \\
T &= 6
\end{aligned}
$$

9. This time, let t be the number of two-seat bicycles and B the number of one-seat bicycles, and from the given information, we have $2t + B = 27$ and $2t + 2B = 40$. From these equations, we can find that there are 7 two-seat bicycles and 13 one-seat bicycles.

$$
\begin{aligned}
2t + 2(27 - 2t) &= 40 \\
2t + 54 - 4t &= 40 \\
-2t &= -14 \\
t &= 7
\end{aligned}
$$

10. Let g be the number of general admission tickets, c be the number of senior tickets, and s be the number of student tickets. Then $g + c + s = 20$ and $6g + 5c + 4s = 100$. Solve the first equation for g and substitute into the second: $g = 20 - c - s$, so

$$
\begin{aligned}
6(20 - c - s) + 5c + 4s &= 100 \\
120 - c - 2s &= 100 \\
20 = c + 2s
\end{aligned}
$$

There are 11 possible solutions to this problem, as illustrated in the following table.

general	senior	student
0	20	0
1	18	1
2	16	2
3	14	3
4	12	4
5	10	5
6	8	6
7	6	7
8	4	8
9	2	9
10	0	10

11. (a) Yes, the customer can use sixteen 3-cent stamps and one 7-cent stamp.
    (b) The customer cannot get exactly 5 cents postage from the stamps available.
    (c) From 1 through 12, you can make the following postages: 3, 6, 7, 9, 10, 12. Any value greater than 12 can be made.

12. (a) All values except $1, $2, $4, $5, and $11 can be made with only 3- and 7-dollar bills.
    (b) All of the values that could not be made exactly can be made giving change. This is analogous to the Measuring Cups Problem, in which water could be removed (subtracted) as well as added.

13. (a) If the available stamps are a and b cents, then the possible postages are those which are of the form $ax + by$, where x and y are counting numbers.
    (b) If you can get every value greater than some value n, you know that a and b have greatest common divisor 1. (That is, they're relatively prime.)

    The challenge question here is asking for the greatest value that can't be created using the two types of stamps. To see this, start with an example where $a > b$, such as $a = 5$ and $b = 3$. Make a chart of consecutive numbers, using a columns:

$$1 \quad 2 \quad 3 \quad 4 \quad 5$$
$$6 \quad 7 \quad 8 \quad 9 \quad 10$$
$$11 \quad 12 \quad 13 \quad 14 \quad 15$$
$$16 \quad 17 \quad 18 \quad 19 \quad 20$$

Now, start with only a-cent stamps. Circle every amount that can be created using those stamps. (In this case, multiples of 5.) They are all the last number in each row. Next, use one b-cent stamp, and circle that amount (3). If you add only a-cent stamps, you will get 8, 13, 18, ... —every number in the third column. So go to two b-cent stamps and circle that amount (6). Again, adding a-cent stamps will give every number in that column *under* that first number. Continue this, until you've circled all the numbers possible.

The last number you circle will be $b(a-1)$, because ab (and every number after it) was already circled. (Because a and b are relatively prime, $b(a-1)$ will remain uncircled until you use $a-1$ of the b-cent stamps. If a multiple rb was in the same column as multiple sb, then $rb = sb + ta$ for some counting number t. But then b would divide ta, which is impossible if $t < b$.) However, you can also get several others before it.

When you circled multiples of b, and in doing so obtained the rest of the column, each multiple landed in a different column. The last value circled is $b(a-1)$, so *all other columns* must already have had a number circled. The last uncircled number, then, must be directly above $b(a-1)$, which is $b(a-1) - a$ or $ab - a - b$.

Notice that the choice of a and b didn't matter. You could have chosen $b > a$ and gotten $a(b-1) - b$, which is equivalent to $ab - a - b$.

(c) You can only create every price possible if a and b have greatest common divisor 1. As noted before, this is analogous to the Measuring Cups Problem.

Pythagoras and Cousins

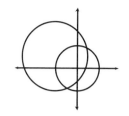

1. The figure in the margin shows two circles. One has a radius of 3 and a center of $(-2, 1)$, while the other has a radius of 2 and is centered at $(0, 0)$. Find the points of intersection of the two circles.

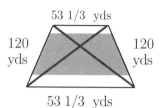

2. Carlos is working on the Homecoming planning committee for Xavier High School and he's going to make a giant **X** out of ribbon, stretching along the diagonals of the football field. The football field is 120 yards long (including the "end zones") and $53\frac{1}{3}$ yards wide. How much ribbon does he need to buy?

3. When you see an advertisement for a 30-inch television set, the 30 inches refers to the length of the diagonal of the TV screen.
   (a) If most television screens are about 1.8 times as wide as they are high, what are the dimensions of a 30-inch set?
   (b) How much larger (in terms of area) is a 30-inch set than a 20-inch set?

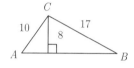

4. Triangle ABC in the margin is *not* a right triangle. Find its area.

5. (a) Make a copy of the square shown below, then partition and cut it out as shown.

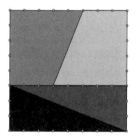 

   (b) Physically rearrange the pieces of your puzzle as shown in the figure below.

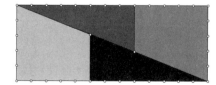

   (c) What are the dimensions and area of the new figure?   *Are you sure?*
   (d) Explain what went wrong. After all, the area of an 8×8 square is *not* 65 square units.

The numbers 5, 8, and 13 are part of an intriguing sequence of numbers—that you may have seen before—called the Fibonacci numbers:
$1, 1, 2, 3, 5, 8, 13, 21, 34, \ldots$
Have you seen them before?

6. *Just for fun:* The dimensions of the figures in the previous paradox were not chosen "out of the blue." You'll now learn to create similar paradoxes (or is it paradoxen?) with other choices for the dimensions.

   (a) Show that a 5×5 square seems to have the same area as a 3×8 rectangle!

   (b) Show that a 13×13 square seems to have the same area as an 8×21 rectangle!

   (c) *Make a conjecture:* Can you find three other numbers with this property? (Other than 5,8,13 or 2,3,5 or 8,13,21, that is).

7. A 3-4-5 right triangle is shown below, with a circle that is "inscribed" inside it (the circle is tangent to the three sides of the triangle). Call the circle's radius r.

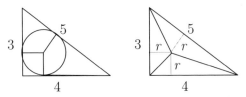

   (a) What is the area of the triangle?

   (b) Compute the areas of the 3 smaller triangles in the figure on the right in terms of r (each of them has an altitude which is the circle's radius).

   (c) Set the two area calculations equal to one another in order to compute r, the radius of the circle.

8. In each of the problems below, a circle has been inscribed in a right triangle. Compute the radius of each of the circles.

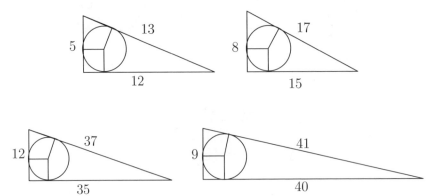

9. ***Make a guess:*** Did you notice something each of the radii had in common? Use the solutions to the previous problems to help you make a guess about what kind of number the radius of the inscribed circle of *any* Pythagorean triangle will be. Be sure your guess agrees with the results of problem 8.

A Pythagorean triangle is right triangle with integer side-lengths.

10. ***Challenge:*** Prove that your guess from problem 9 is correct.

Solutions

1. The equations and graphs of the circles are given below:

$$(x + 2)^2 + (y - 1)^2 = 9$$
$$x^2 + y^2 = 4$$

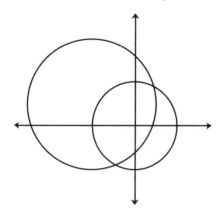

Suppose (x, y) is an intersection point of the two circles. Then x and y satisfy both equations. The first equation expands to $x^2 + 4x + 4 + y^2 - 2y + 1 = 9$, which simplifies to $x^2 + y^2 + 4x - 2y = 4$. Substituting 4 for $x^2 + y^2$ in the first equation (since the second equation is satisfied by x and y, too) and simplifying, we get $4x - 2y = 0$, so $y = 2x$. So, what does that tell us? Any point of intersection of the two circles must be on the line $y = 2x$. Now, substitute $y = 2x$ in the equation $x^2 + y^2 = 4$ to see that $5x^2 = 4$, so $x = \pm\frac{2}{\sqrt{5}}$ and $y = \pm\frac{4}{\sqrt{5}}$. Since we began this solution with an *assumption* (*if* (x, y) is a point of intersection ...), we must check to see if any of our "solutions" are extraneous. Evaluating the two equations of the circle at the points $(\frac{2}{\sqrt{5}}, \frac{4}{\sqrt{5}})$ and $(-\frac{2}{\sqrt{5}}, -\frac{4}{\sqrt{5}})$, we see that both equations are satisfied, so the circles intersect at $(\frac{2}{\sqrt{5}}, \frac{4}{\sqrt{5}})$ and $(-\frac{2}{\sqrt{5}}, -\frac{4}{\sqrt{5}})$.

2. Carlos needs two times the length of the diagonal of the football in ribbon. So the amount of ribbon needed is $2\sqrt{120^2 + (53\frac{1}{3})^2} \approx 262.64$ yards.

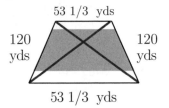

53 1/3 yds

120 yds   120 yds

53 1/3 yds

3. (a) If the 30-inch set has height x, then its width is $1.8x$ so the Pythagorean Theorem gives

$$\begin{aligned} x^2 + (1.8x)^2 &= 30^2 \\ 4.24x^2 &= 900 \\ x &\approx 14.57 \text{ inches} \end{aligned}$$

(b) If the 20-inch set has height x and width $1.8x$,

$$\begin{aligned} x^2 + (1.8x)^2 &= 20^2 \\ 4.24x^2 &= 400 \\ x &\approx 9.71 \text{ inches} \end{aligned}$$

The dimensions of the 20-inch television are approximately 9.71 inches by 17.48 inches.

Since the areas of the 30-inch and 20-inch sets are about $14.57 \times 26.22 \approx 382.03$ and $9.71 \times 17.48 \approx 169.73$ square inches, respectively, the difference in their areas is about 212.3 square inches. Is it surprising that the area of the 30-inch TV is over twice the area of a 20-inch TV even though the ratio of the diagonals is only 1.5:1?

4. To find the area of $\triangle ABC$, we need to find the length of $\overline{AB}$. Let D be the foot of the altitude drawn from C to $\overline{AB}$. Then $AD = \sqrt{10^2 - 8^2} = 6$ and $DB = \sqrt{17^2 - 8^2} = 15$, so $AB = AD + DB = 6 + 15 = 21$. Then the area of $\triangle ABC$ is $\frac{1}{2}(8)(21) = 84$ units^2.

5. (a) It appears that the new figure is a 13×5 rectangle, so its area is 65 square units.

(b) Since the area of the original square is 64 square units, the figure we created cannot be a rectangle. In fact, if you look carefully, you'll see that there's some overlap between the pieces which is not due to cutting errors.

6. (a) Following the same method as with the previous problem, we have the following figures: The "holes" are a little easier to see in this case, but you can almost believe that you get a 3×8 rectangle with this dissection.

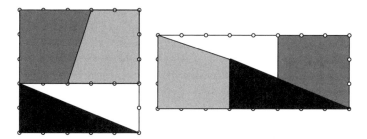

(b) This one looks even closer than the original one, but the rectangle is 1 square unit smaller than the square. It's harder to see the discrepancy, since it's still off by 1 square unit, but in this case, that is a smaller percentage of the whole area ($\frac{1}{169}$ is much smaller than $\frac{1}{8}$).

Note that the figure is scaled to fit the page.

(c) One possible collection of answers comes in the form of consecutive Fibonacci numbers. This is due to the fact that if F_{n-1}, F_n, and F_{n+1} are consecutive Fibonacci numbers, then $F_n^2 = F_{n-1} \cdot F_{n+1} \pm 1$. More precisely, if you define the sequence by $F_1 = F_2 = 1$ and $F_n = F_{n-2} + F_{n-1}$ when $n > 1$, then

$$F_n^2 = F_{n-1} \cdot F_{n+1} + (-1)^{n+1}.$$

7. (a) The area of the triangle is $\frac{1}{2}(3)(4) = 6$.
   (b) Each small triangle has height r, so their areas are $\frac{1}{2}(3r)$, $\frac{1}{2}(4r) = 2r$, and $\frac{1}{2}(5r)$.
   (c) Since the sum of the areas of the smaller triangles is 6, we have
$$6 = \frac{1}{2}(3r) + 2r + \frac{1}{2}(5r) = 6r,$$
   so $r = 1$.

8. Using the method used in the previous problem,
   - $\frac{1}{2}(5)(12) = \frac{1}{2}(5r) + \frac{1}{2}(12r) + \frac{1}{2}(13r)$, so $30 = 15r$, which implies $r = 2$ for the 5-12-13 triangle.
   - $\frac{1}{2}(8)(15) = \frac{1}{2}(8r) + \frac{1}{2}(15r) + \frac{1}{2}(17r)$, so $60 = 20r$, which implies $r = 3$ for the 8-15-17 triangle.
   - $\frac{1}{2}(12)(35) = \frac{1}{2}(12r) + \frac{1}{2}(35r) + \frac{1}{2}(37r)$, so $210 = 42r$, which implies $r = 5$ for the 12-35-37 triangle.
   - $\frac{1}{2}(9)(40) = \frac{1}{2}(9r) + \frac{1}{2}(40r) + \frac{1}{2}(41r)$, so $180 = 45r$, which implies $r = 4$ for the 9-40-41 triangle.

9. It seems that the radius of the incircle of a Pythagorean triangle is always an integer.

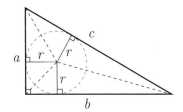

10. Notice that if a, b, and c are the legs and hypotenuse, respectively, of a Pythagorean triangle, then $\frac{1}{2}ar + \frac{1}{2}br + \frac{1}{2}cr = \frac{1}{2}ab$ (as in the problem 8 examples), and therefore $r = \frac{ab}{a+b+c}$, so in order to show that r is a counting number, we could show that $a + b + c$ is a divisor of ab. An alternative proof involves another interesting representation for r (namely, $r = \frac{a+b-c}{2}$), which is derived through another dissection of the Pythagorean triangle (as illustrated below).

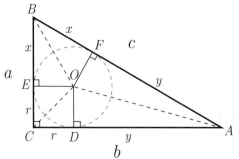

Triangles BEO and BFO are congruent by the Hypotenuse-Leg Theorem, and therefore $BE = BF$, since corresponding parts of congruent triangles are congruent. Similarly, triangles ADO and AFO are congruent, implying $AD = AF$. Letting $BE = x = BF$ and $AD = y = AF$, we see that $a = r + x$, $b = r + y$ and $c = x + y$, so $a + b - 2r = c$, and therefore $r = \frac{a+b-c}{2}$. Now every possibility for the parity (even or odd) of a and b makes $a + b - c$ and even number, as the table below illustrates (recalling that $a^2 + b^2 = c^2$):

a	b	c	$a + b - c$
even	even	even	even
even	odd	odd	even
odd	even	odd	even
odd	odd	even	even

Therefore, r must be a counting number. (An interesting consequence is that $a + b + c$ is a divisor of ab!)

In fact, a and b can't both be odd. If this were the case, c would have to be even. But $(2n+1)^2 + (2m+1)^2$ equals $4n^2 + 4n + 1 + 4m^2 + 4m + 1$, which is 2 more than a multiple of 4, and the square of an even number must be a multiple of 4. Therefore, the two legs of a Pythagorean triangle can't both be odd.

Pascal's Revenge: Combinatorial Algebra

1. If everyone in a group of 4 people shook hands with everyone else in the group, how many handshakes took place, in all? What if there were 10 people? 100 people? Can you come up with a formula that will compute the number of handshakes that will take place among p people, where p can be any positive integer?

2. How can you use the result (and solution method) of the previous problem to derive a closed-form solution (a more concise formula) for $1 + 2 + \cdots + n$, the sum of the first n natural numbers?

3. Shanna has entered the 37th Annual Race to the Statue at City Park, which starts at the park gazebo and ends— you guessed it!—at the statue. There is no specific course for the race; the only rule is that everyone must stay on the sidewalks (no cutting across on the grass), which are laid out in a rectangular grid as shown in the figure below. There are many possible paths from the gazebo to the statue, and Shanna wants to try out each of them before the race to see on which one she runs fastest. She's already decided that she should only run north and east in order to run as short a distance as possible.

Have your students work on this problem in groups and present their findings. You might prefer to have them explain why Shanna should only run north and east to get to the statue and skateboard park (to avoid backtracking, thus minimizing the running distance). Don't dissuade students from trying to "map out" each path in the first part of the problem. Any approach which engages them and allows them to make progress is a good one. They'll soon realize that another strategy is called for in the second part. Depending on the grade level, you might want to create analogous "coordinate" problems and/or ask students to generalize their results.

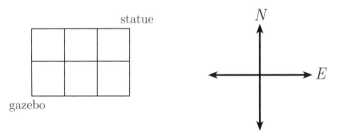

(a) If Shanna tries one path per day, how many days before the race must she begin training?

(b) If the race was to the skateboard park (as seen below), instead, how many different paths are possible?

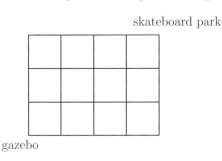

4. There are 10 kids who want to play basketball. In how many ways can they split up into two teams of 5?

5. One form of the lottery is played by selecting 5 integers (in any order) from the set $\{1, 2, 3, \ldots, 50\}$. Cecil P. Moneybags has decided that he wants to win the lottery, so he's going to buy *every* possible number since that's the only way to guarantee that he wins.

   (a) In order for Mr. Moneybags to make any money on this deal, how much does the lottery jackpot need to be?

   (b) What if one other person is lucky enough to also pick the winning numbers? In this case, Mr. Moneybags needs to split the money with the other person.

   (c) What if 5 other people pick the winning numbers?

   (d) How long will it take him to fill out all of those tickets?

6. Sophie and Nikolas have decided to play tic-tac-toe, even though Sophie *always* wins in 3 turns. If Sophie always goes first (since she's the youngest) and plays with **X**, and they play until they repeat a final **X-O** combination, what is the minimum number of games they must play? The figure below shows 3 possible final **X-O** combinations (don't forget that Sophie *always* wins on her third move).

In each of the following problems, *first* make a guess, *then* check to see whether your guess is correct.

7. When 2 dice are rolled, what are the possible sums? In how many ways can a sum of 8 occur? In how many ways can a sum of 5 occur? Which sum is most likely?

8. When 2 dice are rolled, is an *even* or *odd* sum more likely (or are both equally likely)?

9. When 2 dice are rolled, is a *prime* or *composite* (nonprime) sum more likely (or are both equally likely)?

10. When 2 dice are rolled, which is more likely: a sum which is a multiple of 3, a sum which is 1 more than a multiple of 3, or a sum which is 2 more than a multiple of 3?

11. When 3 dice are rolled, what are the possible sums? In how many ways can a sum of 10 occur? In how many ways can a sum of 15 occur? Which sum is most likely?

12. When 3 dice are rolled, is an *even* or *odd* sum more likely (or are both equally likely)?

13. When 3 dice are rolled, is a *prime* or *composite* (nonprime) sum more likely (or are both equally likely)?

14. When 3 dice are rolled, which is more likely: a sum which is a multiple of 3, a sum which is 1 more than a multiple of 3, or a sum which is 2 more than a multiple of 3?

15. When 3 dice are rolled, which is more likely: a sum which is a multiple of 4, a sum which is 1 more than a multiple of 4, a sum which is 2 more than a multiple of 4, or a sum which is 3 more than a multiple of 4?

16. What do you think happens when 4 dice are rolled? 5 dice? *Any* number of dice?

Solutions

1. As in the other problems of this session, this problem can be solved in a variety of ways. Again, it depends on how you organize your work. You might even try getting variously sized groups of students to act out the handshakes.

   - Suppose the names of the 4 people are Anne, Betty, Chiang, and David, and imagine they're all standing in a line, in alphabetical order. Anne gets out of line, shakes the hand of everyone else, then stands on the other side of the room, since she's shaken everyone else's hand. This leaves Betty, Chiang, and David in line. So far, 3 handshakes have occurred. Betty (now at the front since Anne is out of line) gets out of line and shakes the hand of everyone else in line. After shaking hands with Chiang and David, Betty joins Anne at the other side of the room, leaving Chiang and David in line. When Chiang turns to shake David's hand and joins Anne and Betty on the other side of the room, David has already shaken everyone's hand, so we're done. Now, counting the number of handshakes that occurred in each round, we see that there were $3 + 2 + 1$, or 6, handshakes in all.

   Now, how would this play out in a group of 10 people (call them Anne, Betty, Chiang, David, Esteban, Fatima, Greg, Hannah, Irving, and Jada, if you like)? In the first round, if Anne goes first, she'll shake 9 hands. When Anne leaves, Betty will shake 8 more hands. Note that Betty doesn't shake only 8 hands, since her handshake with Anne was counted already in round 1. Thus, in round 2, there are 8 *additional* handshakes; in round 3, there are 7 *additional* handshakes; and so on. Hence, there are $9 + 8 + \cdots + 1$, or 45, handshakes in a group of 10 people.

   - In a group of 4 people, *everyone* shakes hands with exactly 3 others, so it's easy to mistakenly conclude that there are a total of 4×3, or 12 handshakes (after all, there are 4 people each having 3 handshakes). So, why is this incorrect? The answer should *not* be, "We saw before that the answer is 6, so 12 can't be right!" since we could apply that reasoning to the first solution, too (now that the answer is 12, 6 must be wrong). We see we must divide by 2, but why? How did we double count? Each handshake got counted twice because it was made by *both* participants. Alternatively, 4 people,

Teacher note: In your class, be sure that there is enough time for your students to justify this "sum rule" to solve the handshake problem. Why does the sum "start" with 1 less than the number of people in the group? What does each addend represent? Why do we stop at 1? Which handshake is that counting?

each shook 3 hands for a total of 12 hands being shaken. But, since each handshake requires 2 hands, there were actually $12 \div 2$, or 6 handshakes, in all.

So, in a group of 100 people, each shakes 99 hands, for a total of $99 \times 100 = 9900$ hands being shaken in all. But this counts each handshake twice, so there are a total of $\frac{9900}{2}$ or 4950 handshakes.

Thus, in the general case, if there are p people, all of whom shake hands with everyone else, there are two ways of expressing the number of handshakes that occur.

- Using the first method, the first person is involved in $p - 1$ handshakes, the second person is involved in $p - 2$ *additional* handshakes, and so on. Therefore, the total number of handshakes that occur is $1 + 2 + \cdots + p - 1$.

- Using the second method, each of the p people are involved in exactly $p - 1$ handshakes, since they shake everyone else's hand. This gives us a total of $p(p - 1)$ hands being shaken (each of the p people shakes hands $p-1$ times). But then every handshake has been counted twice, since every handshake requires 2 people, so there are actually a total of $\frac{p(p-1)}{2}$ handshakes in all.

These methods arrive at the answer from two very different points of view, which has a very interesting consequence. Namely, the solution to the following problem.

2. When solving the previous problem using the first method, many students remark that $1 + 2 + \cdots + n$ is not really a "formula" because formulas must be "short" (like $\frac{n(n+1)}{2}$). This is a nice opportunity to discuss closed-form solutions, since both of these representations are formulas (or algorithms, if you prefer) for the answer. More interestingly, though, they give rise to a solution strategy for the problem at hand, since $1 + 2 + \cdots n$ is the answer to the "handshake problem" for a group of $n + 1$ people, and we have *another* way to calculate it—namely $\frac{(n+1) \times n}{2}$.

Teacher note: You might also want to discuss the solution of this problem attributed to the mathematician Carl Friedrich Gauss as a boy. The possibly apocryphal story goes that Gauss's teacher was fed up with his class and gave the students a long arithmetic problem to solve – namely, find the sum of the first 100 natural numbers. Gauss reportedly gave the correct answer (5050) in a matter of seconds. When his teacher asked him how he got the answer so quickly, he replied that he noticed $1 + 100 = 2 + 99 =$

$3 + 98 = \cdots = 101$, and since there were 50 such sums, the answer must be 50×101, or 5050. Of course, it is necessary to think more deeply about this method when the 100 is replaced with an odd number, but you get the gist of the method.

3. (a) Students can trace out all 10 paths here, but it might provide a "hook" to lead them to the methods of section 2. (5 "steps" need to be taken—3 to the east and 2 to the north, for a total of $\binom{5}{2}$ (or $\binom{5}{3}$) paths.) No matter how it's solved, Shanna has 10 paths to try, so she must start training at least 10 days before the race.

   (b) This time, Shanna must try all paths involving going 4 blocks east and 3 blocks north. There are $\binom{7}{3} = 35$ such paths.

4. How many ways are there to choose "team A"? There is a set of 10 people, and you need to create a subset (team) of 5. Note that once team A is chosen, the rest of the kids are in team B! There are

$$_{10}C_5 = \frac{10!}{5!5!} = \frac{(10)(9)(8)(7)(6)}{(5)(4)(3)(2)} = (3)(2)(7)(6) = 252$$

ways to choose 5 kids out of a group of 10. But, if you think about it, this answer is too big. Suppose the 10 kids are Andrew, Blaire, Candace, Deshondra, Elvin, Farouk, Giselle, Horace, Isolde, and Jamaal, then team A consisting of Andrew, Blaire, Candace, Deshondra, and Elvin (and then team B being represented by Farouk, Giselle, Horace, Isolde, and Jamaal) produces the same *teams* as team A consisting of Farouk, Giselle, Horace, Isolde, and Jamaal (and team B being represented by Andrew, Blaire, Candace, Deshondra, and Elvin). That is, *every* team division gets counted twice, so the actual number of possibilities is $252/2 = 176$.

5. (a) Mr. Moneybags just needs to know the total number of lottery tickets possible. Since there are 50 numbers to choose from and 5 need to be chosen, there are

$$_{50}C_5 = \frac{50!}{5!45!} = \frac{(50)(49)(48)(47)(46)}{(5)(4)(3)(2)}$$
$$= (5)(49)(4)(47)(46) = 2118760,$$

so Mr. Moneybags must buy 2118760 tickets, which will cost him over 2 *million* dollars ($2,118,760, to be exact)! Therefore, for Mr. Moneybags to not *lose* any money in this transaction, the *Lottery* winnings must be at least $2,118,760.

(b) If two winners must share the winnings, each getting $2,118,760, then the total prize must be $2118760 \times 2 = \$4,237,520$.

(c) If there are 5 winners splitting the winnings, in order for Mr. Moneybags to break even, the prize must be $2118760 \times 5 = \$10,593,800$.

(d) The time it takes Mr. Moneybags to fill out all 2118760 tickets depends on several parameters. Let's say that it takes him an average of 10 seconds to fill out each ticket (or, if you prefer, it takes his chauffeur that long!), which doesn't even take into account how long it would take to generate the list of all of the possibilities. Then it will take him $2118760 \times 10 = 21187600$ seconds, which is $21187600/60 = 353126\frac{2}{3}$ minutes (or $\frac{21187600}{(60)(60)} = 5885\frac{4}{9}$ hours or $\frac{21187600}{(60)(60)(24)} = 245\frac{49}{216}$ days!). Thus, at a rate of 6 tickets per minute, it would take about 8 months to fill enough tickets out – not too realistic, since most lottery drawings are held once or twice a week. Even if he was able to fill out one ticket per second, it would take him 1/10 as long, or about $24\frac{1}{2}$ days! Poor Mr. Moneybags!

6. This seems to be a harder problem than the previous two, until we realize that we can make it much easier by solving a "smaller" problem first. For instance, how many final combinations are there for which Sophie's **X**s all lie on the top row? That's just the number of ways to place Nikolas's two **O**s on the remaining 6 places, which is

$$_6C_2 = \frac{6!}{2!4!} = \frac{6(5)}{2} = 15.$$

Using the same logic, there also 15 final combinations corresponding to Sophie winning with any 3-in-a-row tic-tac-toe. So how many tic-tac-toes are there? There are 3 going across, 3 going down, and 2 diagonals, for a total of 8 winning possibilities. Since each of these occurs in 15 final combinations, there are $15 \times 8 = 120$ final combinations, in all.

7. The possibilities for 2 dice rolls, along with their sums and the frequencies of these sums, are given below. This table was created by listing all of the ordered pairs (with entries chosen from 1–6).

SUM	ROLLS	FREQ
2	(1,1)	1
3	(1,2) (2,1)	2
4	(1,3) (2,2) (3,1)	3
5	(1,4) (2,3) (3,2) (4,1)	4
6	(1,5) (2,4) (3,3) (4,2) (5,1)	5
7	(1,6) (2,5) (3,4) (4,3) (5,2) (6,1)	6
8	(2,6) (3,5) (4,4) (5,3) (6,2)	5
9	(3,6) (4,5) (5,4) (6,3)	4
10	(4,6) (5,5) (6,4)	3
11	(5,6) (6,5)	2
12	(6,6)	1

We may therefore read off the fact that the possible sums are 2–12 (which we could have determined without the table by considering the fact that the smallest number on each die is 1, so the minimum sum of 2 dice is 2, and the largest number on each die is 6, so the maximum sum for 2 dice is 12). See the argument for intermediate sums in the solution to a similar *Activities and Explorations* problem in section 5 of Chapter V. The table also helps us see that there are 5 ways to roll a sum of 8 and 4 ways to roll a sum of 5 (but that could have been determined by considering which pairs have sums of 8 and 5 independent of the table). The table really is necessary, though, to determine that 7 is the most likely sum, occurring in a total of 6 ways.

8. Using the table, we see there are $1 + 3 + 5 + 5 + 3 + 1 = 18$ ways to roll even sums (add up the frequencies of the even sums) and $2 + 4 + 6 + 4 + 2 = 18$ ways to roll an odd sum, so even and odd sums are equally likely. This might be surprising, since 7 is the most likely sum, so one might conjecture that odd sums are more likely.

9. The prime sums are 2, 3, 5, 7, and 11, which occur in 1, 2, 4, 6, and 2 ways, respectively. Thus, a prime sum can occur in $1 + 2 + 4 + 6 + 2 = 15$ different ways, and a composite sum will occur $36 - 15 = 21$ different ways. Thus, a composite sum is more likely. Since 5 of the 11 sums are prime, you might have guessed this.

10. Sums 3, 6, 9, and 12 (the sums that are divisible by 3) occur in $2 + 5 + 4 + 1 = 12$ different ways; sums 4, 7, and 10 (having remainder 1 when divided by 3) occur in $3 + 6 + 3 = 12$ different ways; and sums 2, 5, 8, and 11 occur in

$1 + 4 + 5 + 2 = 12$ different ways; so these types of sums are equally likely. This might be surprising, since 3 of the 11 sums have remainder 1 when divided by 3 (4 each for the other remainders).

11. Using reasoning as above, we see that the possible sums are 3–18. A sum of 10 can occur in 27 different ways, since in order to get a sum of 10 with 3 dice, the sum of the first 2 dice would need to be 4, 5, 6, 7, 8, or 9 (with corresponding third roll 6, 5, 4, 3, 2, or 1, respectively). Using the table from problem 7 above, we see that these sums occur in 3, 4, 5, 6, 5, and 4 ways, respectively, so there are $3 + 4 + 5 + 6 + 5 + 4 = 27$ different ways to roll a 10. If we really want to, we can list the rolls which produce sums of 10 and 15 by adapting the 2-dice distribution table, as illustrated below:

How to get a sum of 10 with 3 dice
(1,3,6) (2,2,6) (3,1,6)
(1,4,5) (2,3,5) (3,2,5) (4,1,5)
(1,5,4) (2,4,4) (3,3,4) (4,2,4) (5,1,4)
(1,6,3) (2,5,3) (3,4,3) (4,3,3) (5,2,3) (6,1,3)
(2,6,2) (3,5,2) (4,4,2) (5,3,2) (6,2,2)
(3,6,1) (4,5,1) (5,4,1) (6,3,1)

Similarly, in order to get a 3-dice sum of 15, the first 2 dice must add to 9, 10, 11, or 12, so there are $4 + 3 + 2 + 1 = 10$ ways to get a sum of 15 with three dice:

How to get a sum of 15 with 3 dice
(3,6,6) (4,5,6) (5,4,6) (6,3,6)
(4,6,5) (5,5,5) (6,4,5) (5,6,4) (6,5,4)
(6,6,3)

Using the methods above, we can create the distribution table for 3-dice rolls:

sum	3	4	5	6	7	8	9	10	11	12	13	14	15	16	17	18
freq	1	3	6	10	15	21	25	27	27	25	21	15	10	6	3	1

Thus, we conclude that the most likely 3-dice sums are 10 and 11 (the "middle" possibilities).

12. There are $1 + 6 + 15 + 25 + 27 + 21 + 10 + 3 = 108$ ways to roll an even sum and $3 + 10 + 21 + 27 + 25 + 15 + 6 + 1 = 108$ ways to roll an odd sum, so even and odd sums are equally likely.

13. The possible prime sums are 3, 5, 7, 11, 13, and 17, which occur in $1 + 6 + 15 + 27 + 21 + 3 = 73$ ways, so the other 143 (that is, $216 - 73$) sums are composite, and we see that composite sums are nearly twice as likely as prime sums.

14. Sums 3, 6, 9, 12, 15, and 18 can occur in $1 + 10 + 25 + 25 + 10 + 1 = 72$ different ways; sums 4, 7, 10, 13, and 16 occur in $3 + 15 + 27 + 21 + 6 = 72$ different ways; and sums 5, 8, 11, 14, and 17 occur in $6 + 21 + 27 + 15 + 3 = 72$ different ways, too. Pretty surprising, huh?

15. Sums 4, 8, 12, and 16 can occur in $3 + 21 + 25 + 6 = 55$ different ways; sums 5, 9, 13, and 17 occur in $6 + 25 + 21 + 3 = 55$ different ways; sums 6, 10, 14, and 18 occur in $10 + 27 + 15 + 1 = 53$ different ways; and sums 3, 7, 11, and 15 occur in $1 + 15 + 27 + 10 = 53$ different ways.

16. There are many possible conjectures, most of which have probably been dealt with in either the text or *Further Exploration* materials.

VII. Answers to Selected Problems
(Chapters I-V)

See the *Further Exploration* CD for complete solutions.

I. *What is Mathematical Investigation?*

1. Problem solving and problem posing

1. Every counting number not equal to 2^n for some whole number n can be expressed as the sum of two or more consecutive counting numbers.
2. (b) Of *two or more* addends.
   (c) The addends must be *counting numbers*.
   (d) They must be *consecutive*.

2. You've got a conjecture—now what?

7. (a) The sum of $4n$ consecutive counting numbers will be even.
   (b) The sum of exactly 2 counting numbers gives all odds > 1.
   (c) Odd prime numbers are the only CNs that have a unique representation as the sum of CCNs.
   (d) Only powers of 2 can't be expressed as the sum of CCNs.
   (f) All multiples of 3 greater than 3 are the sum of 3 CCNs.
   (g) All multiples of 5 greater than or equal to 15 are expressible as the sum of 5 CCNs.
   (h) Sums of consecutive odd numbers, starting at 1, produce all squares.
   (i) Sums of consecutive odd numbers produce differences of two squares.
   (j) Sums of CCNs, starting at 1, produce triangular numbers.
   (k) Sums of CCNs produce differences of two triangular numbers.
   (l) Products of CCNs, starting at 1, produce factorials.
   (m) Products of CCNs produce quotients of two factorials.

5. Discerning what *is*, predicting what *might be*

2.

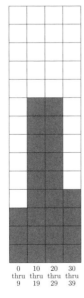

4. (1)

15	0	2	2				
14	3	4	4	4	9		
13	2	3	5	6	7	8	
12	0	5	5	5	5	5	8
11	0	2	4	5	5	5	7	9
10	1	3	4	5	8		

(2) Mean: 126.471   Median: 125   Mode: 125

5.

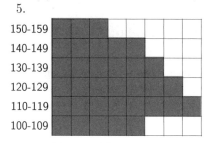

150-159
140-149
130-139
120-129
110-119
100-109

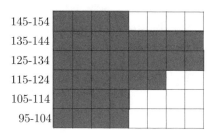

145-154
135-144
125-134
115-124
105-114
95-104

Horizontal histogram by decade   Horizontal histogram by rounding

8. Interval center was varied (width was constant).

12. The mean and median can change by at most a half pound. The range can change by at most a whole pound. The mode, however, can change by as much as 27 pounds.

19. The median will be between 82 and 86.

21. Mean will increase by 4; median will be unchanged.

II. *Dissections and Area*

1. Be a mathematical cut-up

1. 8 square units

2. Making assumptions, checking procedures

1. (a) Here are some pictures teachers could use:

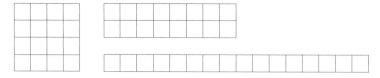

(b) Circles, equilateral triangles, for example

3. The "rectangle" doesn't really fit together (there are gaps).

5. $A = \frac{1}{2}(b_1 + b_2)h$ (b_1 and b_2 are bases, h is height)

6. A triangle is a trapezoid having a base of length 0. A parallelogram is a trapezoid with equal bases.

7. $A = \frac{1}{2}(b + 0)h = \frac{1}{2}bh$

8. $A = \frac{1}{2}(b + b)h = bh$

3. Thinking about area

1. (a) $7\frac{1}{2}$ (b) $4\frac{1}{2}$ (c) $9\frac{1}{2}$ (d) 15   (e) $11\frac{1}{2}$ (f) 25

2. Area$(B) =$ Area$(A \cup B) -$ Area$(A) +$ Area$(A \cap B)$

4. $A = ($maximum $x -$ minimum $x)($maximum $y -$ minimum $y)$

5. $A = (\max x - \min x)(\max y - \min y) - \frac{1}{2}|x_1 - x_2||y_1 - y_2| - \frac{1}{2}|x_1 - x_3||y_1 - y_3| - \frac{1}{2}|x_2 - x_3||y_2 - y_3|$

8. The polygon must be convex.

11. (a) The area measured in hexagonal units should be $\frac{3\sqrt{3}}{2}$ times the area measured in square units.

12. (a) The area measured in triangular units should be $\frac{1}{6}$ the area measured in hexagonal units (or $\frac{\sqrt{3}}{4}$ times the area measured in square units).

13. The triangular units should give the most accuracy.

4. Areas of non-polygonal areas

2. The areas are equal.

6. The parallelogram always has smaller area than the circle.

7. Inscribed octagon has area $8r^2 \sin(\frac{\pi}{8})\cos(\frac{\pi}{8}) \approx 2.828r^2$.

8. Circumscribed octagon has area $8r^2 \tan(\frac{\pi}{8}) \approx 3.314r^2$.

5. Transformations and area

1.

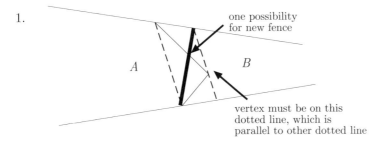

III. *Linearity and Proportional Reasoning*

1. Mix it up

1.–3. Mixture A is bluer.

4. The mixtures are equally blue.

5. Nancy and Sid will always agree but Terry will not agree with either.

7. Sid needs 30 clear beakers.

8. 600 units of dye and 400 units of water

11. A is bluest.

12. No

13. Yes

14. No

15. 60% dye, 40% water

16. The larger the BQ, the bluer the mixture

17. Nancy's mixture is now bluer.

18. No

19. $\frac{7 \cdot (BQ \text{ of } A) + 12 \cdot (BQ \text{ of } B)}{19}$

20. Adding fractions in the usual way doesn't take into account the sizes of the original mixtures.

21. Problem 19

22. How much of each mixture, one with a BQ of $\frac{3}{10}$ and the other with a BQ of $\frac{1}{2}$, must be combined to make a 100 ml mixture with a BQ of $\frac{9}{20}$?

23. If you combine 50 ml of a mixture with a BQ of $\frac{1}{3}$ and 50 ml of a mixture with a BQ of $\frac{1}{2}$, what is the BQ of the resultant mixture?

24. If you make a mixture, $\frac{5}{8}$ with a BQ of $\frac{83}{100}$ and $\frac{3}{8}$ with a BQ of $\frac{39}{50}$, what is the BQ? (Or, if you combine 5 ml of a mixture with a BQ of $\frac{83}{100}$ and 3 ml of a mixture with a BQ of $\frac{78}{100}$, what BQ results?)

25. If you combine 250 ml of a mixture with a BQ of $\frac{3}{10}$ and 70 ml of a mixture with BQ of $\frac{7}{10}$, what is the resultant BQ?

2. Filling in the gaps

3. $1, 1\frac{1}{2}, 2, 3, 4, \ldots$ and $1, \sqrt{2}, 2, 2\sqrt{2}, 4, \ldots$

4. $\frac{1}{3}$ of the way: $1\frac{1}{3}$ or $\sqrt[3]{2}$; $\frac{2}{3}$ of the way: $1\frac{2}{3}$ or $\sqrt[3]{2}$ or $\sqrt[3]{4}$

5. $1\frac{n}{m}$ and $2\frac{n}{m}$ are $\frac{n}{m}$ of the way between 1 and 2.

6. Additively, $2\frac{2}{3}$ is $\frac{1}{3}$ of the way between 2 and 4, and $3\frac{1}{3}$ is $\frac{2}{3}$ of the way between 2 and 4; multiplicatively, $2(2^{\frac{1}{3}})$ is $\frac{1}{3}$ of the way between 2 and 4, and $2(2^{\frac{2}{3}})$ is $\frac{2}{3}$ of the way between 2 and 4.

9.

n	$1\frac{1}{3}$	$2\frac{1}{3}$	$2\frac{3}{4}$
a_n, appr.	1.5	2.75	3.5

11. (a)

n	$1\frac{1}{3}$	$2\frac{1}{3}$	$2\frac{3}{4}$
a_n, appr.	1.25	2.4	3.4

12. The length of each jump is $\frac{1}{3}$ of a unit, so you are at $1\frac{1}{3}$.

17. $\frac{xA+yB}{x+y}$

19. $a_n = a_m \left(\frac{p-n}{p-m} \right) + a_p \left(\frac{n-m}{p-m} \right)$

20. The final zooms look linear.

21. The slope goes to $3x^2 + 3xh + h^2$.

22. (a) slope $= \frac{f(x+h)-f(x)}{h}$

(b) slope of the tangent line $= \lim\limits_{h \to 0} \frac{f(x+h)-f(x)}{h}$

3. Guess my rule

1. Yes

2. $F(0) = 0$, but there's not enough information to determine $F(1)$.

3.

x	$F(x)$	Reason
1	$-\frac{5}{6}$	Given
2	$-\frac{10}{6}$	$F(2) = F(1+1)$
3	$-\frac{15}{6}$	$F(3) = F(2+1)$
any positive integer n	$-\frac{5n}{6}$	$F(n) = \underbrace{F(1) + \cdots + F(1)}_{n \text{ times}}$
0	0	Problem 2
-1	$\frac{5}{6}$	$F(1) = F(2+(-1))$
-2	$\frac{10}{6}$	$F(1) = F(3+(-2))$
any integer n	$-\frac{5n}{6}$	$F(-n) = F(1) - F(n+1)$

5.

x	$F(x)$	Reason
$\frac{1}{2}$	$-\frac{5}{12}$	$F(\frac{1}{2}) = F(1+(-\frac{1}{2}))$
$\frac{1}{3}$	$-\frac{5}{18}$	$F(\frac{1}{3}) = F(1+(-\frac{2}{3}))$
$\frac{1}{n}$, n is an integer	$-\frac{5}{6n}$	$F(\frac{1}{n}) = F(1+(-\frac{n-1}{n}))$
$\frac{m}{n}$, m, and n are integers	$-\frac{5m}{6n}$	$F(\frac{m}{n}) = mF(\frac{1}{n})$; Problem 4

7. No

8. (a) yes   (b) no   (c) no   (d) yes

9. (a) yes   (b) no   (c) no

10. No

12. (a) $T(3) = -12$ (b) $a = -4$ (c) $x = -\frac{3}{4}$ (d) none

13. $P(x) = mx$ for some real number m

15. (a) $n = m + x(p - m)$ or $n = (1 - x)m + xp$

   (c) $0 \le x \le 1$

4. Functions of two variables

(a) The chart shows the cost of any combination of pencils and erasers (using between 0 and 6 of each)

(c)

number of pencils

	0	1	2	3	4	5	6
0	0	5	10	15	20	25	30
1	10	15	20	25	30	35	40
2	20	25	30	35	40	45	50
3	30	35	40	45	50	55	60
4	40	45	50	55	60	65	70
5	50	55	60	65	70	75	80
6	60	65	70	75	80	85	90

(number of erasers)

(d) Erasers cost 10 cents, and each pencil is 5 cents.

(e) For 55 cents, you can buy 1 pencil and 5 erasers, 3 pencils and 4 erasers, or 5 pencils and 3 erasers.

   For 30 cents, you could buy 3 erasers and 0 pencils, 2 pencils and 2 erasers, 4 pencils and 1 eraser, or 6 pencils and 0 erasers.

4. (a) $C(4 + 2, 2 + 5) = 100$

   (b) $C(p_1 + p_2, e_1 + e_2) = C(p_1, e_1) + C(p_2, e_2)$

   (c) $C(8, 4) = C(4, 2) + C(4, 2), C(12, 6) = C(8, 4) + C(4, 2)$, etc.

   (d) $C(ap, ae) = aC(p, e)$

5. (a) Yes

6. No

9. The correct answer to the chicken/egg question is 6 eggs.

	0	$\frac{1}{2}$	1	$1\frac{1}{2}$	2	$2\frac{1}{2}$	3
0	0	0	0	0	0	0	0
$\frac{1}{2}$	0	$\frac{1}{6}$	$\frac{1}{3}$	$\frac{1}{2}$	$\frac{2}{3}$	$\frac{5}{6}$	1
1	0	$\frac{1}{3}$	$\frac{2}{3}$	1	$1\frac{1}{3}$	$1\frac{2}{3}$	2
$1\frac{1}{2}$	0	$\frac{1}{2}$	1	$1\frac{1}{2}$	2	$2\frac{1}{2}$	3
2	0	$\frac{2}{3}$	$1\frac{1}{3}$	2	$2\frac{2}{3}$	$3\frac{1}{3}$	4
$2\frac{1}{2}$	0	$\frac{5}{6}$	$1\frac{2}{3}$	$2\frac{1}{2}$	$3\frac{1}{3}$	$4\frac{1}{6}$	5
3	0	1	2	3	4	5	6

11. (a)–(d) yes

12. $E(3, 5) = 10$

13. $E(H, D) = \frac{2}{3}DH$

5. From cups to vectors

1. Kathryn can measure 2 fluid ounces by filling the 6 fluid ounce cup and pouring from that into the 4 fluid ounce cup until it is full. Two fluid ounces will be left in the 6 fluid ounce cup. She can also measure 14 fluid ounces by filling the 6 ounce cup once and the 4 ounce cup twice. There is no way for her to measure 7 ounces.

2. The solution to $4x + 6y = 2$ is $x = -1$ and $y = 1$ and the solution to $4x + 6y = 14$ is $x = 2$ and $y = 1$.

4. Any even amount can be measured.

6. (a) GCD = 1; any amount can be measured.
   (b) GCD = 3; any amounts that are multiples of 3 can be measured.
   (c) GCD = 4; any amounts that are multiples of 4 can be measured.
   (d) GCD = 1; any amount can be measured.

9. Frank should borrow Kathryn's 4-ounce cup.

10. If GCD = 1, all amounts can be measured.

11. (a) $\frac{b}{12}(2, 12) + \frac{6a-b}{18}(3, 0) = (a, b)$
    (b) $(10, 15)$ and $(2, 3)$ do not span $\mathbb{R}^2$.
    (c) $(1, 1, 0)$ and $(1, 0, 1)$ do not span $\mathbb{R}^3$.
    (d) $\frac{2a-2c+b}{3}(1, 1, 0) + \frac{b-a+c}{3}(0, 2, 1) + \frac{2c-b+a}{3}(1, 0, 1) = (a, b, c)$
    (e) One possibility: $\frac{6a-b}{13}(3, 5) + \frac{3b-5a}{26}(2, 12) + 0(5, 17) = (a, b)$

12. The sets in parts (a), (c), and (d) are linearly independent.

14. (a) $y = -\frac{a_1}{a_2}x$, $y = -\frac{b_1}{b_2}x$
    (b) The two equations are guaranteed to cross at the origin. You cannot make a decision on independence based on that intersection.
    (c) If they cross again, they are the same line.

15. The sets in parts (a) and (d) are each a basis for the stated space.

16. The triples in part (c), $(1, 1, 0)$ and $(1, 0, 1)$, are linearly independent but do not span $\mathbb{R}^3$. They are a basis for the set of triples (x, y, z) in $\mathbb{R}^3$ such that $z = x - y$.

IV. *Pythagoras and Cousins*

1. What would Pythagoras do?

1. $\left(\frac{3}{5}, \frac{4}{5}\right)$, $\left(\frac{4}{5}, \frac{3}{5}\right)$, $\left(\frac{5}{13}, \frac{12}{13}\right)$, $\left(\frac{12}{13}, \frac{5}{13}\right)$, $\left(\frac{7}{25}, \frac{24}{25}\right)$, $\left(\frac{24}{25}, \frac{7}{25}\right)$, $\left(\frac{8}{17}, \frac{15}{17}\right)$, $\left(\frac{15}{17}, \frac{8}{17}\right)$, among others.

2. All (x, y) such that $(x + 1)^2 + (y - 3)^2 = 25$

3. 3-by-4 or 4-by-3 (measured in miles)

4. Obtuse

5. 60 units

6. They are equal.

7. $\cos \theta = \pm \frac{12}{13}$

9. $\sqrt{(a - c)^2 + (b - d)^2}$

10. $(x - a)^2 + (y - b)^2 = r^2$

12. $x^2 + y^2 = 1$

2. Puzzling out some proofs

9. The sum of the areas of the smaller triangles is equal to the area of the larger triangle.

10. The sum of the areas of the smaller rectangles will never equal the area of the larger rectangle.

11. The sum of the areas of the smaller rectangles will equal the area of the larger rectangle in this case.

3. Pythagoras' *second* cousins

1.

$\angle ACB$	$(a^2 + b^2) - c^2$
acute	positive
right	zero
obtuse	negative

2. As $\angle ACB$ goes from 0 to 180° $(a^2 + b^2) - c^2$ must decrease.

3.

$\angle ACB$	$\cos(\angle ACB)$	a	b	c	$(a^2 + b^2) - c^2$
60°	1/2	3	3	3	9
60°	1/2	3	8	7	24
60°	1/2	5	8	7	40
60°	1/2	7	15	13	105
60°	1/2	3	5	$\sqrt{19}$	15
60°	1/2	4	7	$\sqrt{37}$	28
30°	$\sqrt{3}/2$	3	5	$\sqrt{34 - 15\sqrt{3}}$	$15\sqrt{3}$
30°	$\sqrt{3}/2$	4	7	$\sqrt{65 - 28\sqrt{3}}$	$28\sqrt{3}$
45°	$\sqrt{2}/2$	3	5	$\sqrt{34 - 15\sqrt{2}}$	$15\sqrt{2}$
45°	$\sqrt{2}/2$	4	7	$\sqrt{65 - 28\sqrt{2}}$	$28\sqrt{2}$

4. $(a^2 + b^2) - c^2 = 2ab\cos(\angle ACB)$

5. The sum of the squares of the diagonals of a rectangle equals the sum of the squares of the four sides.

6. The sum of the squares of the diagonals of a rectangle equals the sum of the squares of the four sides.

7. 17 inches

8. $d = \sqrt{a^2 + b^2 + c^2}$

9. 3 units

10. $(x - 1)^2 + (y + 1)^2 + (z - 2)^2 = 16$

11. The sum of the squares of the edges equals the average of the squares of the diagonals in a parallelepiped.

4. Pythagorean triples (and cousins)

2. Pythagorean triples must have either 1 or 3 even entries. The hypotenuse can never be the only even length.

3. 54 and 58

5. If k is a positive integer, $(2k + 1, (2k + 2)k, (2k + 2)k + 1)$ is a PT.

7. If k is a positive integer, $(4k, 4k^2 - 1, 4k^2 + 1)$ is a PT.

8. One possible solution:

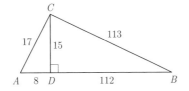

Then the rewritten version of problem 3 is:

Determine the perimeter of $\triangle ABC$, given that $AC = 17$, $CD = 15$, and $BD = 112$.

11.

a	12	35	5	16	9
b	16	12	12	12	12
c	20	37	13	20	15

13. If (a, b, c) is a primitive Pythagorean triple (with b even), then $c - b$ is a square.

14. No

5. Classroom cousins

1. The counting numbers that can be expressed as the difference of the squares of two counting numbers are the odd numbers greater than 1 and the multiples of 4 greater than 4.

2. 60

3. 32

4. 6 and $\frac{105}{4}$ square units

5. 17

6. The problem can be rewritten in two ways:

   Determine the perimeter of right triangle ABC, given that $CD = 60$, and $AB = 125$.

   Determine the perimeter of right triangle ABC, given that $CD = 60$, and $AB = 169$.

8. Here are 3 possible solutions:

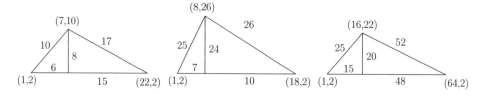

10. The following table gives several 60° triples (the top row and left column show the corresponding d and n value).

	2	3	4	5	6	7
1	(3,3,3)	(8,5,7)	(15,7,13)	(24,9,21)	(35,11,31)	(48,13,43)
2		(5,8,7)	(12,12,12)	(21,16,19)	(32,20,28)	(45,24,39)
3			(7,15,13)	(16,21,19)	(27,27,27)	(40,33,37)
4				(9,24,21)	(20,32,28)	(33,40,37)
5					(11,35,31)	(24,45,39)

11. Some possibilities:

length	width	depth
3	4	12
9	12	8
6	8	24
5	12	84
8	15	144

V. *Pascal's Revenge: Combinatorial Algebra*

1. Trains of thought

1. The only train of length 1 is the single car of length 1, which we'll denote "1".

   The trains of length 2 are denoted 1-1 and 2.

   Trains of length 3: 1-1-1, 1-2, 2-1, and 3.

   Trains of length 4: 1-1-1-1, 1-1-2, 1-2-1, 1-3, 2-1-1, 2-2, 3-1, and 4.

   Trains of length 5: 1-1-1-1-1, 1-1-1-2, 1-1-2-1, 1-1-3, 1-2-1-1, 1-2-2, 1-3-1, 1-4, 2-1-1-1, 2-1-2, 2-2-1, 2-3, 3-1-1, 3-2, 4-1, and 5.

3. There are 2^{n-1} trains of length n.

4.

Number of cars in the train → *Total length of the train* ↓	1	2	3	4	5	6
1	1	0	0	0	0	0
2	1	1	0	0	0	0
3	1	2	1	0	0	0
4	1	3	3	1	0	0
5	1	4	6	4	1	0

5. There are 55 trains of length 12 made up of 3 cars.

7. The sum of the entries in row n is 2^{n-1}.

2. Getting there

1. 12,870 days

2. 10

3.

# of Es, # of Ns	0,5	1,4	2,3	3,2	4,1	5,0
# of such words	1	5	10	10	5	1

4. This is equivalent to creating words with a Es and B Ns.

3. Trains and paths and triangles, oh my!

2. $Pas(6,2) = 15$, $Pas(8,5) = 56$

3. $Pas(n,k) = Pas(n, n-k)$ or $Pas(a+b, a) = Pas(a+b, b)$

4. There are two properties: $\sum_{i=k}^{n} Pas(i,k) = Pas(n+1, k+1)$ and

   $\sum_{i=0}^{n-k} Pas(k+i, k) = Pas(n+1, k+1)$

5. The number of trains of length n with k cars is $Pas(n,k)$.

6. The number of paths from the origin to (a,b) is

$$Pas(|a| + |b|, |a|) = Pas(|a| + |b|, |b|)$$

   and the number of taxicab paths from (a,b) to (c,d) is

$$Pas(|a-c| + |b-d|, |a-c|) = Pas(|a-c| + |b-d|, |b-d|)$$

7. $Pas(12,8)$

8. $\sum_{k=0}^{n} (-1)^k Pas(n,k) = 2^n$

9. $\sum_{k=0}^{n} (-1)^k Pas(n,k) = 0$

10.

Subsets of $\{A, B, C\}$:

$\emptyset$	$\{A\}$	$\{A,B\}$	$\{A,B,C\}$
	$\{B\}$	$\{A,C\}$	
		$\{B,C\}$	

Subsets of $\{A, B, C, D\}$:

$\emptyset$	$\{A\}$	$\{A,B\}$	$\{A,B,C\}$	$\{A,B,C,D\}$
	$\{B\}$	$\{A,C\}$	$\{A,B,D\}$	
	$\{C\}$	$\{A,D\}$	$\{A,C,D\}$	
	$\{D\}$	$\{B,C\}$	$\{B,C,D\}$	
		$\{B,D\}$		
		$\{C,D\}$		

Subsets of $\{A, B, C, D, E\}$:

$\emptyset$	$\{A\}$	$\{A,B\}$	$\{A,B,C\}$	$\{A,B,C,D\}$	$\{A,B,C,D,E\}$
	$\{B\}$	$\{A,C\}$	$\{A,B,D\}$	$\{A,B,C,E\}$	
	$\{C\}$	$\{A,D\}$	$\{A,B,E\}$	$\{A,B,D,E\}$	
	$\{D\}$	$\{A,E\}$	$\{A,C,D\}$	$\{A,C,D,E\}$	
	$\{E\}$	$\{B,C\}$	$\{A,C,E\}$	$\{B,C,D,E\}$	
		$\{B,D\}$	$\{A,D,E\}$		
		$\{B,E\}$	$\{B,C,D\}$		
		$\{C,D\}$	$\{B,C,E\}$		
		$\{C,E\}$	$\{B,D,E\}$		
		$\{D,E\}$	$\{C,D,E\}$		

Subsets of $\{A, B, C, D, E, F\}$:

$\emptyset$	$\{A,B\}$	$\{A,B,C\}$	$\{A,B,C,D\}$	$\{A,B,C,D,E\}$
	$\{A,C\}$	$\{A,B,D\}$	$\{A,B,C,E\}$	$\{A,B,C,D,F\}$
	$\{A,D\}$	$\{A,B,E\}$	$\{A,B,C,F\}$	$\{A,B,C,E,F\}$
$\{A\}$	$\{A,E\}$	$\{A,B,F\}$	$\{A,B,D,E\}$	$\{A,B,D,E,F\}$
$\{B\}$	$\{A,F\}$	$\{A,C,D\}$	$\{A,B,D,F\}$	$\{A,C,D,E,F\}$
$\{C\}$	$\{B,C\}$	$\{A,C,E\}$	$\{A,B,E,F\}$	$\{B,C,D,E,F\}$
$\{D\}$	$\{B,D\}$	$\{A,C,F\}$	$\{A,C,D,E\}$	
$\{E\}$	$\{B,E\}$	$\{A,D,E\}$	$\{A,C,D,F\}$	
$\{F\}$	$\{B,F\}$	$\{A,D,F\}$	$\{A,C,E,F\}$	$\{A,B,C,D,E,F\}$
	$\{C,D\}$	$\{A,E,F\}$	$\{A,D,E,F\}$	
	$\{C,E\}$	$\{B,C,D\}$	$\{B,C,D,E\}$	
	$\{C,F\}$	$\{B,C,E\}$	$\{B,C,D,F\}$	
	$\{D,E\}$	$\{B,C,F\}$	$\{B,C,E,F\}$	
	$\{D,F\}$	$\{B,D,E\}$	$\{B,D,E,F\}$	
	$\{E,F\}$	$\{B,D,F\}$	$\{C,D,E,F\}$	
		$\{C,D,E\}$		
		$\{C,D,F\}$		
		$\{D,E,F\}$		

Since a table is so unwieldy in this case, we'll list the subsets of $\{A, B, C, D, E, F, G\}$ horizontally, arranged by their size:

$\emptyset$,

$\{A\}, \{B\}, \{C\}, \{D\}, \{E\}, \{F\}, \{G\}$,

$\{A,B\}$, $\{A,C\}$, $\{A,D\}$, $\{A,E\}$, $\{A,F\}$, $\{A,G\}$, $\{B,C\}$, $\{B,D\}$, $\{B,E\}$, $\{B,F\}$, $\{B,G\}$, $\{C,D\}$, $\{C,E\}$, $\{C,F\}$, $\{C,G\}$, $\{D,E\}$, $\{D,F\}$, $\{D,G\}$, $\{E,F\}$, $\{E,G\}$, $\{F,G\}$,

$\{A,B,C\}$, $\{A,B,D\}$, $\{A,B,E\}$, $\{A,B,F\}$, $\{A,B,G\}$, $\{A,C,D\}$, $\{A,C,E\}$, $\{A,C,F\}$, $\{A,C,G\}$, $\{A,D,E\}$, $\{A,D,F\}$, $\{A,D,G\}$, $\{A,E,F\}$, $\{A,E,G\}$, $\{A,F,G\}$, $\{B,C,D\}$, $\{B,C,E\}$, $\{B,C,F\}$, $\{B,C,G\}$, $\{B,D,E\}$, $\{B,D,F\}$, $\{B,D,G\}$, $\{B,E,F\}$, $\{B,E,G\}$, $\{B,F,G\}$, $\{C,D,E\}$, $\{C,D,F\}$, $\{C,D,G\}$, $\{C,E,F\}$, $\{C,E,G\}$, $\{C,F,G\}$, $\{D,E,F\}$, $\{D,E,G\}$, $\{D,F,G\}$, $\{E,F,G\}$,

$\{A,B,C,D\}$, $\{A,B,C,E\}$, $\{A,B,C,F\}$, $\{A,B,C,G\}$, $\{A,B,D,E\}$, $\{A,B,D,F\}$, $\{A,B,D,G\}$, $\{A,B,E,F\}$, $\{A,B,E,G\}$, $\{A,B,F,G\}$, $\{A,C,D,E\}$, $\{A,C,D,F\}$, $\{A,C,D,G\}$, $\{A,C,E,F\}$, $\{A,C,E,G\}$, $\{A,C,F,G\}$, $\{A,D,E,F\}$, $\{A,D,E,G\}$, $\{A,D,F,G\}$, $\{A,E,F,G\}$, $\{B,C,D,E\}$, $\{B,C,D,F\}$, $\{B,C,D,G\}$, $\{B,C,E,F\}$, $\{B,C,E,G\}$, $\{B,C,F,G\}$, $\{B,D,E,F\}$, $\{B,D,E,G\}$, $\{B,D,F,G\}$, $\{B,E,F,G\}$, $\{C,D,E,F\}$, $\{C,D,E,G\}$, $\{C,D,F,G\}$, $\{C,E,F,G\}$, $\{D,E,F,G\}$,

$\{A,B,C,D,E\}$, $\{A,B,C,D,F\}$, $\{A,B,C,D,G\}$, $\{A,B,C,E,F\}$, $\{A,B,C,E,G\}$, $\{A,B,C,F,G\}$, $\{A,B,D,E,F\}$, $\{A,B,D,E,G\}$, $\{A,B,D,F,G\}$, $\{A,B,E,F,G\}$, $\{A,C,D,E,F\}$, $\{A,C,D,E,G\}$, $\{A,C,D,F,G\}$, $\{A,C,E,F,G\}$, $\{A,D,E,F,G\}$, $\{B,C,D,E,F\}$, $\{B,C,D,E,G\}$, $\{B,C,D,F,G\}$, $\{B,C,E,F,G\}$, $\{B,D,E,F,G\}$, $\{C,D,E,F,G\}$,

$\{A,B,C,D,E,F\}$, $\{A,B,C,D,E,G\}$, $\{A,B,C,D,F,G\}$, $\{A,B,C,E,F,G\}$, $\{A,B,D,E,F,G\}$, $\{A,C,D,E,F,G\}$, $\{B,C,D,E,F\}$,

and $\{A,B,C,D,E,F,G\}$.   *Whew!!*

11.

$k \to$ $n \downarrow$	0	1	2	3	4	5	6	7
0	1							
1	1	1						
2	1	2	1					
3	1	3	3	1				
4	1	4	6	4	1			
5	1	5	10	10	5	1		
6	1	6	15	20	15	6	1	
7	1	7	21	35	35	21	7	1

12. There are a total of $Pas(n,k)$ k-element subsets in a set with n elements.

4. Binomial theorem connection

1.
$$\begin{aligned}
(a+b)^2 &= a^2 + 2ab + b^2 \\
(a+b)^3 &= (a+b)(a^2 + 2ab + b^2) \\
&= a^3 + 3a^2b + 3ab^2 + b^3 \\
(a+b)^4 &= (a+b)(a^3 + 3a^2b + 3ab^2 + b^3) \\
&= a^4 + 4a^3b + 6a^2b^2 + 4ab^3 + b^4 \\
(a+b)^5 &= (a+b)(a^4 + 4a^3b + 6a^2b^2 + 4ab^3 + b^4) \\
&= a^5 + 5a^4b + 10a^3b^2 + 10a^2b^3 + 5ab^4 + b^5
\end{aligned}$$

2. (a)
$$\begin{aligned}
(a+b)^{10} &= a^{10} + 10a^9b + 45a^8b^2 + 120a^7b^3 + 210a^6b^4 \\
&\quad + 252a^5b^5 + 210a^4b^6 + 120a^3b^7 + 45a^2b^8 \\
&\quad + 10ab^9 + b^{10}.
\end{aligned}$$

(b)
$$(a+b)^{11} = a^{11} + 11ba^{10} + 55b^2a^9 + 165b^3a^8$$
$$+ 330b^4a^7 + 462b^5a^6 + 462b^6a^5 + 330b^7a^4$$
$$+ 165b^8a^3 + 55b^9a^2 + 11b^{10}a + b^{11}$$

3. $(a+b)^n = \sum_{k=0}^{n} \binom{n}{k} a^k b^{n-k}$,

4. (a)
$$(x+y)^7 = x^7 + 7x^6y + 21x^5y^2 + 35x^4y^3 + 35x^3y^4$$
$$+ 21x^2y^5 + 7xy^6 + y^7$$

(b) $(x+2y)^5 = x^5 + 10x^4y + 40x^3y^2 + 80x^2y^3 + 80xy^4 + 32y^5$

5. The coefficient of a^5b^2 in the expansion of $(a+b)^7$ is 21, the same as the coefficient of a^2b^5 in the expansion of $(a+b)^7$.

11. (a) 3^n (b) $(r+1)^n$ (c) 1   (d) $\left(\frac{13}{4}\right)^n$

12. $E = O$

5. Supercalifragilisticgeneratingfunctionology

1. The choices are 1-6, so there are 6 possibilities, each of them equally likely, assuming you're dealing with a *fair* die.

2. 36 possible pairs; 10 possible sums; 7 is the most likely sum

3. 216 possible triples; 16 possible sums; 10 and 11 are the most likely sums

4. 6^n possible n-tuples; $5n+1$ possible sums; the most likely sum for n dice is $\frac{7n}{2}$ $\left(= \frac{6n+n}{2}\right)$ when n is even, and the most likely sums are $\left\lfloor \frac{7n}{2} \right\rfloor$ and $\left\lceil \frac{7n}{2} \right\rceil$ (the two integers closest to the average of the minimum and maximum sums) when n is odd.

5.

sum	3	4	5	6	7	8	9	10	11	12	13	14	15	16	17	18
freq	1	3	6	10	15	21	25	27	27	25	21	15	10	6	3	1

6. $7n - S$

7. $x^2(x+1)^2(x^2+x+1)^2(x^2-x+1)^2$.

10. The coefficient of x^S in the expansion of $\left(x + x^2 + x^3 + x^4 + x^5 + x^6\right)^n$ is the number of ways to roll a sum of S with n dice.

11. 6^n

12. See answer to problem 4.

13. $(x+1)^n = \sum_{k=0}^{n} \binom{n}{k} x^k$

14. $(H+T)^n$; there are 10 ways to get 3 heads and 2 tails when you flip a coin 5 times.

CORWIN PRESS

The Corwin Press logo—a raven striding across an open book—represents the union of courage and learning. Corwin Press is committed to improving education for all learners by publishing books and other professional development resources for those serving the field of K–12 education. By providing practical, hands-on materials, Corwin Press continues to carry out the promise of its motto: **"Helping Educators Do Their Work Better."**